Gentleman Troubadours
and Andean Pop Stars

Chicago Studies in Ethnomusicology

A series edited by Philip V. Bohlman, Ronald Radano, and Timothy Rommen

EDITORIAL BOARD

Margaret J. Kartomi
Bruno Nettl
Anthony Seeger
Kay Kaufman Shelemay
Martin H. Stokes
Bonnie C. Wade

Gentleman Troubadours and Andean Pop Stars

Huayno Music, Media Work, and Ethnic Imaginaries in Urban Peru

JOSHUA TUCKER

The University of Chicago Press
Chicago and London

Joshua Tucker is assistant professor of music at Brown University.

The University of Chicago Press, Chicago 60637
The University of Chicago Press, Ltd., London
© 2013 by The University of Chicago
All rights reserved. Published 2013.
Printed in the United States of America

22 21 20 19 18 17 16 15 14 13   1 2 3 4 5

ISBN-13: 978-0-226-92395-6 (cloth)
ISBN-13: 978-0-226-92396-3 (paper)
ISBN-13: 978-0-226-92397-0 (e-book)
ISBN-10: 0-226-92395-9 (cloth)
ISBN-10: 0-226-92396-7 (paper)
ISBN-10: 0-226-92397-5 (e-book)

Portions of chapter 4 were previously published as "Mediating Sentiment and Shaping Publics: Recording Practice and the Articulation of Social Change in Andean Lima," *Popular Music and Society* 33, no. 2 (2010). Portions of chapter 5 were previously published as "Music Radio and Global Mediation: Producing Social Distinction in the Andean Public Sphere," *Cultural Studies* 24, no. 4 (2010).

Library of Congress Cataloging-in-Publication Data

Tucker, Joshua, author.
   Gentleman troubadours and Andean pop stars : huayno music, media work, and ethnic imaginaries in urban Peru / Joshua Tucker.
       pages cm. — (Chicago studies in ethnomusicology)
   Includes bibliographical references and index.
   ISBN-13: 978-0-226-92395-6 (cloth : alkaline paper)
   ISBN-10: 0-226-92395-9 (cloth : alkaline paper)
   ISBN-13: 978-0-226-92396-3 (paperback : alkaline paper)
   ISBN-10: 0-226-92396-7 (paperback : alkaline paper)
   [etc.]
   1. Popular music—Social aspects—Peru. 2. Huaynos—Peru—Ayacucho—History and criticism. 3. Huaynos—Peru—Lima—History and criticism. 4. Radio and music—Peru. 5. Sound recording industry—Social aspects—Peru.   I. Title. II. Series: Chicago studies in ethnomusicology.
   ML3917.P43T83 2013
   781.640985'09051—dc23
                                                                        2012021910

♾ This paper meets the requirements of ANSI/NISO Z39.48-1992 (Permanence of Paper).

CONTENTS

Acknowledgments / vii

INTRODUCTION / Cities, Sounds,
and Circulation in Twenty-First-Century Peru / 1

ONE / The Distributed Society / 9

TWO / The Andean Music Scene / 35

THREE / Bohemians, Poets, and Troubadours / 79

FOUR / The Commercial Huayno Business / 111

FIVE / Finding the Huayno People / 147

EPILOGUE / Folkloric Frames and Mass Culture / 177

Notes / 185
Bibliography / 205
Index / 221

ACKNOWLEDGMENTS

A project of this kind is made possible by the aid and support of many others, all of whom I would like to thank. I will begin by recognizing Judith Becker, Bruce Mannheim, Andrew Shryock, and Amy Stillman, all of whom guided my initial research efforts, helped me to develop my thoughts, and later formed a sterling dissertation committee. The Quechua language instruction provided by Inés Callalli and Serafín Coronel-Molina, too, proved invaluable in research and analysis.

Financial support for field research was provided at various times by the Wenner-Gren Foundation, the Social Sciences and Humanities Research Council of Canada, the Rackham School of Graduate Studies and Center for Latin American and Caribbean Studies at the University of Michigan, and the Lozano Long Institute for Latin American Studies at the University of Texas at Austin, all of which is gratefully acknowledged, as is the writing support provided by the David Rockefeller Center for Latin American Studies at Harvard University and Brown University's Center for Latin American and Caribbean Studies.

For giving me their time and helping me to understand the dynamics of musical life in Ayacucho and Lima, I would like to thank Lucho Aguilar, Isaac Argumedo, Alex Arone, Daniel Arone, Martín Arone, Pedro Arriola, Keti Bedrillana, María Luisa Bustamante, Ernesto Camassi, Diosdado Gaitán Castro, Otoniel Ccayanchira, Arturo Chiclla, Rosa Chiclla, Fernando Cruz, Ricardo Daryx, Eladio Díaz, Antonio Sullca Effio, Carlos Falconí, Julián Fernández, Óscar Figueroa, Fausto Flores, Ranulfo Fuentes, Amílcar Gamarra, Zoila and Doris García, Raúl García Zárate, Miguel Ángel Huamán, Julio and Walter Humala, Mario Laurente, Alfredo Loayza, Daniel Loayza, Magda Medina, Edy Méjico, Milton Mendieta, Walter Mendieta, Walter Muñoz, Dina Paucar, Carlos Prado, Manuelcha Prado, Marco Tucno

Rocha, Antonio Sullca "Sunqu Suwa," Walter Wayanay, and Juan Zárate. For aiding in this and more informal ways, I thank all of my friends, *compadres*, and godchildren in Ayacucho and Lima as well. For their hospitality in Lima, Jeanine Anderson, Raúl Romero, and Víctor Vich all merit special recognition. In Ayacucho, I received valuable insights in conversation with Jeffrey Gamarra, and would also like to single out the staff at the San Francisco Monastery as well as the Archivo Público Departamental de Ayacucho for their assistance in accessing historical documentation.

Upon returning from the field, I received invaluable commentary on my work from friends and colleagues, including Michael Ferguson, Susan Frekko, Karen Hebert, and Edward Murphy, as well as the Círculo Micaela Bastidas de Estudios Andinos at the University of Michigan. Opportunities for presentation at the University of California, Riverside, Yale University, and the University of Oklahoma proved invaluable in helping me further shape my thoughts, for which I would like to thank Jonathan Ritter (who also deserves special thanks for his long-standing help in many, many other ways), Enrique Mayer, and Alan McPherson and Mandy Minks, respectively. Comments by David Novak and Amy Weidman after a presentation at the conference of the Society for Ethnomusicology are also gratefully acknowledged.

Colleagues at both the University of Texas and Brown University have provided ample support of various kinds during the writing up of this work, and I would like to single out Dana Gooley, Kiri Miller, Robin Moore, Marc Perlman, Sonia Seeman, and especially Paja Faudree. Thomas Turino and an anonymous reader from the University of Chicago Press made suggestions that helped make an initial manuscript much better, as did my editor, Elizabeth Branch Dyson, and I express my deepest thanks to all for their thoughtful comments.

Finally, the support of family and friends, before, during, and after research, is the foundation upon which everything else rests. For various kinds of logistical support in the field, I would like to thank Jeff and Joanna Leinaweaver, as well as Megan Callaghan. My mother and father, Sheila and Michael Tucker, deserve thanks in ways that exceed my capacity to phrase them. Most of all, I give thanks every day for the support, critique, and companionship of my wonderful wife, Jessaca Leinaweaver, and for Leo, whose skills in comic relief have proved perhaps more valuable than everything else put together.

INTRODUCTION

Cities, Sounds, and Circulation in Twenty-First-Century Peru

After years of studying Andean popular music in Lima and Ayacucho, Peru, the thought of either place conjures a wealth of sensory stimuli that define my experience of their city-spaces. The clouds that loom over Peru's desert coast, for instance, shed no rain, but they place Lima under a blanket of damp, heavy air whose weight the visitor perceives immediately upon arrival. They also trap the dirty fumes of city traffic, merging the olfactory and the tactile into a synesthetic sensation of acrid humidity. On the drive in from the airport, past wan palm trees and square cement buildings crowned by thickets of rebar, the view calls to mind peer cities in the Global South. But the word *Escarchado*, painted alongside a phone number on curb after curb, reminds the attentive observer of the way that Limeños stake a visual claim to respectability amid urban blight: by having a mason at that number coat their house in a layer of plaster (*escarchado*), the outward sign of a decent, well-maintained home.

Most indelible are Peru's raucous urban soundscapes. The streets of the capital teem with taxis and buses past their prime, gunning their engines as they compete for every inch of road. Blaring horns combine with the shrieking whistles of traffic cops and the hollering of fare collectors to produce a multilayered din that only abates with the workday's end. On sidewalks, ambulatory vendors insistently hustle clients, who shout in turn into cheap cell phones. Everywhere, sound spills from homes, cantinas, stores, workshops, market stalls, offices, internet labs, and the booths of night watchmen, the sounds of the private sphere engaging those of the public street in polyphonic transgression of any nominal boundary between them. And music pulses at the heart of things, as buskers, transistor radios, car stereos, barroom DVD players, and the external loudspeakers of businesses hoping to lure clients all suffuse the city with a layer of melody and rhythm that leavens the casual cruelty of "Lima the Horrible" (Salazar Bondy 1964).

Lima's musical density is the aural consequence of half a century's unregulated growth. The compact colonial city, squeezed into a narrow coastal strip between the Pacific Ocean and the Andes Mountains, was unprepared when waves of rural migrants began to arrive from Peru's highlands in the 1940s, driving its population from 645,000 to 8.7 million between 1940 and 2008 (Takenaka, Paerregaard, and Berg 2010). Its infrastructure crumbled, settlers sprawled into nearby valleys or barren plains, and Lima became the kind of hypertrophic megalopolis where a certain sonic abundance is to be expected. But Lima's noisiness also obeys a social disposition whereby music is tied to conviviality. This is the sensibility that led the producer and promoter Rodolfo Arriola to harangue me about the impoverished quality of life in the United States, where his relatives cannot play music in the street after 10:00 P.M. Each Sunday it draws blue-collar migrants to marathon concerts featuring popular *huayno* and *cumbia* music at which audience members devote their lone day of leisure to drinking and dancing. It means that places of business, from upscale offices to flyblown market stalls, are filled with workers using companionable radios to ease the daily grind. Most important, the accessible nature of musical creation and distribution, combined with its pervasiveness, means that this is a key conduit whereby Andean migrants have altered the public culture of the capital and of Peru at large.

This book is about the way that Andean music inhabits the country's public sphere, and more specifically about the way that the circulation of particular sounds through particular spaces helps to define the categories of Peru's social imaginary. I approach these issues via contemporary recordings of huayno music from the highland city of Ayacucho. From the early 1990s, performers began to blend the city's guitar-based folk traditions with foreign pop, and with the pan-Andean world music of Bolivia, Chile, and Ecuador (Turino 2007; Wara Céspedes 1984, 1993). I follow the musicians, mediators, and musical ideologues associated with these developments as they define new markets within a changing social landscape, adapting genre ideologies to the emergent conditions of Peruvian life. Different sounds diverge as they move through the national soundscape, and their idiosyncratic paths of circulation carve the public sphere into distinct territories. Some of the publics that these sounds shape build upon older cultures of taste, but others elaborate upon the evolving fault lines of contemporary Peruvian society, revealing and reifying social categories in formation. For this reason, I also situate Ayacucho's evolving huayno style in relation to genres with which it is sociomusically allied and those to which it is opposed. The sounds in play are tailored to consumers' desires for social and cultural capital, but they also provide listeners with identarian clues amidst a sea of uncertainty—because Andean listeners within and beyond Lima face competing challenges to old loyalties. Like audiences everywhere, they parse popular cultural activity, seeking to understand what kind of people they live among and what kind of people they are becoming. Musical discourse informs these deliberations, and acts of musical consumption often manifest the personal conclusions drawn from them.

A trip across Lima might approximate the everyday sonic cartographies available to city residents. My typical journeys began in leafy Barranco, the elegant southern neighborhood where I lived, and ended two hours later at the house of my *compadres* in faraway Lurigancho, a migrant district that sprawls up an arid northeastern valley toward the Andes. Musically, this trip starts with a transition from Barranco's rock clubs and dance bars, where local hipsters rub elbows with tourists, into the sound world of Lima's urban transport, where radios blare salsa, merengue, and cumbia, jangling "tropical" genres that keep overworked drivers alert during long shifts at the wheel. Entering the sunken highway that channels traffic away from tony Miraflores, home to the decorous theaters of the María Angola Hotel and the Instituto Cultural Peruano-Norteamericano, the bus eventually emerges downtown. Here traffic crawls past underground punk clubs and holes in the wall like my preferred *cevichería*, La Buena Muerte, where lunchtime performers belt out the melancholy *valses* dear to Lima's old guard. Farther into the grimy city center, walls along Avenida Abancay are festooned with garish neon-hued posters announcing cumbia or huayno performances, events that are aimed at the commuters who come in from Lima's peripheral migrant districts to work in the nearby central market. Crossing the Rímac River, the bus enters Lurigancho, the largest of these districts, and posters multiply amidst scattered clubs and open-air lots, all of which become centers of nightlife on Sunday evenings. Concert advertising thins out once more as the bus leaves Lurigancho's commercial center, climbing into high desert, where many neighborhoods lack power, water, security, and other basics. Finally, at my destination in the barrio of Cruz de Motupe, I would often arrive to the sound of a household radio, playing none of the markedly proletarian musics heard in nearby venues. Instead, as if to underline media's potential for creative disloyalty to the immediate environs, it would fill the household with contemporary Ayacuchano huayno—a genre that connoted social sophistication and was much beloved by the children of this upwardly mobile household.

This sketch suggests the sonic transformation of a city that has historically been hostile territory for *serranos* (highlanders) and their cultural expressions. Moreover, Lima's musical life increasingly affects that of provincial cities such as Ayacucho as well. These smaller urban centers often appear strangely quiet in scholarly writings, their stasis interrupted only by riotous festivals—or, in the case of Ayacucho, by the bombs and bullets that shook the city during the conflict between the Shining Path and government forces (1980–c. 1993). However, if music was once limited mainly to acoustic performance in the home, the cantina, or the street, then today radio retransmitters, pirated media, and online circulation all make Ayacucho and its peer cities reverberate with the same sounds as the capital. Residents of the sierra face the same sets of musical choices as their coastal peers, and they too put them to work in deconstructing social distinctions.

This book brings into focus the process whereby such distinctions arise, travel, and pass into everyday life, largely through the prism of Ayacuchano huayno. Most of the relevant developments were centered in Lima. The city's concentration of industry and wealth make it a crucible of change, and practices from the highlands are often reworked in the capital before returning home. In the late 1980s, for instance, Ayacuchano huayno was a relatively obscure style with diehard adherents in its home city, a handful of practitioners, and a small recording studio dedicated to capturing wider audiences. Before long, its musicians were packing venues in Lima with audiences from all over the country and entering the restricted world of Lima's FM radio. Only later did it enter national distribution circuits, which is why much of my account focuses on the capital. However, events there depended upon ideas about musical legitimacy that were codified in early twentieth-century highland circles, upon musical changes that transpired during Ayacucho's years of violence in the 1980s, and upon radio disc jockey techniques pioneered within the Andean city. As such, I tack back and forth between coast and highlands in order to convey the full range of processes at play and their effects in both cities.

I begin in chapter 1 by outlining the historical factors that weigh upon the contemporary significance of Ayacuchano music and the theoretical tools that guide my interpretation of its place in Peru's public sphere. It is obvious enough that human spaces are alive with meaningful noise (Bull and Back 2003; Corbin 1998; Erlmann 2004), but in post-industrial cities the public sphere is dominated by media enterprises seeking customers, and the implications of this insight cannot be grasped without a framework for analyzing the circulation of sound's most profitable form. Popular music's pervasiveness, its commercial nature, and its commonsense ties to social identity make it unique. Understanding its effects means accounting for the ways that mediators recruit consumers, and although media scholars have increasingly drifted toward such user-centered technologies as the internet or video games (Howard and Jones 2004; K. Miller 2008, 2012; Turkle 2005), it remains true that "radio and television, which are more evenly distributed throughout the entirety of the city, disseminate information and entertainment to all sectors better than . . . spatially based public venues." Especially where the mastery of more recent technologies remains sporadic, it is "these media—with their vertical and anonymous logic—[that] sketch out the new and invisible links" binding communities of consumption (García Canclini 2001: 53). Group sentiment depends upon circulatory loops (cf. Larkin 2008), stable pathways along which products go gathering adherents, marking consumers as members of a distinct market with a recognizable historicity and thereby encouraging a sense of intersubjectivity. Here, I outline an analytical approach to the sonic topography of the public sphere, designed to describe how mediators guide listeners toward particular sounds and to particular conceptions of self and other.[1]

Such an approach is indispensable for understanding musical activity in contemporary Peru, where different styles compete for audiences by engaging distinct visions of Andean identity. The notion of an Andean subject position can be traced to colonial times, when a contrast emerged between the coastal strip settled by Europeans and the conquered mountain region populated by indigenous and *mestizo* ("mixed") peoples. As an unselfconscious label for the diverse highland area, the idea of an Andean identity is impermissibly essentialist. It conflates peoples of various cultural backgrounds, and it typically glosses a stereotyped vision of the mountains as a bastion of archaism, peopled by Indians hewing to premodern lifeways (Starn 1991). Nevertheless, as a label that calls attention to shared histories of oppression and disrespect, it can also become a sign of solidarity, and the ongoing transformation of *lo andino* (roughly, "the Andean") has long been central to Peruvian scholarship.[2] By the 1960s it was already clear that evolving music and dance styles tracked the changing identities of migrants in Lima and other cities (Lloréns Amico 1983; Mendoza 2000; Núñez Rebaza 1990; Romero 2001; Turino 1990, 1993). However, inherited distinctions of class, region, and race are transformed amidst Lima's chaos, differentiating subsectors of the Andean community in ways that are linked to the capital's ramifying means of cultural production. Musical developments are no exception, though it has rarely been noted that many stylistic options tend to coexist at any given time, presenting different models for the value of Andean heritage (but see Romero 2002).

Attentive to this fact, chapter 2 presents an overview of key popular styles including *chicha*, pan-Andean music, *indigenista* folklore, and especially huayno. Huayno is often treated as a general term for Andean folk music in Peru, but it encompasses many stylistic variants associated with different kinds of audiences. The contemporary Ayacuchano variant that is central to this book is a self-conscious hybrid pioneered by performers from Ayacucho during the 1980s and 1990s and largely understood as a modernized version of an antecedent traditional style from the highland city. A musical response to changing demographics, it took advantage of international sounds to tap new markets during a moment of social transition, and it was part of a broader transformation in Andean performance, which in turn changed the aesthetic categories through which Peruvians establish a sense of self and other. It combines Ayacuchano and foreign elements but draws its meaning from its relationship to other genres; together they map out the heterogeneous social field within which Andeanness moves today. As such, this chapter sets different sounds and musical experiences in dialogue with one another, limning the background against which contemporary Ayacuchano huayno acquired its unique profile.

Chapter 3 turns to early twentieth-century Ayacucho, when local discussions about the city's traditional huayno style set the terms in which future generations would interpret it. These discussions took place in intellectual spaces, including the journals and public events of an organization called the Centro Cultural Ayacuchano, which was tied obliquely to Peru's contemporaneous indigenista movement. *Indigenismo* saw highland intellectuals challenge Lima's dominance by promoting an alternate vision of Peruvian nationality, one rooted in Andean cultural patterns (de la Cadena 2000; Mendoza 2000, 2008; Turino 1993). Its ideologues adopted symbols and modified cultural practices from Indian communities to express their sense of difference from the capital's European-descended elite, but it was organized by nonindigenous elites and reflected their thirst for a role in Peru's national development; it was not a project of indigenous revindication per se.[3] Ayacuchano intellectuals were sympathetic to some but not all aspects of indigenista thought, and they mainly turned to the mestizo music of the city's elite, forging an interpretive scheme based upon their self-image as guardians of an Andean Hispanist heritage. Billing themselves as the inheritors of an erudite musical tradition that set them apart from their Indian neighbors, they created a series of racialized tropes related to intellectualism and refinement, which subsist in contemporary conversations about musical legitimacy.

Chapter 4 shows how these tropes were reworked in the late twentieth century as musicians and mediators sought to cultivate markets within Lima's rising Andean middle class. Traditional Ayacuchano huayno was seen as a sophisticated but archaic pursuit of highland gentlemen, and its revival depended upon the way that determined agents rerouted its urbane associations through contemporary signifiers of musical cosmopolitanism. Here I focus on the activities of the record label Dolby JR (later renamed Dolly JR), which was centrally important in making contemporary Ayacuchano huayno successful in the 1980s, 1990s, and 2000s. Their savvy use of the technological tools at their disposal, as well as their skill at reading and gratifying the emergent dispositions of Andean audiences, underwrote the style's success. Most important, their actions did not merely bring a fading music back to life: in fostering its uptake among Peru's new migrant bourgeoisie, they outlined the initial parameters of an Andean middle-class subject position that had yet to be effectively defined and inhabited.

Chapter 5 focuses on radio, the main channel through which most Peruvian citizens access musical sound and the key medium in promoting the virtues of contemporary Ayacuchano huayno to its fans. As the agents who sit at the heart of Peruvian musical distribution, radio DJs have a central role in shaping huayno's public meanings, and I examine the way that their on-air performances, their musical ideologies, and their working conditions structure those interpretations. Indeed, it is largely here that the contemporary notion of huayno as a leisure product suitable for bourgeois listeners met inherited notions of huayno as an elegant musical object, blending signifiers old and new to produce an aesthetic experience particular to those young Andean listeners who were the objects of commercial interpellation.

My account is meant to place media workers on a par with performers as contemporary sociomusical agents. Analyses tying distribution patterns to musical communities remain rare within music studies, even as accounts elsewhere show how often the social efficacy of artistic endeavor depends upon the labor of circulation (see Abu-Lughod 2005; Himpele 2008; Hirschkind 2006). In the case of popular music, its efficacy depends more particularly upon the way that agents harness available technologies to connect sounds and ideologies with the kind of listenership that they seek. In the case of Ayacuchano huayno, scholarly writers, radio DJs, and record producers all took advantage of changing socioeconomic conditions to produce new kinds of Andean listeners, musical consumers invested in their own notion of bourgeois respectability. Especially as mediated experience continues inexorably to muscle out other possibilities for musical interaction, it is imperative that scholars develop effective tools for describing the process whereby such mediators shape the public life of musical style.

In the spirit of Romero's call to "de-essentialize the Andean *mestizo*" (2001: 132), this account also calls renewed attention to the social construction of elite identities in Andean Peru. Accounts of Andean music making usually emphasize the sound world of indigenous subalterns, and mestizo subjectivity is understood, if at all, through top-down movements such as indigenismo and related expressions of Andeanness. Propagated by nonindigenous elites, these have rightly been criticized for appropriating Indian images and displacing subaltern voices while claiming to speak in their name. However, Andean mestizo identities are too often placed in simplistic opposition to those of their indigenous alters. In fact both positions exist in mutable, evolving tension with one another, and the notions of Andeanness associated with the privileged are no less powerful for their bearers than is the depurated Indian subject position to which nonindigenous identities are usually opposed. Especially given that "internal and external boundaries constantly shift, and ethnicity has to be constantly redefined and reinvented" (Yelvington 1991: 165), the identity work performed in claims to indigeneousness or Andeanness should not be judged by whether they hew to notions of difference rooted in ancestral Indian culture. Rather, the task for the analyst is to account for the reasons that particular visions of Andean selfhood become organizing tropes at the moment they appear.

ONE

The Distributed Society: Andean Sounds, Mediated Scenes, and Urban Space

Ethnographic work tying media use to subjectivity has yielded accounts of great subtlety over the last decade, as constructivist notions of identity have engaged the "experience of mass-mediated forms in relation to the practices of everyday life" (Appadurai and Breckenridge 1995: 4) and revealed the fluid popular uptake of the social identifications in circulation.[1] At the same time, these very works have made the task of media ethnography seem more vexed than ever, insofar as the genre at its best helps to illuminate "the contingent way in which all social categories emerge, become naturalized, and intersect in people's conception of themselves and their world" (Rofel 1994: 703). The sheer profusion of media forms, each bringing new points of reference to large, dispersed groups and transcending culturally or territorially bound models of shared substance, defies attempts to align one system of symbols and meanings with a single class, culture, or nation. It has become hard to specify the range of categories and discourses available within a given situation, and it is increasingly clear that consumers are promiscuous and fickle, using different media forms for different purposes at different moments. The very language of identity, with its connotations of deep psychosocial convictions that guide character and action, seems inadequate to describe the transient, ephemeral bonds that accrue to contemporary media objects. In short, there is still no single, all-encompassing "means of theorizing the formation of collectivities that cross ruptures of space and are outside formal definitions of 'culture'" (Ginsburg, Abu-Lughod, and Larkin 2002: 5).

My approach rests ultimately upon Jürgen Habermas's ([1959] 1989) seminal study of the public sphere, and more proximately upon its resonance in recent work on public culture. His account of the public as a type of collective that arose with democracy, and specifically via rational-critical discussion about the priorities of civil society, provided an elegant, anti-essentialist model of the way that people come to share a sense of commitment and common cause.[2] The ties that bound the emergent public were built through mutually engaged discourse about collective rights and obligations, and they grew from the mutual recognition of evolving interests rather than from antecedent categories of culture or class. Insofar as such discussions moved dialogically, the bases of group sentiment were elaborated collectively; they were the creation of all and none, and their very anonymity gave the public its air of legitimacy. And if group sentiment was contingent, then the principles of identification were very real for the actors involved.

However, Habermas's idealized model depended upon the independence of communicative channels from forces that might bend public discourse to their interest. He condemned the colonization of the commons by commerce, arguing that the promotion of consumer goods had split the public into competing constituencies of style and reduced its role to that of spectator, choosing among "products designed to please various tastes . . . none of [which] reaches the whole of the public" (Calhoun 1992b: 25). Though accurate enough, this account pathologized the mediated transactions that make up much of contemporary life without offering an analysis of their generative particularities. If consumption rarely promotes rational-critical discussion, for instance, then it is powerfully implicated in the growth of shared investments (Appadurai 1986; D. Miller 1994, 1995; García Canclini 2001). Commercial media also channel images or sentiments dear to subcultural groups who lack the social capital necessary for rational-critical discussion, building subaltern "counterpublics" (Warner 2002) that act through the resources of the corporatized public sphere (Fraser 1990).[3] Later accounts deploy Habermas's processual insights against the grain of his own theory, describing publics as social bodies organized around "folk notions about groupness, interest, and communication" (Gal and Woolard 2001: 7), and emphasizing the sense of mutuality that develops when people are identified as members of markets—that is, consumers with common investments in material culture—and understood to have a historical endurance as such (Kunreuther 2006; Mazzarella 2004; Pinney 2001; Warner 2002). Habermas's critique of the public sphere's undemocratic topography remains compelling, but taking it seriously cannot mean abandoning analysis of the publics produced by the actual conditions of the media landscape. Instead, it means accounting for the conditions that grant certain individuals the capability to speak and act publicly and analyzing the means by which their models of groupness become persuasive.

Simon Frith's model of genre, which describes the way that the popular music industry stabilizes the relation between sound and market, echoes many of the concerns raised by these theorists of public culture. Here industry workers read the purchasing patterns of consumers, seeking to determine the persuasive elements of successful recordings. They use the insights gleaned thereby to develop a set of "genre worlds," which shape the sound and imagery applied to future productions, and which are in turn marketed to the same consumers who generated the initial series of discourses (Frith 1996: 88). Audiences, in other words, are initially defined in relation to an amorphous set of musical attributes and later serve as the basis for the consolidation of those attributes as a genre, as mediators and artists refine them in ways that they think will satisfy emergent tastes. Markets and genres gradually become defined in terms of one another, and though everything has the appearance of a spontaneous social manifestation, production is part of an ongoing and commercially negotiated dynamic involving listeners, who make their will known through acts of consumption; media workers, who help musicians create sounds that win audience approval; and musicians, who may or may not resist such imperatives.

To be fully effective, Frith's model needs to be placed into a broader context, because musical genres are ineluctably defined not only in relation to their listenerships, but also against one another. Useful here is the concept of the scene as defined by Will Straw, who describes it as a "cultural space in which a range of musical practices coexist, interacting with each other within a variety of processes of differentiation, and according to widely varying trajectories of change and cross-fertilization" (Straw 1991: 373). The styles that define a scene are mutable and stand in constant, transformational dialogue with one another, but the structure of the scene may be elucidated by specifying the elements that differentiate genres and their devotees at any given moment in time. The task of the analyst is to explain the "specific forms of connoisseurship central to an involvement in" a given music culture, and the social institutions that disseminate those forms of connoisseurship (Straw 1991: 372).

Straw's model allows that differentiation may be articulated in terms of cultural or class-based identities. This is certainly the case in Peru, where such social distinctions are aspects of everyday interaction. Here his ideas are most useful when they are placed in dialogue with Pierre Bourdieu's account of the field of cultural production (Bourdieu 1984, 1993). Departing from the insight that "a class is defined as much by its being-perceived and . . . by its consumption—which need not be conspicuous to be symbolic—as by its position in the relations of production" (1984: 483), Bourdieu shows how notions of good and bad taste both derive from and reproduce existing class relationships. His ideas depend upon the notion of cultural capital, which may be thought of as "an internalized code or a cognitive acquisition which equips the social agent with empathy towards, appreciation for or competence in deciphering . . . cultural artifacts" (Johnson 1993: 7). Such competence is rarely acquired through formal schooling. Instead, it is learned gradually over time, in myriad everyday rituals that, owing to their unremarked nature, come to inhabit a subconscious realm (the habitus; see also Bourdieu 1977). However, precisely because its acquisition is mystified and understood as innate, this nebulous sense of propriety makes the aesthetic habits of different social classes seem like instinctive tastes. In this way, performances of musical taste classify listeners according to the position of the evaluated style, product, or art object within the overall social field (Bourdieu 1984, 1993), and "by discriminating among the world of goods, people distinguish among each other and naturalize their position in a class-divided society" (Colloredo-Mansfeld 1999: 200).

It is precisely such modes of differentiation that act to produce distinction within the contemporary Andean music scene, and the insights of these theorists provide a nuanced way to approach the changing dynamics of Andean popular music in Peru. Highlanders inhabit a deeply overdetermined ethnic category, and persistent reminders of that fact lead most to adopt a particular stance toward Andean heritage. However, the interpretation of what it might mean actually to be Andean is more volatile than ever. Music provides a way of anchoring a conception of this subject position, but different musics compete for the right to capture it, using very different sounds and cultural discourses. As contemporary performers of Ayacuchano huayno fused local folk and international popular styles, for instance, their music became a site of identification for those who valued highland ancestry, but not its traditional terms. Their targets in Lima and, later, the highlands increasingly recognized themselves as the objects of radio broadcasts, news reports, and buyers of concert tickets or CDs. Insofar as its fans share other attributes, including ancestry and class, their style retained the aura of a spontaneous manifestation. But "consumers must be made rather than found in order to create a market" (Ang 1991: 32), and the identification between style and public depended upon the capacity of media actors to stabilize relationships between sound, audience, and a kind of social capital that is understood in relation to transnational cultural savvy.

Music and Media Work

Musical sounds may acquire social markers at several distinct sites of mediation, ranging from club advertisements aimed at a particular clientele (Thornton 1996), to the A & R department of record companies, where performing careers are designed in light of preexisting genre discourses (Negus 1999). In the case of contemporary Ayacuchano huayno, record producers and radio DJs were central in crafting the style's image and tying it to images of social progress and upward mobility. As elsewhere, such mediators have received little scholarly attention in Peru, owing to the long shadow cast by the Frankfurt School and its vision of an artless, avaricious culture industry herding consumers toward bland, easily replicable musical parameters.[4] However, in light of ample evidence that consumers actively negotiate the meanings of the media products they use, and that artistic, personal, or societal commitments inflect the actions of industry workers, serious consideration of "the many human mediations which come in between the corporate structures and the practices . . . of musicians" (Negus 1999: 16), not to mention between all of these actors and their audiences, seems long overdue.[5]

Mediators are liable to have especially wide leeway in places such as Peru, where changes in recording technology have brought production into the hands of smaller enterprises. It is an amply supported truism that creative freedom can increase outside large corporate structures, with their need to maximize profits and minimize risk (see Greene 2005; Manuel 1993). Independent labels often empower musicians whose limited markets do not fit the economies of scale that govern large businesses, giving them unprecedented access to the public sphere and greater control over production than might be granted by a major studio. As it happens, contemporary Peru houses many independent (and often pirate) media channels, but even these nominal independents are constrained by structures of aesthetic hegemony and find themselves driven to draw upon genre discourses that are defined at more powerful studios. Furthermore, their challenge to the dominance of major labels often grows not from a democratizing instinct, but rather from the desire to tap the very markets that powerful media actors have defined. As such, their actions should be treated "neither as pure corporate manipulation nor as grassroots expression, but as contested territory where hegemonic and oppositional values symbolically or explicitly engage one another" (Manuel 1993: 10).

Ethnographic attention has already shown how the recording process, which involves manipulating and imbricating marked musical categories, stages "poetic representations of the self and others in relation to one another" (Meintjes 2003: 259).[6] Recordings make publicly available possible models of social interaction in the proxy realm of style, acting as synecdoches for broader debates about what kinds of sounds, and hence what kinds of subjects or discourses, "go together"; moreover, they are understood to do so by creators and consumers. Recordings are driven by the need to capture audiences, but they also reflect and constitute larger debates about social and musical propriety. However, although the studio is the place where new sociomusical relations are affixed in the form of recordings, consumers are more properly recruited for those recordings in the process of distribution. And despite a dearth of research on music radio, it is often the most effective means of organizing markets, particularly where the listening public is larger than the record-buying public (Hennion and Méadel 1986).

Radio is an omnipresent force within Peruvian life and the central means whereby most people interact with music, but as elsewhere it is typically dismissed as a mere technology for delivering listeners to advertisers (Alfaro et al. 1990; Bolaños 1995).[7] This is a mistake. In one of the few studies to seriously consider radio work, Debra Anne Spitulnik has argued that "when radio listeners have an awareness of one another and a sense of simultaneous participation, they are more than just a social aggregate of listeners who happen to use radio. They have a sense of intersubjectivity" (1994: 19). Moreover, by showing how the unique metadiscursive markers of radio broadcasting create the categories through which listeners interpret the materials that they hear, she demonstrates the analytical potential of greater attention to broadcast form. Radio workers hierarchize musical styles by positioning them variably over the day or within individual programs (Berland 1998; Hendy 2000), and DJs index the values of the music they play by linking it to other kinds of materials over the course of a broadcast (Hennion and Méadel 1986). A realistic portrait of radio's role in musical life should account for these tasks as well the structure of local radio businesses, which may encourage employees to organize musical sound according to uniquely local principles, pressures, and parameters.

The record label Dolby JR and the radio station Frecuencia A Record were both instrumental in structuring the public meanings of contemporary Ayacuchano music. As performers incorporated international sounds beyond their traditional competencies, they grew to rely heavily upon studio players, sound engineers, and multitrack recording. Recording huayno music became an exercise in piecemeal, studio-based composition under the eyes and ears of recording personnel, rather than a matter of placing a mic before a well-honed group to capture a live performance. And as new experts helped musicians tailor artistic choices to audience tastes, records came to tack between existing musical values and the bottom line, navigating between artists' respect for tradition and the "modern" sound that they believed would attract listeners. Studio workers also built links to broadcasters that could be trusted to promote the style appropriately, while DJs and radio managers chose broadcasting techniques that would attract likely audiences. The shape of the public associated with contemporary Ayacuchano music depended on the network that linked all of these actors, and most of all on the motivations of those who directed the traffic of sound through these networks. Following Lila Abu-Lughod's dictum that the goal of media ethnography is to show "how particular communities and individuals both have been subjected to and have responded to the calls of [the culture industry]" (2005: 11), then, their actions sit at the heart of the analysis I present in this book.

The main sociomusical distinction that was reworked through contemporary Ayacuchano recordings was that between tradition, understood as clinging to Andean people and to cultural manifestations such as huayno music, and modernity, tied instead to foreign climes and to such international genres as rock, pop, and the pan-Andean music of neighboring countries. Hackneyed as this dichotomy may be to scholars, it remains very real and very pressing to most people. Where those who bear the burden of "traditional" status seek to redefine their place in the world, the successful mastery of "modern" aesthetics has often proved to be a useful strategy. Here recent approaches to globalization and cosmopolitanism are helpful in understanding Peruvian musical developments.

Globalization and Cosmopolitan Sounds

In its knowing ambivalence, Anna Tsing's use of "friction" as a figure for transnational cultural dynamics is a felicitous coinage (2005: 1). Nodding to the physics of two discrete bodies in contact, whose meeting creates heat and light but also irritation, it captures the productive yet fraught nature of the processes gathered under the rubric of "globalization." It has provided local actors with an unprecedented range of social, cultural, and material resources to use in managing their lives, and these are often put to work in productive ways. But just as often globalization hastens the waning of local cultural specificities, which are forced to compete on unequal terms with the products of transnational commerce. The angst, bewilderment, and outright rebellion that may arise in response to such circumstances are worthy of accounts that recognize the anxious register in which they are lived.

If the voluminous ethnomusicological literature on the subject has furnished a single grand lesson, it is that globalization does not create a uniform global village, but rather fosters "disjuncture and difference" as objects and discourses move variably across distinct contexts (Appadurai 1996: 27).[8] Traveling sounds are welded together in variable ways, and accounts of their transmission increasingly attend to the fine mechanics of the way that they take root. Showing how individuals acquire the capacities to engage such unfamiliar materials, and how determined agents harness them to more familiar cultural manifestations, they instantiate Thomas Turino's admonition to combine "large, overarching structuralist analyses" with attention to the question of "why and how people can do what they do in relation to given sets of objective conditions" (2000: 352).

Accounts of this kind show that transnational idioms and cultural hybrids are often used to make new sense of changing local worlds. They may be used to shore up local patterns, further reifying the boundaries of national or subnational groups, or they may drive new processes of social differentiation. In either case, the process whereby they are indigenized depends upon the means through which they circulate, and their effects "are worth tracing to particular configurations of power, education, age, and wealth in particular places" (Abu-Lughod 2005: 50). This processual injunction is critical, because any given mediascape allows for the constitution of many publics. The discrepant forms of global modernity that locals experience arise from the configuration of local networks, and more particularly from the actors who direct objects through them, linking consumers in ways that are specific to the network itself.

Because so much of globalization's cultural work happens in the realm of consumption, it is the emergent middle classes of the Global South that have typically taken center stage in work on transnational public culture (Appadurai and Breckenridge 1995; Liechty 2003; Mazzarella 2003; Pinney 2001). Their rising wealth and power, their access to technology, and their search for forms of identification that transcend the hierarchies dear to national elites have all made these new bourgeoisies uniquely important as originators and objects of public cultural discourse. Many of these discourses aim to secure local identities that are nevertheless intelligible in terms of cosmopolitan experiences associated with an elsewhere, to mutually imbricate categories of local and global experience in a way that is "neither purely emancipatory nor entirely disciplined but is a space of contestation in which individuals and groups seek to annex the global into their own practices of the modern" (Appadurai 1996: 4).[9] Contemporary Peru is no exception, and the imperative to "modernize" Andean music traverses all levels of society, generating different configurations of style and audience, each one drawing upon aspirational images of cosmopolitan cool and middle-class leisure that are in turn driven by a growing facility with transnational popular forms. But this trend is also transected by a growing public pride in Andean heritage. Under these conditions, musicians and mediators experiment constantly with the limits of genre, seeking to satisfy the consumerist desires of an audience whose tastes are permanently emergent. And as subjects struggling to mitigate the local hegemony of global cultural discourse, they become the agentive nodes through which the terms of the global and the local are remade in everyday life.

Indeed, insofar as it produces vibration, friction creates sound, in addition to light, heat, and pain, and its easy mobility, its ability to signify in multiple registers at once, and its rapid response to changing patterns of consumption all make popular music a particularly effective bellwether of developments in the global order. Contemporary Ayacuchano huayno might be seen as one genre of noisy, globalizing friction, insofar as its success has depended upon its engagement with the dichotomy between "local tradition" and "foreign modernity." Its musicians and mediators have sought to create a "vernacular modern" style (Neyazi 2010: 908; see also Donham 1990; Knauft 2002), a musical "translation of sites . . . which confuses what is the general and what is the specific, what is the part and what is the whole" (Bhabha, cited in Pinney 2001: 14), and by allowing listeners to demonstrate their mastery of modernity's sonic categories, musicians and mediators allowed listeners to claim the right to be treated as modern people. However, if the style incited new kinds of Andean subjectivity, then the process also involved the preferential selection of certain local experiences over others. Rather than challenging hegemonic categories, those involved in this discourse often simply redistributed their terms, pitting new forms of cosmopolitanism against new kinds of parochialism. It is for this reason that a history of recent Andean popular music must move beyond the generality that fusion is inevitable, to show how new hybrids depend upon local histories of representation and power.

The Country of *todas las sangres*:
Race, Power, and Geography in Perspective

Peru has long been divided along parallel lines of race, culture, and geography, and the very notion of a Peruvian nation-state has been called "nothing but a semantic excess" (Macera, cited in Cotler 1978: 16). The country is usually conceptualized according to a division between the western Pacific

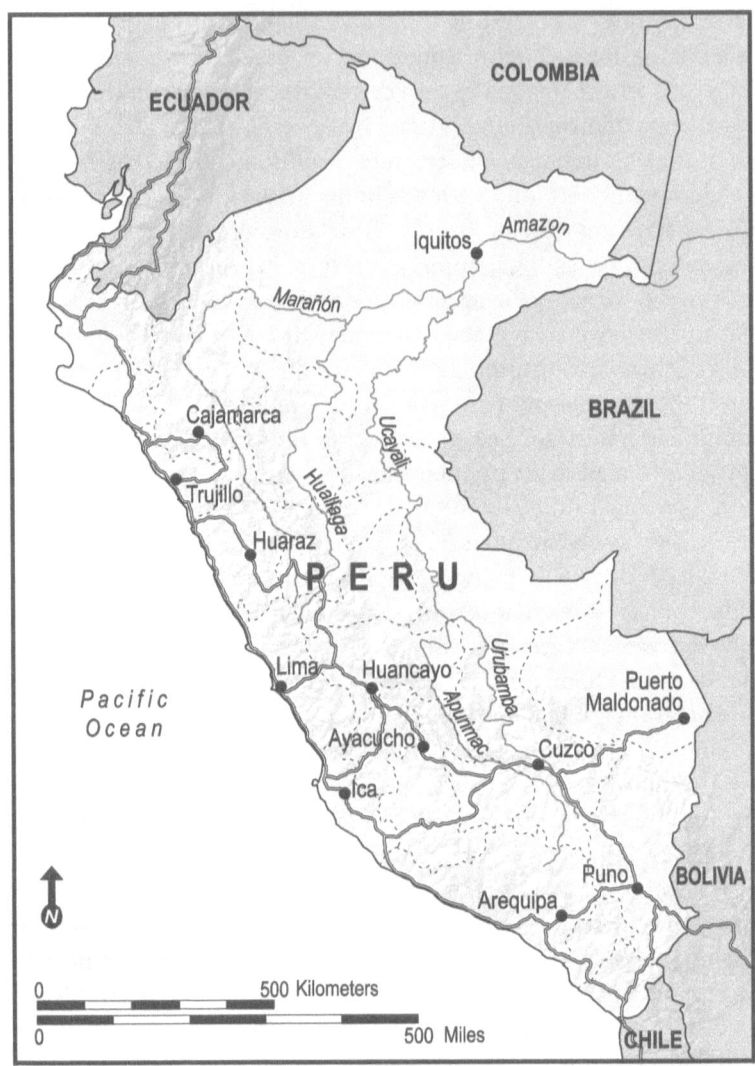

Map 1. Peru

littoral, the Andes Mountains, and the Amazon basin, a tripartite model that glosses coincident demographic distinctions (see map 1). The eastern jungle lowlands have always been sparsely populated, and today they house only 10 percent of the country's 29 million inhabitants. Instead, the Andes Mountains held most of the population before and after the Spanish arrival in 1532, when the invading Europeans overthrew the ruling Inca and pressed the large, complex indigenous communities of the highlands into service. Iberian immigrants began to settle in the Andes, extracting wealth in the form of tribute labor, but the Spanish capital was established at faraway Lima, in the coastal desert between the Pacific Ocean and the mountains, and this template, pitting the coastal European seat of power against subordinate Andean and Amazonian regions, guided Peru's development until well after independence in 1821. From within opulent Lima, Spaniards and *criollos* (Americans of Spanish descent) governed indigenous polities they rarely came to know—unless they gained political posts in one of the Andean towns where settlers kept European houses, customs, and centers of governance. Meanwhile, Indians became either impoverished peasants, peons living in indentured servitude, or migrant workers clustered around the edges of cities. Nor were disparities limited to political and monetary matters: indigenous cultural manifestations were widely reviled by colonists, who sought to civilize the locals.

This social structure was neither monolithic nor static.[10] But from the standpoint of Lima, the Andean region has always stood for backwardness, its isolated cities only dimly lit by the light of Western civilization. Other Latin American countries eventually created narratives of national identity centered on the celebration of diversity (see Turino 2003; Wade 1997), but Peruvian elites largely refused to transact a common sense of nationhood with their subalterns. Instead, their notion of progress "rested upon the assumption that . . . the alien world of the rural majority was one of marginal importance, which civilization would sooner or later cause to disappear" (Matos Mar 1984: 100). Nation-building focused on coastal criollo interests, and Andean peoples were recognized mainly through praise for the achievements of the ancient Inca—an easy and meaningless rhetorical concession, since they were long dead and did not trouble postcolonial hierarchies (Méndez Gastelmundi 1993).

This dichotomous vision gave an uneasy place to highland mestizos, who typically lived apart from the sphere of indigenous culture and belief, but who were liable to be considered Indians by those who looked down on the Andean region. Although the term "mestizo" denotes mixture, and although mestizo traditions combined elements of European and Andean provenance, these have never been considered signs of Indianness by mestizos themselves. Over the colonial and early republican periods, mestizos instead strove to enter the cultural orbit of the criollo elites and force a blurring of the line between themselves and those of "pure" European extraction. On the whole, it is difficult to draw clear lines between indigenous, mestizo, and coastal criollo cultures, especially given that indigenous

Andeans too adopted nominally "European" cultural practices long ago. Here, a sense of historical context is useful.

The foundational binary of the Andean colonial scheme made Indians juridically inferior to Europeans (Gootenberg 1991). However, terms such as "Spaniard," "criollo," and "Indian" quickly became complicated, as interaction between settlers, subjects, and slaves created people whose mixed ancestry defied such neat schemes. The term "mestizo" came to be widely used in this context, first as a simple label for people of mixed Spanish and Indian ancestry, who enjoyed a status superior to that of Indians. But miscegenation created ever finer gradations of Spanish and Indian descent, and the capricious nature of genetics made appearance unreliable as a gauge of a person's status, since mestizos might as commonly have "typically indigenous" as "typically European" features. Finally, "mixed" individuals made various lifestyle choices, adopting the lifeways of either Spanish settlers or colonized Indians with equal facility. Under these circumstances, ancestry and physical traits became unreliable gauges of social identity on their own. Determinations of ethnicity came instead to involve a combination of "genetic heritage, phenotypic attributes, or deliberate adoption of clothing and occupations reserved for persons of mixed blood" (Wightman 1990: 95; cf. Sturm 2002: 140).

In practice, this ethnoracial scheme of classification meant that highland residents were considered mestizos to the extent that they mastered the mores and practices that marked one as a "decent person [*decente*]" (Mendoza 2000; see also de la Cadena 2000). Axes of distinction included residence (rural vs. urban), occupation (peasant, laborer, or artisan vs. bourgeois or landowner), language (Quechua, Aymara, or bilingual vs. Spanish monolingual), and other customs and habits, such as attire and gustatory preferences, understood as more or less "Indian" in nature. Furthermore, since a mastery of "decent" habits entitled one to social mobility, wealth itself became a sign for mestizo status, and the term came in circular fashion to denote the "[superior] position of an individual in the social division of labor [rather] than . . . any specific biological or phenotypic characteristic" (Mendoza 2000: 12). In the most general sense, then, the term "mestizo" has come to denote Andean elites, whose superiority might rest upon riches, social capital, or cultural capital, but rarely upon "race" per se, considered in isolation.

Since individuals and family lines might accrue sufficient capital to shed a stigmatized Indian identity, commentators long treated Andean society as race-blind: terribly riven by prejudices of class and culture, but indifferent to descent (e.g., van den Berghe and Primov 1977). Recent theorists, however, have shown conclusively that the everyday categories used to define "decency" remain rooted in, and help to sustain, race-based understandings of behavior even when they operate in ostensibly nonbiological realms (Mendoza 2000; Poole 1997; Weismantel and Eisenman 1998). In a powerful analysis, Weismantel (2001) has considered archetypes of Andean storytelling, including Indian-killing monsters that take the form of white men and *mestiza* women who are at once dirty, proud, and sexually available. Such tropes are rarely used as labels for real people, but they keep age-old notions of white power and Andean abjection available.

The persistence and power of these categories is exacerbated by national-level colonial legacies: whatever privileges mestizos command in the highlands, the Andes remain negatively racialized in the Peruvian imagination, "classed down" before a connotatively European coast (cf. Parker 1998: 233).[11] Mestizo elites always considered themselves peers of Lima's criollo aristocracy, but visitors often insist on singling out their dark skin, high cheekbones, and "mixed" cultural practices as evidence that they are something less than that.[12] The humiliation involved with becoming the object of racism leads Andean mestizos to perform constant, often unconscious identity work aimed at repairing the boundary between Indian and non-Indian and ensuring that they stand on the comfortable side of it.[13] *Mestizaje* (mestizoness), then, might be understood as a discursive technology for mitigating the effects of racialization, a compendium of devices that allows individuals to secure a relatively advantageous place within a hierarchical scheme even as it sustains the inequalities upon which hierarchy depends.[14] It is urgent to clarify the way that this discourse works, but unless denunciations are matched by effective accounts of the way that Andean elites come to adopt and express their identities, it will remain impossible to fully grasp the pressures at work (cf. Hale 2006; Romero 2001). Studies that decry without situating elite ambivalence about indigeneity do little justice to the complex position inhabited by mestizos, who may feel their Andean specificity deeply, but who also seek to construct identarian projects distinct from both Andean indigenous and coastal criollo premises, which of course are not their own (cf. Mendoza 2008; Tarica 2008; Turino 1984).

This book aims to clarify such performances of Andeanness, and this means specifying the rhetorical categories in play—no easy task, since in Andean Peru, people avoid the use of explicit ethnoracial terms (Fuenzalida 1970) and instead rely upon the implications of other, often community-specific words to convey difference (Romero 2001).[15] I draw upon labels specific to Ayacucho, especially the term *huamanguino*, which derives from the colonial name of the city (Huamanga), but which also connotes social distinction and a connection to the Hispanophilia of the city's old bourgeoisie. Allied terms include the adjective *señorial* (gentlemanly) and the quality of "sentiment," which is something of a folk-musicological term describing the bittersweet feeling that infuses Ayacuchano performance.

Rarely, however, do I describe real people as "mestizos" or "Indians," even though I have been using the terms heuristically thus far as an aid in sketching the racial ideologies that subsist in contemporary Andean social interaction. This is because very few of the people involved describe themselves in those terms. Andean ethnographies often portray "mestizos," "Indians," and their behaviors, and elsewhere I too have written about indigenous performers who adopt such terms of identification (Tucker 2011). However, in the research upon which this book rests, I heard them used as personalized labels in only three contexts: conversations with a decided minority of scholar-activists, who assumed them in a pointedly political fashion; tense social situations where men used them to insult one another; and uncomfortable conversations near the beginning of my research, where I naively asked friends about them, misled about the taboo nature of such frank talk by the casual treatment of racial terminology in Andeanist literature. I quickly learned how rare and rude such explicitness is among upwardly mobile people such as those who are the subject of this book, and by now the reason for this should be clear: self-ascription to the mestizo category means public acceptance of a possible indigenous ancestry that is widely seen as a hindrance to personal advancement.[16]

Precisely because open discussion is so rare, it is worth specifying the categories that are used instead, the racialized genealogies behind them, and the way that they collude in the perpetuation of colonial hierarchies. Like Weismantel, I am more interested in the tropes that distinguish respectable and undesirable identities and the ways in which they are deployed than in fixing identities that they do not claim upon people who have not asked me to do so.[17] I do use terms such as "mestizo" in discussing sites of discourse where they actually appeared, including historical and literary documents or the occasional interview, and to describe cultural artifacts, which are indeed regularly characterized in these terms. However, insofar as this account is not about "mestizos" or "Indians," but about people seeking dignity and the cultural tropes that are useful in claiming it, I am loath to reify categories that are more fluid in practice than in print.

This in turn raises thorny questions of subaltern representation. Especially given that my account focuses on people and ideas with a relationship to indigenous Andean culture that is ambivalent at best, it is reasonable to ask whether the voices of Indians lie anywhere in the text, even after this exegesis of fluidity. In fact, many of the people who appear in these pages would be described, by scholars in print and by everyday Peruvians in private, as Indians or perhaps as *cholos*, a word that describes urban migrants seen as being in transition away from an Indian identity. Such individuals unite the diacritics of rural origin, membership in the working class, and bilingualism that furnish the bases of these identities. However, because I am mainly interested in the way that cultural tropes enable social advancement irrespective of background, it is no more sound to specify who is "really indigenous" than it to specify who is "really mestizo."

I do occasionally discuss the point of view represented by *huayno norteño* artists such as Dina Paucar and connoisseurs of the style such as the radio director Fernando Cruz, who appear along with a few of their fellows in the pages that follow. All of these individuals resist the notions of artistic superiority associated with Ayacuchano huayno and instead speak through discourses of subalternity, often by arguing that their preferred style, in its themes of marginality and its closer ties to dance, reflects the life world and habits of Peru's working class with much greater fidelity than the esoteric, cerebral world associated with Ayacuchano music. Again and again, I was told by such people that the Ayacuchano style was "nice," in certain circumstances, but terribly boring and not suited to the kinds of dancing and emotional catharsis that they sought from a weekend's entertainment.

However, insofar as they do not demand the label, these people should not be taken as speaking for Indianness, the social and musical aesthetics of which have already been explored in many excellent works.[18] Instead, they should be taken as inhabitants of one position in the changing scheme of identarian oppositions that subtends Andean daily life. If Peru's Andean popular music scene was and is marked by a binary divide, it is not one that distinguishes indigenous from non-indigenous listeners. Rather, it places on one side those who stake their right to respect upon the public mastery of the qualities of decency, intellectual seriousness, and educational uplift historically associated with Ayacuchano music and allied styles, and on the other, those who define an ethics of taste in relation to artists who embody an ethic of hard work and personal advancement, and whose music also appeals to embodied pleasure. These paths to respect are rooted in colonial ideologies that once marked the difference between Indians and their alters, and insofar as they still mark the difference between respectable (*decente*)

Andeanness and a version of Andeanness which is not, they continue to sustain old distinctions in a new register. However, this does not mean that they are always or even primarily deployed in order to classify the self or the other as Indian or nonindigenous.

Finally, I do not mean to claim that there is an easy correlation between a person's identity, however ascribed, and the music that is considered to represent that social position: of course many people listen to music that seems to go against type, and not every listening act is part of a strategy. Contemporary Ayacuchano huayno sometimes echoes through proletarian barrios, and well-off citizens sometimes listen to chicha or huayno norteño, because either the melancholy of the former or the lively nature of the latter suits the momentary recreative needs of listeners. I do, however, claim that Andean musical genres have become useful in emblematizing and arguing for status, and that musicians, mediators, and audiences all employ them accordingly as aspirational technologies of the self. During the time that I conducted research in Peru, contemporary Ayacuchano huayno was widely treated and understood as such a resource, and it lies at the heart of this book because its association with a self-aware discourse of sociocultural transformation made it an unparalleled window into the role of Andean art in Peruvian life. Overall, I mean to show how those who follow it locate themselves and their art forms within evolving systems of social relations, and to demonstrate how Andean public culture becomes differentiated as traditional sources of cultural authority get displaced by the operations of the popular-culture industry. Here old boundaries are undone and new musical distinctions are used to classify artists as well as the audiences they gather. Lima has been a uniquely important location for these processes, both because of its position as the national capital and because of its recent demographic history.

Bourgeois Andeans and New Limeños: Migration and Class Formation

In the 1940s Lima entered a period of industrialization, attracting massive numbers from the stagnant highlands and making it into Peru's biggest "Andean" city. Rapid growth brought infrastructural challenges, and by the 1970s the capital had been transformed from the garden city described by earlier visitors into an overcrowded warren choked with shoddy public transportation. The "official" economy was strained beyond capacity, so newcomers turned to the "informal" sector, trading goods of dubious legality or quality in the central market. Meanwhile Lima grew laterally as migrants seized desert land on its outskirts, spreading south, north, and east from downtown to fill three expanding "cones" that became synonymous with economic misery (Meneses Rivas 1998). Finally, its old elites withdrew from the city center, taking shelter in nearby seaside resorts or new subdivisions against the flanks of the Andes, all of which were eventually incorporated into the capital itself.

The demographic shift was paralleled by a cultural transformation as migrants recreated practices from home, filling Lima with unfamiliar sounds, sights, and smells.[19] Solidarity clubs tied to regions of origin were centers of such activities, and Andean cultural adaptation therefore followed inherited lines of community differentiation at first (Altamirano 1984; Lloréns Amico 1991; Turino 1993).[20] But new, pan-regional cultural forms soon transected these parochial retentions and grew to dominate the life of the city, leading Matos Mar to posit that "the culture of the elite is retreating [and] a new Peruvian culture begins to form" (1984: 107; see also Franco 1991; Sandoval 2000). Intrigued, scholars increasingly sought out and examined emergent patterns in political tactics, work ethics, comic performances, soccer fandom, and popular music, everywhere finding evidence of new identities and behaviors that were grounded in neither Andean tradition nor the hegemonic terms of criollo society.[21]

However, the process of social realignment was not as linear as predicted, and the "new Limeños" have never coalesced into a unified group with a common sense of purpose. Andean Lima is widely recognized today as the protagonist of Peru's ongoing national narrative, but its "forms of representation are very partial, and strongly anchored in the microsocial dimension" (DESCO 2005: 55). Despite this fractured character, the Andean bourgeoisie has acquired a special role in the ongoing involution of Limeño society, for if the informal marketplace represented a second-class path to prosperity, it also gave hardworking migrants a way to earn capital. It placed them in a financial position to demand representation and drive the city's public culture. Fuller's definition nicely captures the parameters of this emergent social group, composed of

> urban people who are grouped in mid-level commerce, artisanal guilds, liberal professions, the state and private sectors, technocrats, and medium entrepreneurs. They are characterized by the fact that work they perform is not manual, and their levels of specialization and education allow them to aspire to the status of "gente decente" [decent people] in contradistinction to a "plebe" dedicated to manual work and with lower levels of education. (Fuller 2002: 420)

Among this ascendant Andean middle class, consumption has become a key realm for demonstrating reserves of cultural capital commensurate with their claims to social distinction. In fact, given Peru's severely unequal distribution of wealth, the public performance of good taste has long been an important way of establishing one's pedigree, allowing an individual of little means to become "as respectable as he could convince the world he was" (Parker 1998: 27). Over the 1980s and 1990s, a new demand for symbols of distinction led media entrepreneurs toward the rising consumerist desires of the Andean middle class, making them "transmitters *par excellence* of urban lifestyles, [and providing] migrants with decisive elements for situating themselves in the city" (Balbi 1997: 20).

The materials that circulate in this milieu usually mediate inherited and emergent criteria of social distinction, pursuing an Andean bourgeoisie whose cultural identity is "not exactly something that is discovered, but invented via selective memory" (Fuller 2002: 437). The objects that compete for the attention of the Andean public at any given time include old practices with a limited regional audience and newer cultural forms that seek to capture the entire Andean community, as well as others that are aimed to emergent fragments of that community. The success of Ayacuchano sounds and performers in this process depended on the values that had become attached to Ayacucho's musical style in the early twentieth century, on one hand, and upon recent sociopolitical events in the highland city, on the other.

Ayacucho: Conflict and Recovery

Today Ayacucho is indelibly associated with Peru's brutal dirty war between Shining Path guerrillas and government forces, which grew out of the city's university and engulfed most of the country by the late 1980s. However, those grim images have not entirely replaced others of longer standing. Probably all citizens can cite the Battle of Ayacucho, which sealed the country's independence in 1824, and after which the city is named: before this date the city was called Huamanga, and locals still tend to use the colonial name, reserving "Ayacucho" for the department (a national subdivision, equivalent to a state) of which it is the capital. Other Peruvians might mention the city's celebrated Holy Week, which involves lavish but emotionally severe processions reenacting the passion of Christ. These are organized around the city's famously large number of churches, constructed between 1540 and the end of the eighteenth century, when colonial Huamanga was an affluent manufacturing center—a fact dimly recalled in the city's moniker as the "Handicraft Capital of Peru." Together with the city's colonnaded plaza, historic mansions, and cobbled streets, the churches lend Ayacucho an aura of stately dignity. But they also stand as sad reminders of its long-lost economic vigor.

The city sits at a moderate altitude in the south-central Andes, within a temperate valley lauded for its blue skies and mild temperatures and lamented for its broken, barren landscape. Unsuited for industrial agriculture, the region was seized by stagnation when the axes of trade shifted in the late colonial period. The economic decline that took root at that time has never really relented, and Ayacucho's hinterland remains impoverished even by the dismal standards of the Andes. The department has long been one of the poorest in the country, its scattered, Quechua-speaking peasant majority eking out a living via subsistence farming, herding, and the petty cash generated by bringing the products of those activities to market. Even for relatively privileged city dwellers, physical isolation impeded participation in the national economy, and no paved roads linked the city to the coast until 1998.

Despite widespread underdevelopment, Ayacucho's urban middle classes have historically found steady mid-level employment in law, education, government, and regional commerce. This bourgeois sector increasingly became a local elite over the late nineteenth century, when the last remnants of Ayacucho's colonial nobility and its tiny landowning class fled to the coast.[22] As elsewhere in the Andes (see Mendoza 2000), the gentlemen of the city center were able to adopt the niche abandoned by their erstwhile social superiors because their relative enculturation to criollo lifeways granted them credibility as "decent people" (see Fuller 2002: 429). Their status derived more from their command of symbolic capital than from their acquisition of wealth, and in Ayacucho no symbol of social standing was as important as education (Gamarra Carrillo 1996; Degregori 1997). Absent other resources for mobility, formal learning has long been both an index for and means of attaining social rank, and although the city's white-collar jobs earned scant pay, they allowed learned citizens to distinguish themselves from the laboring Indian plebe.

Indeed, prior to the emergence of the Shining Path, Ayacucho's most important sociopolitical movement was the one that led to the reopening of its state university, the Universidad Nacional San Cristóbal de Huamanga (UNSCH), founded in 1677 and shuttered in 1886. Residents of the early twentieth century agitated for the institution's refounding, arguing that it would stimulate the economy and grant poorer citizens access to educational capital. When it finally reopened in 1959, it attracted distinguished researchers and students from well beyond Peru, and it had a decisive effect on the city. The sudden influx of young scholars made sleepy Ayacucho a bustling university town even as Andean peasants began moving en masse to urban centers, and Ayacucho's population rose from 17,000 to 43,000 between 1940 and 1972 (Caballero Martín 1995). Together, changing demographics and the presence of the university fostered deep attitudinal shifts. Bohemian intellectuals brought relaxed moral and sartorial codes, challenging the reserved tenor of social interaction. They also brought new visions of social equality forged in Latin America's leftist intellectual circles, admixtures of socialism and ethnic politics that threatened age-old hierarchies. As a state university, the UNSCH was free to any who passed its entrance examinations, and within its halls people from different social classes gathered on newly egalitarian ground. Taken together, these intellectual, political, and demographic trends "fostered a modernizing spirit, capable of transforming social structures," and by 1974 it could be asserted that "no one remembers the surnames of the old [elite]: the [new] bourgeoisie now dominate the city" (Diez Hurtado 2003: 98).

Still, this increased mobility never created the interethnic and interclass leveling that many had anticipated. University activities encouraged respect for rural-indigenous society, but social distinctions were still defined "in terms of 'decency' and 'culture'" (Diez Hurtado 2003: 140), and poor migrants remained marginalized to the extent that they hewed to their heritage rather than adopting Ayacucho's mestizo customs. Living conditions for most remained precarious, and as in Lima, migrants resorted to informal labor and land seizure, their rough adobe barrios clustering along the roads leading out of the city and eventually climbing the valley's steep western wall. The persistence of inequalities helped foster frustrations that provided the conditions for the emergence of the Shining Path.

A hard-line Maoist group dedicated to destroying Peru's capitalist state, the Shining Path was incubated in the halls of the UNSCH beginning in the mid-1960s under the leadership of Abimael Guzmán, then a professor of philosophy and an expert on Kantian thought.[23] He and his allies recruited acolytes from among the students, forming a guerrilla cadre that would spread the group's ideology throughout the countryside as the students were assigned to rural teaching posts. This ideology was grounded in a view of violence as a cleansing fire, laying waste to the "feudal" order and forcing peasants to seek refuge among "liberated" communities.[24] When the group initiated armed actions in 1980, it lived up to its rhetoric, eliminating shopkeepers, town mayors, utility workers, government employees, unsympathetic villagers, and others who might be construed as agents of capitalism. The armed forces, meanwhile, assumed that they faced a ragged, generalized ethnic-nationalist revolt rather than a minoritarian, systematically Marxist political movement. Puzzled and afraid, stationed in an alien landscape among people who often spoke a different language, soldiers made grievous decisions, failing to discriminate between insurgents and bystanders, committing atrocity after atrocity in their attempts to cow the local population.[25]

Between 1982, when Ayacucho was placed under martial law, and the mid-1990s, when the violence subsided following the capture of Guzmán, the combatants devastated the Andean region. Seventy thousand Peruvians were killed, an indeterminate number were disappeared, and migrants poured into relatively secure cities, leaving rural Ayacucho littered with ruined villages. Fields, army barracks, and soccer stadiums continue to reveal mass graves dug by both sides, while highland cities suffer such lingering pathologies as gang activity and partisan resentments. And Ayacuchanos are painfully aware that they are widely considered "reds" or "terrorists," especially if they have attended the UNSCH—which retains something of a radical, though moderately so, image.[26]

A side effect of the conflict was the revival of traditional Ayacuchano music. The city's old huayno style had been considered both patrician and dowdy by the 1970s, a formal art associated with the salons and soirees of the city's old elite. However, during the 1980s young local musicians took it up once more as a means of communicating their feelings about the violence that raged around them. Their considerable talent, combined with a nationwide hunger for accounts from the combat zone, ensured that Ayacuchano songs traveled far beyond the local milieu, and the city's musicians were increasingly drawn to Lima, with its large, ready-made fan base of Andean listeners. After the end of the conflict, artists returned to traditional themes of love and longing, but the style only grew in popularity after musicians and mediators repackaged it as a self-conscious symbol of cosmopolitan chic and marketed it to Lima's Andean bourgeoisie. In this form, too, the style returned home, and there it was put to similar use. Ayacucho remains a small, economically marginal city with a population of about 125,000, but like Lima it is socially stratified, and social mobility, largely afforded by the university, has driven the emergence of a precarious middle class. The legitimacy that Lima has bestowed upon determined forms of Andean public culture, in turn, leads such ascendant citizens to seek out those forms. In this sense, media circulation increasingly obviates the very division between coastal and Andean spaces that has been so fundamental to Peruvian discourse, bringing citizens throughout the country to repertoires of class and cultural identity unprecedented in their scope and influence.

Latter-Day Indigenismo: Popular Music and Ethnic Discourse in Twenty-First-Century Peru

Developments at the turn of the twenty-first century intersected with all of these structural changes to place the relevance of old social categories under new scrutiny. The growing political use of multiculturalist rhetoric, for instance, fostered intense discussion about the relationship of Andean peoples to Peru's national idea. Such conversations crested during the presidency of Alejandro Toledo (2001–6), modern Peru's first Andean leader. Toledo's performative Andeanness, with its "peculiar and erratic appropriation of the indigenous imaginary," may have remained "blind and deaf before indigenous problems" (Pajuelo 2007: 29; see also Green 2006), but by playing up his origins and using highland sound and imagery in his public appearances, he gave bearers of Andean culture a platform of no small visibility.[27] The neoliberal policies of Toledo and his predecessors also helped to foster an efflorescence of Andean imagery by largely devolving state involvement in cultural discourse to the private sphere (Vich 2006b). Even as the rhetorical recognition for multiculturalism grew, independent cultural producers faced a deregulated mediascape, and with barriers to participation lowered they increased production, seeking to capture consumers newly enjoined to recognize the highland heritage of themselves and their fellow-citizens.

These developments dynamized Peruvian conversations over culture and representation, but they failed to significantly alleviate Andean inequality.[28] In this sense they provided a modern-day echo of indigenismo, Andean Peru's most influential, if ultimately unsuccessful, movement for cultural revindication. Indigenismo flourished in the early twentieth century (c. 1910–40), and although its ideals varied across time and space, its intellectuals were united in calling for a version of national identity that would recognize Peru's Andean majority. Despite the name, it was a concern of Andean elites, mostly bypassing the direct input of indigenous peoples. This class had been weakened in the late nineteenth century as the Peruvian state centralized industry and government in the coastal capital. Languishing, and stung by the prejudices of Lima high society, intellectuals reacted by developing a counterhegemonic national project. In pursuit of their goals, they documented, adapted, and disseminated indigenous practices in virtually every field of endeavor. They conducted field research, publishing their findings in scholarly journals. They painted, photographed, and wrote sympathetic fiction about indigenous subjects, arguing against injustice and for the richness of Andean culture. All of these efforts were directed at producing a body of knowledge that could be used in developing the region, but they were also a means of defining the practices and symbols that would be used as the building blocks of a new national culture.

The indigenistas achieved few concrete results within the political and economic realms, but they were successful at forging a vision of regional identity based on the symbolic valorization of indigenous lifeways. Aspects of it were taken up readily by government ideologues, who found in the patronage of Andean culture an easy way to demonstrate sympathy for Andean concerns while avoiding serious investment in fixing Andean problems. However, given the assumptions that underlay indigenismo, its widespread success is also its most dubious legacy. It was defined by the attitude that vanguardist intellectuals were uniquely qualified to forge a collective identity for Peru and a political project on behalf of indigenous peoples. It reduced the latter to the raw material of a nascent, putatively shared nation, rather than distinct communities interested in self-determination or interlocutors of equal stature. Worse, the images and practices singled out for acclaim were either those identified with the vanished Inca or those that were refined for presentation by educated folklorists, rather than those performed and valued within contemporary indigenous communities.

The contemporary relationship between Andean popular music and ethnic discourse should be understood partly in light of this inheritance. Discussions of highland heritage continue to revolve around the priorities of nonindigenous elites, and to the extent that their preferred forms are promoted as "Andean culture," they displace indigenous alternatives. Indeed, contemporary mestizo performance and consumption often act as a kind of surrogate indigeneity, a means of inhabiting a newly valued ethnic subject position, without requiring that adherents bear the burdens associated with indigenous status. Overall, developments within the Andean music scene demonstrate the ongoing diversification of the mestizo imaginary and clarify the developing parameters of debates about Andean heritage, but they give little cause for optimism. Peruvian citizens feel a growing sense of comfort with declaring and defending an Andean subject position that has always been that of the marginalized majority. But instead of promoting common cause, records, DJs, liner notes, broadcast contexts, and performance venues all differentiate the Andean public into competing subsectors, pitting the bourgeois, upwardly mobile audience for contemporary Ayacuchano music against the distinct sociomusical culture of Peru's Andean proletariat. As fluctuating social boundaries become reified in and through musical consumption, they not only reinscribe old distinctions in new terms, but also subsume finer distinctions among the highly diverse peoples and regions of the Andes, creating overly broad categories of Andeanness differentiated primarily by class.

The contemporary Andean music scene also clarifies the stakes involved in treating popular music as a manifestation of cultural identity. An overwhelming emphasis on identity in recent literature has led to calls for a hiatus in the discussion of a term that is often assumed to explain musical action in a rather facile manner (Samuels 2004). Indeed, the theoretical reduction of all musical activity to acts of identity work neglects much of what makes music important. But this does not mean that people fail to recognize the notion of a meaningful relationship between the two. Neither does it displace the insight that people find musical activity to be an effective way to realize various aspects of their personalities. It is, to the contrary, abundantly clear that people often use cultural forms in this way. For this reason, it seems more fruitful to couch the development of social categories in more precise and realistic terms, while going "beyond identity" (Brubaker and Cooper 2000) to recognize the way that everyday interactions with material culture motivate a sense of self.

In this sense, this book does not show how contemporary Ayacuchano huayno "stood for" the social group with which it became associated. Instead, it seeks to describe how the work of mediation makes shared symbols available for people seeking to understand a changing social milieu. The outstanding contribution of recent public cultural studies is their attention to the processes of distribution and circulation, which draw people into conversations about the stuff of everyday life, sharpening their awareness of social categories. The figures that animate public cultural discourse alert even casual consumers to locally meaningful terms of debate, whether or not they identify directly with the materials they encounter. Treating media circulation as a way to build communities of shared reference rather than shared substance allows us to specify how popular culture generates mutual recognition, without positing that these communities depend upon clear boundaries, internal coherence, or essential attributes. The task of public cultural analysis, in other words, is to show how media objects become sites of identification and recognition. It is to ask how particular individuals are gathered into overlapping circuits of consumption, which thicken through repeated engagement, thereby fostering a sense of shared investment amidst the heterogeneous social and physical spaces of real life.

In the case of contemporary Peru, musicians and mediators made patent the possibility of an ascendant Andean, bourgeois subject position and invited listeners to inhabit it by harnessing it to a variety of national and international sounds. The identification between sound and society was not merely a logical culmination of tendencies latent within Peru's changing climate, and its success did not depend upon the way that the music "represented" a preexisting social group. Rather, the artists and mediators associated with particular sounds and circuits of production organized audiences within Lima's migrant community, and it was their actions that drew people to share the very points of reference that constituted a sense of distinction in the first place.

TWO

The Andean Music Scene

My friend Ana has probably taught me more than anyone about musical consumption in Andean Peru. A student at Ayacucho's national university during the time that I lived there, she spent a lot of time hanging out at my house and listening to music. She asked about my research, interested to learn aspects of local history that were obscure to her generation, and she kept me up to date about what she and her peers made of ongoing musical developments. We attended concerts together and she borrowed CDs from me, so I knew her listening habits well. I found her an excellent guide to the distinctions that mattered and was grateful for her insights.

I was left somewhat perplexed, though, after a formal interview with her. As she listened to the songs that I had selected for discussion, she told me that any music worth one's while grew from the soil of local history and captured the emotional tenor of real events. She upbraided contemporary Ayacuchano artists for fusing the city's huayno style with foreign pop genres, complaining that the musicians vulgarized the style and diluted its specificities. She had even harsher words for chicha, a tropical Peruvian bricolage associated with proletarian migrants, and for huayno norteño, which drew in turn upon elements of chicha. I already knew that she, like most of her university peers, disliked these latter genres. However, her dismissal of contemporary Ayacucho huayno was puzzling, since this was precisely the kind of music that she most often solicited from me.

This gap was dimly illuminated when she asked me to collaborate on a project for her music appreciation course. The professor, a staunch traditionalist, had assigned her group a presentation about the 1980s, and they asked me to bring my guitar and accompany them as they sang. After we performed before a room full of bemused students, Ana's professor launched into a diatribe about cultural etiolation. He pointed to my presence as evidence of traditional huayno's superior qualities, erroneously describing my research as a project in defense of it and using me as a foil for railing against the violence that contemporary performers were visiting upon it. At the time I doubted that this classroom harangue had a significant effect on listening habits, and it is possible that it did not even ring true to its speaker, for when I later recounted the experience to a friend who ran one of Ayacucho's corner store-*cum*-cantinas, she gave a derisive laugh and said, "Oh yeah? Then why is he in here drinking to those songs every Friday night?"[1]

I was initially frustrated by such discrepancies between word and deed. They made it hard to discern the neat congruence that I expected to find between style, ideology, and listenership. Indeed, listeners' reports of their preferences are often poor guides to their actual habits, since learned categories of aesthetic legitimacy and shame determine the image that people seek to project in public. But precisely for this reason, these everyday performances of taste revealed the extent to which distinct values have accrued to different Andean styles, and they suggested the risks to personal standing run by those whose preferences traduced established categories. It is possible that, like Ana's professor, some listeners framed their habits in terms that they believed were important to me. But clearly a hierarchy of taste, distributed through institutional sites of authority, left people embarrassed to acknowledge that they were invested in music that had been declared trivial.

In this chapter, I survey the main genres that animated the Andean music scene over the twentieth century and into the twenty-first. Popular and academic sources often present the Andean scene as homogeneous, but it is fractious and full of contending musics, and its evolving oppositions are key to understanding its social efficacy. This is no simple matter: even the brief sketch given above indicates the bewildering confusion of styles and substyles that compete for attention. Huayno itself can be subdivided into a number of regional styles, some of which have also acquired extraregional connotations. Because of this complexity, I do not present an overview of all Peru's styles. I largely leave aside, for instance, the transnational dance music, rock 'n' roll, *balada*, and other popular genres that fill Peruvian airwaves and Andean lives. Neither do I treat the valses, *marineras*, and related Afro-Peruvian genres, collectively dubbed *música criolla*, that are historically associated with Lima's criollo community.[2] This not because they have disappeared, nor because they lie outside the purview of the people who appear in these pages. A visit to an Andean household around lunchtime is as likely as not to reveal a television tuned to the daily television show *Mediodía criollo*, probably the dominant venue for the style's continuing dissemination. And all of these styles appear peripherally throughout the book, because they are often points of comparison and competition for artists working in Andean styles—indeed, Ayacuchano artists have always used the renowned elegance of *vals* music as a point of comparison for their own style. Rather, I leave them aside because otherwise they fall outside the series of oppositions that motivate musical development within the Andean scene.

I begin with an overview of huayno before describing two key musical movements of the early twentieth century, each related to the indigenista movement, and the pan-Andean music that descends from them. I then return to huayno, describing the way that the recording industry stabilized relations between regional styles and their social connotations at mid-century, an account that emphasizes the Ayacuchano variant. I then move on to discuss its latter-day transformations. I end by describing chicha music and huayno norteño, which are the musical figures against which artists associated with Ayacuchano music and allied styles have been contrasted in recent times. My narrative is largely drawn from my own observations and experiences as a student, consumer, and observer of Andean musical practice in Peru between 2000 and 2008. However, it is enlivened by the insights of the popular musicians, listeners, and media workers from whom I learned to think about musical value and fandom.

"The Spiritual Story of the Mestizo People": An Overview of the Huayno Genre

Huayno is the most widespread musical genre in the Andes, transcending every boundary of race, class, region, and language. For generations it has been Andean Peru's principal music, a cherished vehicle for emotional expression and the background hum of leisure and celebration.[3] It varies by region, class, context, and era, but common structures provide an underlying matrix that links the Andes as a musical unit—indeed, other Andean genres are similar to it in structure, and while the term is often used as a gloss for all traditional music of the highland region, aficionados of the huayno music that is dominant in urban-mestizo settings point to a series of structural principles and musical traits that distinguish huayno proper from this everyday metonymic usage.

Huayno in this sense, and in the sense that I follow here, is always organized strophically, with the melody and text of verses usually organized

1. Huayno "Chipillay Prado"

in an AABB pattern.[4] Melodies tend to proceed in undulating fashion from a higher to a lower register, and most tend toward pentatonicism, though many do not, and even those that do incorporate passing and ornamental notes from outside the pentatonic scale. Most important, they almost always involve a certain modal ambivalence, which typically arises from the way that a melody's A phrase ends in the area of its major tonic triad, while the B phrase ends in the area of the relative minor triad (see fig. 1).[5] The sensation is one of continual shift between related major and minor modes, and the effect is amplified in performance, where instrumentalists articulate the notated phrase endings with cadences that use the relevant harmonies. Given the tendency of Western ears to associate the minor mode with gloom, this property explains the many accounts that describe huayno music as poignant, nostalgic, and haunting—or deride it as depressing.

This appreciation also arises from the nature of many huayno texts, which explore sadness, uncertainty, loss, abandonment, grief, separation, and yearning—a trait that is hardly universal across space and time, though it is widely held to be so by outsiders to the tradition, and has become very closely associated with Ayacucho's huayno style. Such huayno lyrics typically strip away details extraneous to the speaker's interior state, leaving only the bare contemplation of an emotional or personal crisis. They rarely name particular incidents or personages, and they are hardly ever narrative, though they are often situated in space by reference to a river, mountain, town, or other landmark. Their appeal lies instead in their anonymous exteriorization of internal turmoil: usually, the feelings arising from love or lost love, and the pain of poverty or social exclusion. Understood to represent private agonies, they nevertheless describe common, recognizable experiences. They provide a means of expressing one's own pain, identifying with

2. Standard huayno rhythm

others who suffer, and taking comfort in the knowledge that one's torments are part of a shared human condition.[6]

None of this means that huayno performance is as downbeat as widespread caricature would have it, especially in indigenous communities, where it is often treated as a dance genre. Rhythmically, huayno is organized in binary fashion, and accompaniments tend to emphasize an eighth-and-two-sixteenths figure while placing the rhythmic accent on the off-beat (see fig. 2). Further rhythmic interest may be generated by the unevenness that often enlivens huayno lyrics, where poetic lines may or may not be symmetrical: the genre's one-beat rhythmic accompaniment accommodates such irregularity, allowing an instrumentalist to simply repeat the pattern until the end of a thought. Frequently, especially in Ayacucho, the guitar acts as the main accompanimental instrument, strumming harmonies that are typically limited to the tonic and dominant of a minor key (usually A minor) and the tonic, dominant, and occasionally subdominant of its relative major as well, though others may be used as passing chords. Texts are set in syllabic and highly syncopated fashion over these basic patterns, and in performance songs are frequently enlivened with a *fuga*, a faster, more rhythmic section tacked onto the end.[7]

Insofar as its strophic texts often follow Spanish poetic forms such as the romance and its musical materials are based on the Western scales and harmonies that came to the Andes with Catholic missionaries, huayno bears a strong colonial stamp.[8] Other elements, however, are clearly indigenous in provenance. Until recently, most were sung in either Quechua or a combination of Quechua and Spanish, and many songs use poetic devices that echo linguistic forms common in other indigenous speech genres (Mannheim 1986). Overall, it is best described as a product of the unique cultural cross-fertilization that the colonial encounter produced in the Andes.

Of course, such clinical descriptions fail to capture what huayno means to its public. For this, it might be best to turn to a song that became one of my favorite huaynos the first time that I heard it.

> Romance de guitarrero, pasa su vida cantando (*bis*)
> Canta penas ajenas, olvida sus alegrías (*bis*)

> Maypiraq Chipillay Prado, llakiyllay takiykunanpaq
> Maypiraq Chipillay Prado, llakiyllay tocaykunanpaq
> Icha pay takiptin, qawkallay kawsakullayman
> Icha pay tocaptin, llakiyllay chinkarullanptin
>
> [Ballad of the guitar man, spends his life singing (*bis*)
> He sings the sorrows of others, and forgets his own happiness (*bis*)
>
> Where has my dear Chipi Prado gone, if he were here he could sing my sadness
> Where has my dear Chipi Prado gone, if he were here he could play my sadness
> Maybe if he sang, I could find the peace of mind to continue living
> Maybe if he played, my sorrow would disappear]

Written by the Ayacuchano musician Carlos Falconí, a well-known composer and my main instructor, "Chipillay Prado" commemorates a real person, a guitarist who was already an elderly man when Carlos came to know him in the 1960s or 1970s. It wasn't his most famous piece, and it has been recorded only once as far as I know. However, it has a haunting melody (see fig. 1), and its melancholy text, rendered in lyrical Spanish and Quechua, nicely captured the traditional role of huayno musicians in Andean life. When I asked Carlos about the song in 2002, he explained that it "describes how [as a musician] you are here to serve, to sing other people's pains and forget your own happiness. It's my idea of the role of the composer, the artist, the singer. It's my cultural conception of what musical art is for."[9]

Years before Falconí and Chipi Prado shared songs in Ayacucho, the Andean writer, scholar, activist, music lover, and ethnologist José María Arguedas called huayno "the clear and meticulous footprint that the mestizo people have left on their road of salvation and creation," an art form that "has gathered all of [their] moments of pain, happiness, terrible struggle . . . [to] speak [their] spiritual story" (Arguedas [1940] 1989: 45–46). The resonant pomp of these phrases indicates something of the ideological load that huayno bears today, and indeed the genre in its current form can be read deep into the past. Although it was probably consolidated no earlier than the late colonial period, reliable attestations date from at least 1872, when the Ayacuchano writer Luis Carranza described huayno music in terms that, if vague, remain recognizable.[10] Elsewhere, the transcriptions of the composer Daniel Alomía Robles, dated largely between 1893 and 1895, include songs that are still played today (Alomía Robles and Robles Godoy 1990), as does *La musique des Incas et ses survivances* (The Music of the Inca and Their Descendants; d'Harcourt and d'Harcourt 1925).[11]

This musical continuity is important for many huayno aficionados who, like folk enthusiasts everywhere, treasure the genre's deep locality, its ability to connect past and contemporary experiences.[12] Ana told me that local huayno music "transmits experiences from Ayacucho itself. What I like most, what I most identify with, is something like when Sila Illanes sings 'Flor de retama.' It's a sad song, but it also makes us remember." And Percy, another young listener, observed that "traditional huayno always deals with the past, real things that have happened to a person, a people," distinguishing it from other, less profound kinds of popular music that he also enjoyed.

Musicians, too, often describe how they inherited their musical knowledge from elders who were active around the turn of the century, staking their musical authority upon their capacity to draw from a deep well of collective experience. By recalling a figure from that generation, "Chipillay Prado" highlights the process of transmission that makes huayno a living link to the past. In addition to a statement about music's emotional life, Falconí told me that the song was "a description of what I see as the guitar tradition of Ayacucho that came before me" and an effort to rescue from fickle memory a musician he admired, "because otherwise, [his name] would be lost to time." In fact, the song looks back not only through its imagery, but also in its very musical structure, which Falconí received from Prado himself in roundabout fashion. Prado was an outstanding performer in a city famed for its guitarists, and he took Ayacucho's guitar technique with him when he was posted as a schoolteacher to the southern town of Puquio.[13] There he left a coterie of followers, among them the contemporary virtuoso Manuelcha Prado, Falconí's sometime collaborator in the 1980s. Manuelcha Prado taught Falconí a melody that he had learned from his mentor Chipi Prado, and it struck Falconí as both beautiful and archaic, well worth putting back into circulation. It became the basis for "Chipillay Prado," his homage to the old master and to the huayno tradition itself.

"Chipillay Prado" also thematizes huayno's power to serve as an emotional palliative, and though its commemorative aspect marks it as a modern composition, it is resolutely traditional in voicing the pleas of someone who seeks relief from anguish. The elevated language of Falconí's song, the "almost bookish" (*casi libresco*) tone that Josafat Roel Pineda (1959) observed in urban-mestizo huayno music, is the quality that would most centrally come to identify Ayacucho's variant of the genre. In this tradition, poetic devices and evocative word play are used to amplify a song's emotional impact. One common method is linguistic parallelism, where lines are repeated with the substitution of a single lexical item, such that central

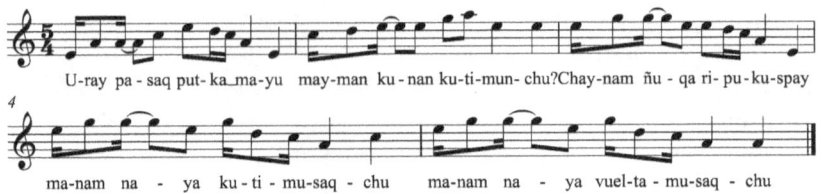

3. Huayno "Chiki tuku"

concepts are emphasized—such as the twin pairings of singing/playing, and of peace of mind/sorrow's disappearance, that appear in "Chipillay Prado." This device echoes other Quechua-language speech genres and is almost certainly an indigenous inheritance. Missing here, however, are the nature metaphors that saturate huayno texts, particularly in indigenous communities. Through long use many nature figures have acquired a deep resonance, signifying to listeners through a wealth of accumulated associations. The most common is undoubtedly the representation of a female love interest as a dove (Quechua: *urpi* or *cuculí*; Spanish: *paloma* or *torcaza*), a warm image that echoes tenderly across hundreds of Andean love songs. Other figures resonate more starkly with their social context. Thus in an impoverished region where outmigration and the uncertainty of fortune at the road's end have been a pervasive reality, travel has become a trope for the grim possibility of death.

Via these tight knots of metaphor, traditional huayno music produces affective links across disparate experiential domains. The song "Chiki tuku" (Barn Owl—see fig. 3), recorded by Manuelcha Prado in his early days as a solo artist, provides a particularly good example:

> Uray pasaq putka mayu
> Maytaq kunan kutimunchu?
> Chaynam ñuqa ripukuspay
> Manam ñaya kutimusaqchu
> Manam ñaya vueltamusaqchu
>
> Wasi tiyasqay esquinapim
> Chikituku qachwallachkan
> Imapaqraq chay chikiqa
> ripunaychu, pasanaychu
> ripunaychu, chinkanaychu

Qaqamantapas paqariqhina
Puqyumanatapas puqyariqhina
Sapachallay kay mundopi
Manay mamayuq manay taytayuq
Runap mamanta mamachakuspa
Runap taytanta taytachakuspa

[Swollen river, passing below
Where does it go?
It will be the same when I go
Never to return
Never to come back

In the corner of my house
A barn owl sings a *qachwa* [festival song]
What is that bird talking about?
Could it be my parting, my passing?
My parting, my disappearance?

Like someone born from the rocks
Like someone sprung from a spring
I am alone in this world
Without mother or father
Calling others' mothers my own
Calling others' fathers my own]

The river that runs on, signifying travel and death, and the call of the barn owl, omen of ill fortune, are common figures of dread. However, this song is especially powerful in using them to shade the connection between marginality and exile, themselves drawn together via the trope of the orphan (*wakcha*). In a region where people have typically lived among large extended kin groups, relations who provide succor in the case of emergency, the true orphan, the only individual with no one to count on, has long symbolized the most pitiful dispossession. Deprived at once of familial love and economic prospects, the orphan makes clear the intertwined nature of social being and material sustenance, stands as a figure of poverty and social disconnection, and metaphorizes the frightening possibility of outmigration. Prado learned this song from Falconí, who in turn learned it from his father, and he interpreted it in this way:

In the first strophe, the speaker compares himself to a river. Just so, he will never return. This could be due to economic need, or it could be a sentimental problem. In the second strophe, an owl's singing in the corner of my house: why? Am I to leave, or am I to die? In all songs, the idea of leaving is linked to death, and the owl is the bird of bad fortune. There are two possibilities: maybe he'll only leave physically, but maybe he'll die. Now, the third strophe. This is not a direct reference to death of his parents, but rather it refers to economic difficulties. It's his poverty that obliges him to leave: he has no means of material support.

The use of Quechua in both songs speaks to the enduring perception that it is "more feelingful" (*más sentido*) than Spanish, and thus better suited for the expression of deep sentiment. In Ayacucho, as in other highland cities, Quechua was never the exclusive idiom of indigenous peoples. It was widely spoken in the houses of the urban elite, and if some were ashamed of the language, others participated in a flourishing tradition of Quechua verbal art that included poetry, drama, and music (Itier and Zúñiga Cazorla 1995; Itier 2007).[14] Many composers and performers still view Quechua as the proper idiom for huayno, and though spoken Quechua has declined significantly in urban areas and among younger people, it is widely understood, and I regularly heard people declare that they treasured its "sweetness," its warm, tender, vibrant emotionalism.

Despite the melancholy of such songs as "Chipillay Prado" and "Chiki tuku," the genre's dourness is not a straightforward matter. Protesting the glum reputation, Raúl Garcia Zárate, Ayacucho's emblematic guitarist and a Living Cultural Patrimony of the Peruvian Nation, explained to me that huayno listeners "take pleasure in their own sadness" (*gozan de su propia tristeza*). And though Carlos Falconí told me that the artist's purpose is to "dissipate the pain" (*gastar sus penas*) of a listener, it might be more accurate to say that huayno appreciation often involves a kind of joy in the contemplation of emotional truth. Moreover, not all huayno is thematically gloomy. The dominance of grief in certain strains of huayno music appears to be recent, and while it is central to music from Ayacucho and the northern Andes—Peru's two dominant traditions since the 1990s—it is not central to the huayno of Cusco, Puno, Cajamarca, or indigenous communities throughout the Andes.[15] Indeed, most huaynos everywhere are songs of love, and bald statements of affection or attraction are nearly as common as complaints of love denied. Finally, local listeners do not really hear the minor mode as sad, and anyone who has spent an evening dancing to huayno music with a group of beaming, laughing friends will attest that even ears trained into a Western bias can easily come to hear modal qualities as affectively neutral (cf. Turino 2008).

The description that I have essayed thus far relies upon works from the city of Ayacucho, but the traits that I have enumerated are common to huayno performance throughout the Andean region. Beginning around mid-century, these shared patterns of performance would increasingly be cross-cut by local differences as the recording industry began to promote regional styles as distinct, often mutually opposed subgenres of huayno music. I will return to a discussion of this process below, but before considering the role of recordists and record labels in the development of huayno, it is necessary to specify the characteristics of the indigenista music and related genres that preceded or coincided with their rise, and against which their efforts were often framed.

From Indigenismo to Pan-Andean Music: Sounds of Surrogated Indigeneity

Huayno was one of many cultural manifestations that indigenista activists of the early twentieth century mobilized in seeking to establish the legitimacy of Andean claims upon the nation-state. In point of fact, the most prominent indigenista compositions were parlor pieces that invoked either contemporary Indian life or the ancient Inca in a very romanticized way. The most famous is Daniel Alomía Robles's "El condor pasa," which the composer claimed to have derived from an ancient Indian tune (Varallanos 1988), though it hardly resembles any indigenous genre. Its thumping rhythms, based on plodding figures that long connoted savagery in Western art music (Pisani 2005), its structural resemblance to Western two-part form, and its very un-Andean melodic contour all suggest the extent to which composers sought musical representations of indigeneity in the Western canon, rather than in local communities. The same can be said for compositions such as Jorge Bravo de Rueda's "Vírgenes del sol" (Sun Virgins), which is further exemplary in its heavy pentatonicism, a trait that indigenistas described as diagnostically Indian despite the prominent use of tritonic, tetratonic, and diatonic scales in indigenous music.[16] Such pieces quickly became Peruvian warhorses, widely performed upon piano, guitar, or harp, as well as *kenas* (end-blown notch flutes) or the small eight- or ten-stringed *charangos* (small lutelike chordophones), Indian instruments that indigenistas made into vehicles for virtuoso performance.

Alongside these activities, indigenista musicians made arrangements of songs that they collected in Indian communities, albeit stylized and altered to fit Western aesthetics. And although they were not tied exclusively to indigenista activities, highland ensembles called *estudiantinas* played all of these compositions, alongside huaynos and other songs in the regional repertoire, promoting a certain cross-fertilization between indigenista fare and the more properly vernacular traditions of the highlands. The estudiantina format brings together a heterogeneous group of instruments, usually including guitars, mandolins, violins, charangos, and kenas, and perhaps other instruments such as harp, *laud*, and *bandurria*. In a typical performance, violins, kenas, and mandolins usually carry a piece's tune in parallel thirds, while guitarists strum along or wind bass lines in counterpoint to the main melody and charangos jangle in the center of the texture. The space between verses might be filled with quasi-improvised runs on any melodic instrument, but otherwise performances tend to be fairly formal, departing little from arrangements that are determined beforehand (see fig. 4 for a mockup of a typical estudiantina arrangement).

Because of their frequent ties to indigenismo, it has often been argued that estudiantinas promoted the elitist formalization of earlier popular traditions (see, for example, Lloréns Amico 1983). There is some truth to this claim, but by implying that estudiantina performances were pale imitations of livelier vernacular sounds, it also equates authenticity with subalternity, denying Andean elites their own cultural particularities and investments. In fact, musical traffic across social boundaries always made it difficult to

4A. Huayno "Chullalla sarachamanta," in estudiantina arrangement

4B and 4C. Huayno "Chullalla sarachamanta," in estudiantina arrangement

4D and 4E. Huayno "Chullalla sarachamanta," in estudiantina arrangement

4F. Huayno "Chullalla sarachamanta," in estudiantina arrangement

separate Andean elite and popular spheres in the first place. Many urban elites had a long-standing investment in traditions that overlapped with those of the indigenous lower classes, and the estudiantinas became one more vector for such processes. Indeed, it might be more accurate to state that the discourses of authenticity used to decry estudiantina performance grew from within the later commercial huayno industry, where activities were often designed to counter the pseudo-Indian abuses of indigenista performance.

Estudiantinas remain active in contemporary Peru, though they are mainly of antiquarian interest. By contrast, indigenista music is widespread, due in part to its association with folkloric dance. Many indigenista tunes were put to use in the early twentieth century by organizations such as the Centro Qosqo de Arte Nativo, which schematized Andean dance forms for choreographed presentation by urban-mestizo dance troupes. These in turn became very popular during the regime of President Augusto B. Leguía (1919–30), who found investing in indigenista performance to be an expedient way of mollifying Andean demands for recognition. Later politicians followed Leguía's lead, and indigenismo's performative precepts eventually became semi-institutionalized during the leftist dictatorship of Velasco Alvarado (1968–75). His government established a state-run National School of Folklore, where students undergo a rigorous training in traditional music and dance, usually in preparation for a job teaching schoolchildren about national diversity. The mandate of the school has expanded to include Andean mestizo, coastal criollo, Afro-Peruvian, and Amazonian dances, but staged indigenousness still dominates the field, and generations of Peruvians have learned that appreciating these cultural artifacts constitutes an act of respect, an identification with an Andean cultural heritage seen as a birthright of all citizens.

Many aspects of indigenista performance subsist in pan-Andean music, which emerged after the mid-twentieth century and came eventually to dominate the Andean slot in world music record bins. A transnational, cosmopolitan style from the moment of its inception, it was created largely by Chilean, Bolivian, Argentinean, and Swiss intellectuals fascinated with the sonorous possibilities of indigenous instruments, and it developed across sites ranging from La Paz and Santiago to Buenos Aires and Paris (Ríos 2008). Directly or indirectly influenced by the sounds and social politics of indigenismo, its musicians refined the earlier movement's basic premises. They drew upon traditions from all over the Andes, stylizing indigenous musical forms for onstage performance and redesigning Andean instruments so as to approximate the technical resources of Euro-American art and popular musics. Responding to the political tenor of their Cold War context, they added healthy doses of anti-imperialist rhetoric, playing up their music's roots in the culture of the continent's oppressed Indians and projecting a non-specific "Andean" identity as a symbol of resistance to U.S. cultural hegemony. Erudite, sophisticated, and rife with revolutionary lyrics, pan-Andean music became and remains a favorite of audiences in the Global North, especially those who identified with Latin America's struggles against American intervention.

Pan-Andean performers adopted a fairly standard ensemble, a shared set of instrumental techniques, and common principles of arrangement over the 1970s and 1980s, and these have changed but little. The style is largely identified with groups of poncho-clad performers playing a deep *bombo* drum with an animal-hide head, pan flutes, kenas, guitar, and the small, ten-stringed charango. As instruments considered typically indigenous, winds and charangos tend to be foregrounded, with guitar reserved for a supporting role. However, kenas and pan flutes are typically played with a wide vibrato, rounded tone, virtuosic ornaments, portamentos, and other sophisticated techniques that distinguish pan-Andean performances from the tinnier, breathier interpretations favored in indigenous communities. The charango, which indigenous performers typically treat with a simple strummed style, took on a much more active role as both accompanist and soloist, alternating cross-string arpeggios with complicated solo passages. In general, pan-Andean tunes tend to remain faithful to the structures and basic rhythms of folk genres while enlivening them with flashy instrumental runs, rich harmonies, and marked instrumental contrast—for example, using different flutes in a call-and-response fashion—all of which are low priorities in traditional Andean performance.

Like its indigenista predecessor, pan-Andean music represented a politicized, metropolitan reimagining of Indianness by and for those who might find traditional Indian music too dreary for uninflected engagement. In each case, performers claimed and may have legitimately believed that their actions validated indigenous contributions to their respective societies, but usually this involved little real dialogue with Indian performers. Indigenista and pan-Andean musicians have consistently delivered an idealized, celebratory vision of indigenous experience that is mostly inconsistent with the lived realities of the countryside, and its uptake in the rural Andes was always sporadic at best. Of course, performers never claimed to interpret authentic indigenous music. They explicitly described their work as an attempt to generate an inclusive national vision from a mestizo perspective, and their ideas remain available as a performative language with which to decry Andean disenfranchisement.

The converging, diverging resonance of these traditions can perhaps be best extrapolated from a pair of experiences that I had in Ayacucho. When I first moved to the city, I occasionally walked by a doorway near the main plaza, noting that the space housed the Estudiantina Municipal de Ayacucho. The group seemed to meet irregularly, though, and the door was always shut when I set aside time to visit. Finally, one evening in 2002, I found it open and poked my head inside, asking if I could come in. Surprised, one of the two middle-aged men in the room assented before turning back to the news program that was blaring on a nearby television. The other turned back to his cards, and neither was interested in my attempts to converse—an understandable attitude, given my unexpected intrusion into a space that functioned as a sort of club. I wandered self-consciously around the sparsely furnished room, reading newspaper clippings posted on the walls, and I learned that the group had been founded in October 1937. Many of its members had gone on to careers as recording stars, and it had even recorded some 45s for the IEMPSA record company in 1961 featuring traditional huaynos from the city, thus antedating all of the artists who made Ayacuchano music famous in later years. In fact, the lead voice on those 45s was "El Pajarillo" (The Little Bird), Nery García Zárate, who, along with his guitarist brother Raúl (also a former member), recorded many of Ayacucho's definitive huayno LPs.

Eventually men and women began to trickle in, cordially greeting their colleagues and me, some opening large wooden cabinets and removing instruments. Mandolins and guitars were tuned, short snatches of melody were run under fingers, and finally a goateed young man asked if I played anything. When I responded that I had been studying huayno a little, he handed me a guitar, and soon the music began: old huayno tunes such as "Chullalla sarachamanta" (see fig. 4), played in a light, upbeat style that bespoke years of ensemble experience. I was not familiar with all the songs, but traditional huayno relies upon a limited series of harmonic patterns, and I followed along with few problems. Conversation became general and amiable, and I asked how the group's playing style had changed in their long decades of existence. Smiling broadly, several members declared that it had changed "not at all" (*en nada absoluto*), positioning themselves as devotees of a style that had largely passed from the world of contemporary performance. Indeed, soon the music ceded to a formal discussion, largely concerning some members' feelings that the group was outrageously marginalized, despite their self-appointed role in safeguarding Ayacuchano musical history. I left during these deliberations, but before I did I heard the lament of one particularly invested woman, whose calls for municipal support was framed as an existential dilemma: "If we are not here to be heard, then why are we here? Why should we continue to exist?"[17]

Judging by extant recordings of comparable ensembles from the 1940s, the Estudiantina Municipal de Ayacucho has indeed maintained an archaic style of performance, and this might be part of the reason for its marginalization.[18] Indeed, indigenismo's contemporary resonance appeared somewhat more dynamic at Ayacucho's San Antonio secondary school, which, like schools all over Peru, stages an annual folkloric show, each classroom presenting a choreographed dance learned from a teacher trained in traditional performance. San Antonio's evening performance took place in the school's central courtyard, with parents seated around the edges. The accompanying musicians were members of Los Warpas, the house band at a local club devoted to the pan-Andean musical style. They were far outnumbered by the various instruments sitting before their amplifiers, testament to the diversity of genres that they played during such gigs. One by one each classroom emerged from the school building, and beginning with an Afro-Peruvian *festejo*, each performed a routine of several minutes' duration, now choreographing themselves into geometric patterns such as lines and circles, now pairing off to execute couples dances. One of the night's highlights was the interpretation of an indigenous *yarqa aspiy* (canal cleaning) ritual put on by a parents' association. Shovels in hand, they mimed the actions of the workers who annually remove the accumulated grit from village waterways, moving to the rhythm of a tune played on the kena, and enlivened their performance with a skirt-chasing priest character, whose connection to the action was unclear.

As the show progressed, I was surprised to hear and see things that I recognized not from Peru's classic canon of folkloric performance, but rather from the pan-Andean repertoire. My sense of incongruity was amplified toward the end of the evening, when a classroom of older children performed their version of a *tinku*, an indigenous combat ritual that has been prohibited throughout the Andes. At local pan-Andean clubs and on the radio I had heard tunes called tinkus that resembled the one that accompanied these students. Loud, fast-paced songs with a driving drumbeat, they seemed like a pan-Andean imitation of heavy metal aesthetics and bore little relation to the ritual genre.[19] The dance performance that I witnessed powerfully echoed this disconnect. A rather tame evocation of the real tinku, which has regularly resulted in injury or death, it instead featured bare-chested adolescent boys who squared off and danced aggressively at one another, jumping and colliding in a way that recalled nothing so much as the celebratory chest bumps performed by professional athletes in the United States.

In retrospect, little is surprising about the appearance of pan-Andean performance in San Antonio's folkloric dance show. Though pan-Andean and indigenista musics date from different historical moments, the former is a lineal sociopolitical and performative descendant of the latter. Each style retains overtones of intellectuality, and appreciation marks connoisseurs as cerebral, serious people devoted to Andean uplift and personal betterment. In fact, when Martín Arone, a broadcaster who cohosts one of Ayacucho's only pan-Andean radio shows, sought to characterize for me the nature of his own listening audience, he told me it was made up of "young people, adults from the 1970s and 1980s who lived through the heyday of this music, some university types, some adolescents. I guess maybe the occasional listener who wants to better himself."

The Sound of Ayacucho: Regional Huayno on Record

As pan-Andean music was emerging between La Paz and Paris, Peru's recording industry became a driving agent in huayno's musical development. Earlier, I relied upon Ayacuchano examples in illustrating the general melodic, rhythmic, and structural properties of huayno music. But huayno is hugely varied in terms of instrumentation, vocal style, and lyrical content. The advent of recordings helped to fix variants of huayno music, making what had been fluid associations between stylistic resources and geographic distribution into a system of regional classification that has become common sense for contemporary performers and analysts (see Olsen 1986).

On the most basic level, there is a broad distinction between urban-mestizo and rural-indigenous huayno performance. Indigenous communities have historically favored either a harp and violin duo or a consort featuring many different-sized instruments of one type. Whatever its resources, the aesthetic of indigenous performance tends to differ from its mestizo counterpart, favoring buzzing, pinched, tinny timbres such as steel strings or nasal voices, sounds that are high in pitch, and a strong rhythmic pulse, reflecting the indigenous version's tight connection to dance. Taken as a whole, indigenous huayno performance often sounds strident and monotonous to untutored ears, a factor that weighs heavily in prejudiced dismissals of "savage" indigenous performers.[20]

Huayno records focused almost exclusively on urban-mestizo variants during their heyday, and it was these that became codified as representative regional sounds. Ayacucho's style may stand at the furthest remove from indigenous stylistics. When it appeared on recordings it was already regarded as uncommonly elegant, suited to concert hall and corner store alike, and by 1983 this reputation had led Lloréns Amico to describe Ayacuchano guitar performances in particular as "export quality" (Lloréns Amico 1983: 140) Andean music. Arguedas had written some time before that Ayacucho's "gentlemanly" caste was foremost among all the Andean cities in developing its own vernacular art forms, including a unique huayno style (Arguedas [1958] 1977: 170). However, if the perceived elegance of Ayacucho's huayno music derives in part from the social class of its interpreters, it derives more specifically from the intensely literary nature of its lyrics, its audibly Hispanic instrumental resources, and its genteel manner of vocal interpretation. Ayacuchano composers have long written songs that make dense, bilingual (Quechua and Spanish) use of poetic devices. Performances have always been accompanied by a variety of instruments, but nylon-stringed Spanish guitars and its relatives, such as the mandolin or charango, are the preferred resources by any measure, and Ayacuchanos have gained fame as guitarists of formidable expertise. Finally, the emotionally expressive yet restrained nature of Ayacuchano vocal interpretation, with its controlled vibrato and throaty timbre, most resembles that of música criolla and other refined musical forms, rather than competing Andean genres.

Indeed, in conversations about Ayacuchano aesthetics, nothing is weighted as heavily as *sentimiento,* a term that describes the musical techniques through which it achieves emotional resonance. Musicians and non-musicians alike struggled to define it, and more than once I was told that as the investigating musicologist, it was really my job to figure it out. But all agreed that a discreet infusion of melancholic nostalgia made Ayacuchano songs emotionally satisfying. Vásquez and Vergara have noted that "to perform without glissandi, appoggiaturas, adornments, anticipations and delayed notes is to play an anodyne melody, flavorless, without character or essence, 'without sentiment'" (Vásquez Rodríguez and Vergara Figueroa 1988: 145), and these kinds of figures provide the key to achieving *sentimiento* instrumentally. But such ornamentation is meant to evoke huayno singing and should be understood as an imitation of the human voice's phatic capacities. In sung performance, *sentimiento* lies in the strained, wistful tone that is adopted by good singers, who augment a song's emotional charge with sighing portamento, "bent" notes, and cracks in the voice, suffusing it with the delicate expressivity that is a hallmark of the Ayacuchano style.[21]

This stands in stark contrast to the qualities of competing regional variants, such as the widely influential style of the Central Andes. Centered in the department of Jauja, the Central Andean (*wanka*) style is famous for singers who belt out boisterous, full-throated songs, accompanied by noisy, rhythmically active *orquestas* of saxophone, clarinet, harp, and violin, and generous helpings of *guapeo* (encouraging shouts; see Romero 2001).[22] This energy means that Central Andean groups are in demand at dance parties throughout the southern Andes, and they have helped establish a stereotype of *wankas* as festive, happy-go-lucky extroverts. Other regional associations include the uptempo string bands of northern Áncash, the pan pipe troupes of Puno, and the ensembles of harp and vocalist from the highlands of Lima, all of which both have been popular throughout Peru at one time or another.[23]

All of these distinctions amount to regional tendencies rather than hard-and-fast rules, and a quick glance beyond the recordings of the late twentieth century reveals a far greater diversity. Foreign record companies, for example, produced 78s of Andean music as early as 1927 and 1928, when teams from RCA Victor visited Lima's annual Indian Day music competition, an event that Leguía had founded in 1921 under indigenista influence. The performances captured by RCA engineers included typical indigenista compositions, including an improbable "war dance" for piano and kenas, but the 1928 recordings also captured a variety of urban-mestizo huayno music from Ayacucho. The female duo Las Lindas Satankas were recorded singing "Peras perascha," a picaresque staple of the city's huayno tradition that praises the virtues of single life. The Estudiantina Típica Ayacuchana performed as well, featuring none other than Chipi Prado on guitar.[24] And the harpist Tani Medina, who went on to record several LPs in Venezuela, performed the huayno "Adiós pueblo de Ayacucho," already a classic and still the unofficial anthem of the city.[25]

These foreign productions had a limited circulation in highland Peru, and the full impact of recording would be felt only after Peruvian companies emerged in the mid-1940s. In 1949 Arguedas convinced the young Odeón company to produce a test run of four Andean records; they quickly sold out, revealing an eager Andean market with serious purchasing power.[26] The major Peruvian record companies (Odeón/IEMPSA, Sono Radio, and Virrey) began to produce massive numbers of discs, and by the 1970s huayno was outselling all other genres. Recordings were broadly similar in some ways, featuring singers with "a wide Western vibrato [singing in] parallel thirds, an Iberian legacy . . . and [ensembles playing] 'hotter' instrumental breaks" than was typical in household performance (Turino 1988: 136–37), but they did showcase vernacular regional styles that had gone largely unrecorded during the earlier estudiantina era.

More important, these regional styles soon became fairly standardized, thanks in part to Arguedas's influence. Distressed by what he saw as the falsified dross of indigenista performing troupes and newly empowered by a post within the Ministry of Education, Arguedas established an apparatus to regulate Andean musical authenticity. His review board had the power to veto performers who violated the musical and sartorial style deemed typical of the region they claimed to represent, barring them from recording or live presentation. The wide adoption of this attitude toward the policing of authenticity helped make relatively narrow trait lists into reflexes of geography, and the associations produced thereby were then amplified through their continual reiteration in recording, marketing, and performance, repeated across the thousands of records through which Peruvians learned the musical truth of other regions.[27] However, if records presented selective visions of regional typicality, they featured existing practices from the places they purported to represent, and it is difficult to see them as the work of people seeking to "westernize" Andean music.[28] Especially since huayno has always been a shared genre, forged in dialogue between Indians and others, never primordial and always already "westernized," it is not clear that the recordings of the era represented a radical shift in Andean musical development.

By the time I arrived in Peru in 2000, Ayacucho's huayno style had gone through three distinct waves of popularity: first, in the 1960s, as a symbol of Ayacucho's distinct urban-mestizo culture; second, in the 1980s and early 1990s, as a vehicle of protest against violence; and third, in the late 1990s, as the basis of a musical fusion that catered to the consumerist desires of an emergent Andean bourgeoisie. Throughout, the music and its makers have traded upon its qualities of refinement and emotional weight, elements that are inseparable in the public understanding of the style and are probably approached best through a performative context.

One of my first experiences with traditional Ayacuchano huayno took place in 2000 at a club in Lima's central Lince district called El Rinconcito Ayacuchano (The Ayacuchano Nook). Arriving early in the evening, my wife and I sat at a table covered with a striped shawl of the kind used by highland peasants. We ordered a pitcher of beer, which I later learned was priced for the club's upwardly mobile clientele. The audience, which filled a dozen tables or so, was mixed and casual, mostly couples in the global urban uniform of jeans and jackets, and all adults, ranging perhaps from their mid-twenties to their sixties. Over the next few hours a series of soloists, progressing from unknown to moderately well-known, sang with a house band of guitars and bass on a small, low stage before a large mural of Andean scenery. The crowd remained seated, sometimes conversing, sometimes singing or clapping along, applauding politely, and occasionally exchanging pleasantries with the performers. Vocal participation was occasionally avid, especially during the traditional tune "Pirwalla pirwa," with its call-and-response refrain, but mostly this was an occasion for listening.

The evening's climax came toward midnight, when the singer Kiko Revatta took the stage. Nicknamed "La Voz Señorial de los Andes" (The Gentlemanly Voice of the Andes), Revatta had been a huayno luminary in the early 1990s.[29] As his moniker suggests, his reputation was built upon a quasi-operatic vocal style, and his performance featured a full-throated, theatrical delivery with stylized bodily gestures, pregnant with emotion. The audience hung on every syllable as he ran through earnest love songs such as "Para un viejo corazón" (Song for a Broken Heart), but eventually he paused to say some words about memory and survival. He spoke of the migrant condition that united the crowd and the circumstances that had driven many of them to the capital. He ended by announcing "Flor de retama," an angry denouncement of military abuse that had been closely tied to revolutionary politics throughout the 1980s, but which is now understood as an anthem of Ayacuchano solidarity and resilience. The crowd emitted a murmur of approval and from the first word joined him en masse.

He finished in dramatic fashion, his muscular vibrato sustaining the song's final syllable over its instrumental coda, his clenched fist held high. Calls of "otra, otra" (encore, encore) rang out as Revatta left the stage, waving and beaming as he passed out of the club and on to another show.

I received a different kind of education in Ayacuchano aesthetics from Carlos Falconí, who I met upon arriving in Ayacucho in 2001. I knew that he had been a member of the huayno group Trio Ayacucho during their 1960s glory days, and that he had become a respected composer in the years since. I hoped that he would teach me some representative songs and help me master the techniques that made Ayacuchano huayno speak to its audience. He began with the basics of Ayacucho's solo guitar style, where a dynamic bass line, outlining huayno's off-beat accompanimental pattern, complements expressive, highly ornamented melodies, rounding off its virtuosity with elaborate runs that are placed between sung lines and verses. Indeed, there is perhaps nothing else that distinguishes Ayacuchano huayno music as fully as these *floreos* (flowerings), which in their endless variability allow a performer to enliven the melodic profile of an otherwise repetitive piece, and not incidentally to demonstrate his or her prowess.

By the time of my third or fourth lesson, I was convinced that things were going poorly. Falconí had started me off with the old Quechua-language huayno "Umpa rosas," a romantic allegory in which the narrator proposes to revive a desiccated garden by watering it with his tears. The lessons proceeded by rote, one phrase at a time, and Carlos focused insistently on the ornaments he wanted me to play. Over and over he highlighted passages where I misunderstood the cross-string figures and anticipatory grace notes that he favored, throwing the core melody out of sync with the bass line. I could sing the song competently and strum along in huayno rhythm, but I seemed incapable of rendering it properly in solo performance. Time after time Carlos shook his head, demonstrated a version of the melody with new ornaments, and then told me to work on it while he tended to his garden. Finally, out of sheer frustration, I stopped trying to mimic him and simply played the melody as I saw fit, embellishing it with a combination of figures that I had seen him use and things that I had heard on CD. It was the first time he approved, and I soon discovered, in sharing music with other friends from the city, that the spontaneous use of idiomatic ornaments was the surest way to elicit positive reactions.

This traditional huayno style, rooted in the urban middle class and centered on guitar playing, poetic involution, and attention to affective technique, had largely receded before newer genres by the twenty-first century. Artists such as Trio Ayacucho and the García Zárates were remembered fondly, but their music was largely confined to the occasional early morning radio show. It had been honored by governmental decree, with November 2—the birthday of Nery García Zárate, who died in 1982—declared the official Day of Ayacuchano Song, but resources for commemorative events were scant. It was still treasured by older listeners and younger traditionalists, who filled the few remaining venues, small and select, where it was performed. Full-scale concerts of this older tradition were rare, though, and when it was heard, it was typically in a staid and often upscale venue, designed for attentive, decorous listening, rather than in the open lots that attracted mass audiences for weekend events.[30]

Even those few institutions dedicated to the maintenance of traditional Ayacuchano huayno were regarded with some ambivalence. Ayacucho's small conservatory, Lima's National School of Folklore, and the university's resident estudiantina were all places where students could study a formalized version of Ayacuchano guitar performance. Such institutions were often deemed to represent the triumphant entry of Ayacucho's vernacular style into the hallowed halls of various academies, but many musicians were convinced that they reduced a dynamic popular style to rote repetition. However, the creeping classicization of traditional Ayacuchano huayno might be seen as befitting what was always an elitist form of vernacular art. Older listeners often dubbed it "salon huayno," distinguishing it from the music heard in rural festivals, seedy cantinas, and raucous concerts. In an interview with me, one middle-aged radio manager explained that Ayacucho's artists had been successful "because they are educated men, teachers, and they know how to interpret the words, they read things very carefully, and sing songs as they ought to be sung," while another emphasized the educational attainment of the fans, stating that the music of García Zárate and his peers was listened to by the "20 or 30 percent of the population with an adequate level of culture— teachers, professors, and students."

Together, these parameters place Ayacuchano music on the ascendant side of a familiar binary between music for cerebration and music for leisure, sounds that edify and sounds that pander, that runs through the history of Western musical thought. Its reputation as a superlative music is tied to its quiet sentimentalism and its self-conscious literariness, best appreciated via contemplative engagement that bespeaks a cultivated mind, rather than through the ebullient bodily engagement demanded by mass-popular styles. According to this stance, the erudite poetry of songs such as "Chipillay Prado" and "Chiki tuku" lift Ayacuchano music above the level of simple diversion. Most important, the disposition that seeks edification, rather than mere escape, in artistic consumption is explicitly tied to education, and this makes the style inseparable from deeply sedimented notions of social hierarchy.

As a representation of the department, or even the city, of Ayacucho, this reputation for sentimental, guitar-based music is more than a little misleading. Each town in Ayacucho's rural indigenous hinterland claims its own variation on the huayno genre: these are performed on a bewildering variety of instruments, usually guitar and charango variants but also including ensembles of kenas, and they typically hew to indigenous Andean aesthetics in their emphasis on shrill timbre, high pitch, and rhythmic intensity (see Ritter 2002). In both rural and urban areas, the harp remained central to huayno performance until well into the recording era, and outside of the city it remains so.[31] The charango and kena, too, straddled the line between rural and urban spheres, and many performers from Ayacucho department, such as Jaime Guardia, are regarded to this day as among the country's most outstanding charanguistas—although, as a performer from the far south of the department, he and his group, the Lira Paucina, are regarded as ambassadors of that region's style, and not the distinct style of the huamanguino elite. As for uniquely urban genres, estudiantina-like groups continued to perform huayno music on household ensembles of mandolin, kena, violin, and charango during the early twenty-first century, and ensembles associated with the Sullca, Camasca, and Medina families were widely recognized as bearers of this living, if fading, tradition.

Notwithstanding the past and present diversity of Ayacucho's soundscape, which has always far outstripped the vision that appeared on commercial recordings, a musical discourse of elegance, formality, and introspection became inextricably tied to the city in the public sphere of the late 1960s, when Peru's record companies turned their attention to Ayacucho and selected the salon style of Ayacucho's gentlemanly elites as the region's musical token. Notions of Ayacuchano musical exceptionalism had circulated throughout the early twentieth century, but beginning in 1965, with an album of solo guitar music by the guitarist Raúl García Zárate, they spilled across books and articles, record jackets, liner notes, concert patter, everyday conversations, and television specials, tightening the binds between style, belles lettres, and social exclusivity. García Zárate was followed in short order by the Duo Hermanos García Zárate (1966), Trio Ayacucho (1967), Trio Voces de Huamanga (c. 1967–69), Edwin Montoya (c. 1968–70), and the university's *tuna* ensemble (1966), all of whom maintained active careers until the early 2000s, and all of whom released records that were stultifyingly similar, except for the Tuna, the style of which is based on the estudiantina model.[32]

In their own time, these recordings undoubtedly had a larger impact on the national reputation of Ayacuchano huayno than they did within the city, where the style was no revelation. Indeed, like other huayno performers, Ayacucho's artists garnered success by playing on Sundays in Lima's *coliseos* (open-air performance venues), which catered to nostalgic Andean migrants seeking diversion on their weekly day off from work. These had been a staple of urban life since the 1940s, launching highland performers to fame and recording careers. In the 1960s, however, the elitism of Ayacucho's huayno style ran up against Lima's widespread disdain for the highlands in these populist spaces. The Andes remained emblematic of inferior social and ethnic status, and testimonies indicate that discrimination was keenly felt by huayno performers and listeners alike. According to Amílcar Gamarra, lead guitarist of Trio Ayacucho,

> there were lots of doctors, lawyers, and engineers who couldn't enter the venue though they were dying to, because a decent person couldn't go in there with their maids and so on. So they'd be waiting in the street when we came out, and they'd take us to their houses, where everything was ready. There we'd find people of another social class, drinking . . . that's how it was, Ayacuchanos were embarrassed to listen to it in public.

Even during its boom years, then, the self-ascribed superiority of Ayacuchano music contended with lingering prejudice about Andean culture. Soon these boom years were over, and the style nearly disappeared. What saved it was the violence, which left perhaps its only generative effect in the rebirth of the city's huayno style.

Huayno Testimonial: Music in the Time of Fear

As Ayacucho wound itself into a bloody spiral of violence centered on the Shining Path, a handful of established artists and university students began to reinvigorate the local genre, turning it to political ends. Composers expanded their expressive palette to include daringly abstruse metaphors and new musical devices that departed from traditional guitar techniques. In the process these musicians established a new audience for local huayno.

Some of these figures, such as Falconí, stuck to traditional huayno aesthetics and simply treated unprecedented political issues in their lyrics. Others, such as the composer Walter Humala, introduced new harmonies and borrowed melodic figures from foreign sources such as Argentinean *zamba* or Bolivian *takirari* music. Carlos Huamán, the youngest of the group and

5. Huayno "Flor de retama"

an accomplished poet, used bizarre and evocative imagery in his lyrics, leading many to dub him a "surrealist" composer.[33] Óscar Figueroa, the movement's master guitarist, introduced solo passages that went well beyond traditional huayno introductions, setting mood and tone with melodies that were either brooding, aggressive, or sorrowful, as required by the song's lyrics. There was also a turn to slower tempos, along with an exacerbation of the genre's legendary sadness in vocal performances.

One of the most emblematic huaynos of the era, upon which other songs were modeled both musically and lyrically, was "Flor de retama" (Broom Flower), by the poet and professor Ricardo Dolorier. Penned in 1970, it was Dolorier's enraged response to a massacre in the town of Huanta, where authorities gunned down a group of students protesting an increase in educational fees. Its revolutionary fury inspired supporters of the emergent Shining Path movement, and by the early 1980s it had become something of an insurgent anthem. Later, as popular opinion turned against revolutionaries and military forces alike, the song became a way to channel a more general lament against the indiscriminate atrocities unleashed upon highlanders of all political persuasions.

Musically and lyrically, the song departed from the traditional huayno model in important ways. Eschewing anonymity, its lyrics detail the original massacre and point toward a solution—revolution—rather than focusing on the speaker's emotional response. It avoided the standard melodic cells of traditional song, and it complicated huayno's AABB formal pattern (see fig. 5). And while it is faithful to huayno tradition in its use of metaphor, its emphasis on a single central figure is distinctive. In Dolorier's hands, the inexterminable broom flower that covers the rural Andes represents an oppressed people's growing discontent, watered and fed by the murderous actions of the state:

Vengan todos a ver,
Ay vamos a ver

En la plazuela de Huanta, amarillito,
Flor de retama
Amarillito, amarillando
Flor de retama

Por cinco esquinas están,
Los sinchis entrando están
Van a matar estudiantes, huantinos de corazón
Amarillito, amarillando
Flor de retama

Donde la sangre del pueblo
Ay, se derrama
Allí mismito floreces, amarillito,
Flor de retama
Amarillito, amarillando
Flor de retama

La sangre del pueblo tiene rico perfume
Huele a jazmines, violetas, geranios y margaritas
A pólvora y dinamita, carajo
A pólvora y dinamita, carajo
A pólvora y dinamita

[Everyone come and see
Ay, let's go see
In Huanta's plaza, little yellow
Broom flower
Little yellow, yellowing
Broom flower

At Five Corners
The *sinchis* [secret police] are coming
They're going to kill students, *huantinos* through and through
Little yellow, yellowing
Broom flower

Where the blood of the people
Ay, where it's spilled
Right there you bloom, little yellow

> Broom flower
> Little yellow, yellowing
> Broom flower
>
> The people's blood smells beautiful
> It smells like jasmine, violets, geraniums, and daisies
> Like gunpowder and dynamite, goddamn it
> Like gunpowder and dynamite, goddamn it
> Like gunpowder and dynamite]

By 1983 Carlos Falconí and dozens more composers had begun to write similar songs, creating a pool of politically engaged anthems that spread by word of mouth within the city and beyond.[34] Overall, the movement resuscitated a local tradition that had lost ground among young Ayacuchanos. Everyone involved described it to me as a musical "renewal" (*renovación*), and soon it spread well beyond the city. The singers Martina Portocarrero and Nelly Munguía recorded songs in the mid-1980s, and before long a live album of political huayno entitled *Testimonio ayacuchano*, featuring Falconí and Manuelcha Prado, was released with the support of human rights organizations. These recordings sent the new huayno style traveling all over Peru, bringing attention to the local political situation and giving Ayacucho a reputation as a city whose composers and performers were on the leading edge of Andean music.

The style heard on *Testimonio ayacuchano* had an enormous effect on popular notions of Ayacuchano authenticity. Whenever I asked young people to name traditional songs, they singled out "Flor de retama" as the most emblematic of the city's huaynos, despite its radical novelty a generation before. However, as the violence eased in the 1990s, the political music of the 1980s itself came to seem dated. It was viewed as an important musical moment, but by and large listeners had been sated by horror and protest, and political songs were displaced by lighter fare.

Contemporary Ayacuchano Huayno: Transnational Fusion in Erudite Terms

Since contemporary developments in Ayacuchano huayno occupy the latter part of this book, I will essay only a brief and provisional description here. The hybrid music that began to appear in the mid-1990s, as young artists began to turn away from huayno testimonial, can be characterized as a fusion of Ayacucho's traditional huayno style with nontraditional music, and traced to performers' desire to attract new audiences weaned on global pop. Pan-Latin American balada music, with its tales of heartbreak and its romantic vocals, was one logical choice, given its congruence with the standard themes and stylistics of traditional Ayacuchano huayno. However, pan-Andean music was the dominant thread unifying the new sound and artists began to dub the style's kenas, pan flutes, charangos, and bombo drums over Ayacuchano guitars on their huayno records. Later, they increasingly began to perform pan-Andean genres from Bolivia, Chile, and Ecuador as well. By the mid-2000s industry professionals regularly expressed hesitancy about the proper terminology to use when describing the work of these artists. Most commentators took the term "huayno" alone to be insufficient, since pan-Andean and pop elements distinguished recent recordings so clearly from their antecedents, but it did not match their understanding of pan-Andean music either, given its audible traces of Ayacuchano guitar playing and the consistent inclusion of songs from the highland city.[35] Here, I often characterize the combination of pan-Andean and traditional Ayacuchano music that dominated between the mid-1990s and the mid-2000s using the compound term "contemporary Ayacuchano huayno," a label that, as far as I am aware, is not used by Peruvian commentators. Indeed, dense stylistic exchange between the nominal spheres of pan-Andean music and huayno renders problematic the very notion of a separate genre called "contemporary Ayacuchano huayno," and in recognition of this dynamism, such huayno music came by 2012 to be grouped together with pan-Andean music under the all-encompassing rubric *fusión* in record stores and broadcast media. Nevertheless, the invented label remains useful as a means of distinguishing the work of the artists responsible for creating this crossover from that of Ayacuchano musical traditionalists, many of whom maintained viable careers during and after its decade and a half of ascendancy, and that is the sense in which I use it here.

These musical choices were hardly unprecedented. Instruments such as the kena and the charango had been played in and around Ayacucho long before pan-Andean performance became widely popular in the 1990s, though their manner of interpretation was distinct from that of the latter.[36] Moreover, visitors have long been welcomed to the city of Cusco, tourist capital of the Andean region, by pan-Andean performers, who have correctly surmised that most foreigners imagine local music through the filter of the pan-Andean street performers and world music recordings that circulate in the Global North, and that there is money to be made by catering to those expectations. These and other pan-Andean bands had occasionally recorded huaynos in the past, too, perhaps attempting to draw local sounds into the sphere of cosmopolitan Andeanness represented by their more well-known brethren in Bolivia or Chile, and thereby prefiguring the moves made by Ayacuchano performers later on.

Notwithstanding such precursors, the widespread adoption of pan-Andean elements by Ayacuchano performers was startling, given the enduring antipathy that huayno musicians bore toward the style, and it demands to be understood in relation to Peru's emergent Andean bourgeoisie. Pan-Andean music had gained a large following in Bolivia, Ecuador, and Chile, from which such groups as Los Kjarkas, Inti-Illimani, and Quilapayún rose to world fame. Within Peru, though, it enjoyed a very small, select listenership until the 1990s. Its leftist politics and intellectual rigor made it attractive on university campuses, and Andean students provided a limited but devoted fan base throughout the 1970s and 1980s, but huayno artists and their devotees by and large hated it, finding its metropolitan aesthetics threatening to local Andean traditions. As Pedro Arriola, formerly of the pan-Andean group Yawar, explained to me, they were not wrong to be suspicious: "Since it was more elaborate, more meaningful, with a greater literary, harmonic, [and] melodic development, we thought that it was more interesting."

Over the 1990s pan-Andean music became less politically strident in tone, moving conspicuously toward an emphasis on Bolivian dance genres such as *saya*, tinku, and *tobas*, much to the chagrin of many committed fans. It never lost its highbrow cachet, but within Peru this more populist version allowed the style to expand from its initial base in the intelligentsia, and it became a fixture of middle-class dance clubs. It was this sudden combination of accessibility and lingering intellectual prestige that made the style attractive to Ayacuchano musicians, who were interested in reinvigorating Ayacucho's huayno style but wary of vulgarizing the tradition too deeply. Indeed, when musicians spoke of their efforts to modernize Ayacuchano huayno, they often explicitly compared their judicious aesthetic choices with those made by chicha and huayno norteño musicians, styles widely viewed as being in grievous violation of Andean tradition. As contemporary Ayacuchano huayno developed over the 1980s and 1990s, it would be positioned relative to these genres in media space.

Chicha: Peru's Proletarian Pop

When fans and performers describe the low state that Ayacuchano huayno had reached in the early 1980s, they always single out chicha music as the culprit. A distinctly Peruvian blend of Caribbean dance music, rock 'n' roll,

6. Standard cumbia rhythm

and huayno, chicha coalesced between the 1960s and the 1980s. It was incubated in a variety of places, ranging from the Central Andean highlands to the cities of the jungle to the concert venues of the capital. However, it became closely associated with migrant Lima by the late 1970s, when artists began to draw more heavily on Andean idioms and to describe the effects of the capital's dismal socioeconomic situation on its Andean proletariat. From there it spread throughout the highlands, displacing local sounds wherever it found youths hungry for cultural expressions that reflected their changing society.[37]

Chicha music ranges widely in style, but it can be concisely defined as a blend of antecedent popular sounds, performed by a group combining electric guitars and tropical percussion, laid over dance rhythms derived mostly from Colombian cumbia (Tucker 2013). The wailing wind sections and simple, binary rhythms of big-band cumbia had become chic all over Latin America during the 1950s, and Central Andean groups were soon using its distinctive backbeat to accompany huayno performances (see fig. 6). Rock 'n' roll had meanwhile taken root in Peru's cities, and during the 1960s artists began to place cumbia rhythms beneath twinned electric guitars, their sound colored by distortion, reverb, delay, tremolo, and wah-wah pedals. Individual songs by such ensembles drew upon Cuban *son*, mambo, *bugalú*, salsa, psychedelic rock, and other styles that entered the Peruvian mediascape, in addition to rock and huayno music. This unique local synthesis was eventually dubbed "chicha," after the traditional corn beer of the highlands, and the label seemed increasingly appropriate over the 1980s as performers began to foreground the Andean aspects of their style's musical bricolage.[38] Performing songs that increasingly sounded like and sometime were huaynos with electrified cumbia accompaniment, marquee artists such as Los Shapis and Chacalón became the style's public face, dominating ticket sales and airplay until its decline in the 1990s.

Chicha's frank lyrics and its marginal thematics were often as appealing as its musical cosmopolitanism, and they too marked a significant departure from earlier styles. "Soy provinciano" (literally, "I'm from the Provinces," but connotatively, "I'm a Migrant"), a 1978 hit that Chacalón recorded with his band La Nueva Crema, is perhaps as pure a distillation of these qualities as any other song. Despite its declarative title, the song dwells not on ethnic or regional pride, but upon the harshness of proletarian life, in the plain and unadorned language typical of chicha lyrics. Over electric guitars and light Caribbean percussion, the narrator describes his struggle to succeed and his grueling work schedule, his lonely days enlivened only by his faith in hard work:

"Soy provinciano"
Soy muchacho provinciano
Me levanto bien temprano
Para ir con mis hermanos
Ay ay ay ay, a trabajar

No tengo padre ni madre
Ni perro que a mi me ladre
Sólo tengo la esperanza
Ay ay ay ay, de progresar

["I'm a Migrant"
I'm a migrant kid
I get up real early
To go with my brothers
Ay ay ay ay, to go to work

I have no father or mother
No dog to bark at me
All I have is my dream
Ay ay ay ay, to achieve]

The style had less sanguine dimensions as well. Chacalón and his peers chronicled love lost, domineering jealousy, and alcoholism alongside hard work and triumph, tracing a grim portrait of both the possibilities and the hardships of life on Lima's social periphery. Such songs were especially attractive to Lima's second-generation Andean majority. Lacking their parents' lived connection to a specifically Andean soundscape and deeply invested in the transnational youth styles that dominated the city's media channels, these children of migrants were nevertheless largely unable to enter the upscale venues that staged cumbia, salsa, and rock shows. Chicha was a way to domesticate them within their own community, and concert venues spread apace, while huayno broadcasters began shifting to the newer style. By the 1980s cultural commentators, rushing to understand the new Lima and its emergent values, had made chicha a pillar of what Pablo Sandoval has called the "optimistic vision" (2000: 303): the idea that the rise of a distinct, interstitial migrant ethos would foster a new national identity, one that spanned and reconciled Andean and coastal cultural formations.[39]

Lima's middle classes, however, took chicha to stand for everything that was distasteful about a migrant sector they blamed for the capital's entropy. Most observers read it as a sonic parallel to the disorder of Andean Lima, a condition that in turn was blamed upon a putative incompatibility between Andean mentalities and the modern life of the city, rather than the privative conditions under which migrants made their lives. Read in this light, chicha was an inept attempt to master the musical signifiers of modernity itself, a derivative and artless imitation of foreign youth culture.

Its growing prominence also riled the Andean middle class, where condemnation was organized along two different lines of critique. First, its marginal stance attracted a kind of scorn that is often directed at pointedly subaltern musics from within the communities they purport to represent.[40] For those who had achieved a measure of respect by mastering the cultural codes that made them into "decent people," chicha's image of proletarian anomie was one-sided and reductive. Its many songs chronicling the alcoholism and criminality rampant in Lima's hard-bitten migrant quarters hampered efforts to combat stereotypes, belied the economic diversity of Andean Peru, and promoted bad habits. To this day, huayno fans associate the style with moral failing and physical hazard. In an interview, one experienced broadcaster blamed chicha for a decline in standards of behavior, telling me "when that music came young people began to go bad, drink liquor, get drunk, [and] party." Indeed, many chicha artists cultivate a tough persona that is easily taken for thuggishness, and the style does attract a certain number of aspiring hoodlums, who perhaps find personal justification in songs such as Chacalón's "Por maldad" (Because I'm Bad). In fact, this song treats criminality as the last resort of the unjustly excluded, but insiders and outsiders alike often willfully overlook such subtleties.

A second critique indicted chicha in terms of cultural alienation, holding that it threatened an Andean cultural distinctiveness that is properly voiced by huayno music. This rather predictable reaction to musical change intersected with changing demographics in ways that made chicha fandom an overdetermined marker of class distinction. When I asked the broadcaster cited above to explain why it had become so popular in the early 1980s, he told me that it was "mostly because the lower classes, people who come from outside [the city], feel that they suffer, that they have more needs, hunger, and the songs are about that. That music is more for those kinds of people." Another broadcaster went further, framing chicha as a problem to be solved through instruction. Describing his goals as a huayno DJ, he told me that "60 percent [of Ayacucho's population] is from outside the city, and they aren't very educated. They like chicha, and that's fine, but what we have to do is to educate via the media, so that tomorrow that 60 percent can be 30 percent."

Such statements traffic in the deep-seated elitism characteristic of the Peruvian Andes, where metropolitan learning has long been a key marker of social attainment. However, these statements should also be interpreted in relation to past battles over dignity. For generations, highland intellectuals had fought to legitimize Andean culture by using ethnological tools of analysis to argue for the worth of folk traditions. According to this interpretive apparatus, Andean culture was a self-contained and rational system, organized according to a logic that was distinct from but no less worthwhile than that of the criollo sphere. Preserving it from corruption was tantamount to promoting cultural survival, and early strategies of legitimation were radical in their defense of people dismissed as immutably backward by Peru's prejudiced elite. Insofar as the defense of authenticity became a sign of intellectual enlightenment, it marked its champions as discerning aesthetes, and while it is easy to critique their essentialist hypostatization of Andean and non-Andean social spheres, this was secondary in a time before the postmodern order made a mockery of the cultural holism thesis.[41]

Chicha, then, appeared to challenge the hard-won legitimacy of Andean tradition itself. Its sonic hybridity affronted idealized notions of cultural integrity, its blunt lyrics and pedestrian musical choices neither conveying truths about Andean heritage nor achieving the sensitive figuration of huayno composition. Naturally, the boundary between consuming communities is permeable, and these stances should be understood as discursive positions rather than accurate representations of individual listening habits. However, they reveal a significant divide within the Andean listening community, one that rests upon an underlying opposition between educated sectors with the capacity to speak for Andean identity and citizenship, and an alienated underclass that is easily led astray by the mass media.

Despite this unremitting background of critique, chicha was on the verge of a sea change when I lived in Peru. In 2006 the television station Frecuencia Latina aired a biographical miniseries entitled *Chacalón: El ángel de los pobres* (Chacalón: The Angel of the Poor). A heavily fictionalized version of the singer's life and posthumous pseudo-canonization, the miniseries, which featured "Soy provinciano" as its theme song, was a clear attempt to tap the purchasing power that has accumulated in Lima's eponymous migrant community. Even so, its premiere on a mainstream television channel was astounding, since the social sector reflected in Chacalón's songs had "never generated a new bourgeoisie in Max Weber's terms, that is, not only people with money but also 'spiritual goods' . . . [they never became] a new guiding elite" (Neira 2004: 170). Their pecuniary muscle stood in contrast to a lingering disdain for migrant popular culture so severe that the term "chicha" has long been used as a slang term for anything crass, makeshift, or unrefined.

Later events suggest that the series presaged a change in the public status of chicha music (see Tucker 2013), but I am not sure that it signaled a significant shift in the attitudes of huayno fans, who continue to use the two styles as markers of social difference. The Sunday after the series premiere I found myself in a bus owned by my compadres, migrants who had worked their way up from street vending into Lima's middle class to become homeowners and business proprietors. One of them was a fervent huayno fan, and I was curious to find out what he thought of Frecuencia Latina's attempt to place Chacalón back into the public ear. When I asked him if he had watched the program, he snorted, wrinkled his nose, and demurred. Pressed further, he responded with a flat refusal to take the topic seriously, drawing in sociomusical terms a clear distinction between himself and his family, on one hand, and the program's intended audience, on the other: "Nooo, that's not for us. We're more huayno [*nosotros somos más folclór*]."

My friend Ana, meanwhile, underlined her aversion in more concrete terms, telling me that fans "drink with that music, and they drink a lot. Mostly it's gang members who listen to it, and in their concerts there are fights, or riots." Indeed, this image clings resolutely to the style, and watching fictionalized scenes of the young Chacalón teetering between legal work and Lima's criminal underworld reminded me of the many times that friends had warned me away from chicha shows, where liquor ran freely among gangs of toughs and concerts were always liable to end in violence. I often heard these attitudes from huayno artists, but accounts from listeners who were drawn to its tough tales of marginality spoke more compellingly of chicha's public image. In narrating his personal music history, from the standpoint of a grown man with a deep love of huayno music, my friend Fausto set chicha within a discursive field marked by ignorance, danger, and the threat of cultural dissolution. His days as a *chichero* began when he moved to Ayacucho from the countryside as a young boy to learn the craft of weaving, and he recalled them as a regrettable phase. Telling me about life in the textile workshop, he said that "everything was different, and I suffered a lot. I was completely green, I didn't even speak Spanish, and all of my roots were being destroyed. Sometimes I went out to look for records, and I almost lost myself, because in the street I would meet bad people, and they would say, 'Hey, Indian, let's go steal some stuff!' And that's when I started to like chicha."

Fausto's otherwise perplexing comment about losing his roots shows the extent to which chicha is still viewed as a threat to the integrity of huayno and all it stands for. These concerns were greatly exacerbated in the 1990s, when chicha aesthetics began to appear in the music of certain huayno artists themselves.

Huayno Norteño: Chicha Values in a Folkloric Register

Chicha entered a steep decline in the 1990s, ceding its audience and its attendant debates over social worth to another genre that I call "huayno norteño," following the usage of Ayacuchano musicians.[42] Huayno norteño represented a turn away from chicha's sound and imagery and back toward traditional markers of Andeanness, but only in part. It is based upon the traditional huayno style associated the north-central highlands of Áncash and Lima, where the harp has historically been a dominant accompanimental instrument.[43] However, it also borrows key elements from chicha, and just as some contemporary huayno musicians infused a traditional Ayacuchano style with pan-Andean elements, huayno norteño might best be understood as a contemporary version of north Andean huayno inflected by chicha aesthetics.

Huayno norteño is distinguished from other huayno styles through its unique instrumentation, the unassuming vocal style of its mainly female singers, its lyrical particularities, and its mode of presentation. It largely follows patterns laid down on recordings of the 1970s and 1980s by such performers as Tomás and Lucio Pacheco, or Totito Cruz and Mina González. Unlike earlier northern artists such as Pastorita Huaracina, who sang with lively string bands, all of these later performers sang in unassuming voices to the spare accompaniment of a steel-stringed harp. Today's performers retain the harp, which doubles the vocal line and fills breaks with ornamented melodies derived from old recordings. However, the style is also meant for dancing, and it is driven by a distinctive trochaic rhythm played in the harp's bass register, doubled by the electric bass, as well as the repeated eighth- and-two-sixteenth-note figure common to huayno styles across the Andes

7. Standard huayno norteño rhythm

(see fig. 7). This figure might sometimes be carried by Caribbean percussion instruments, such as timbales or guiro, but more typically it is played by a drum machine, which also provides extravagant fills at seemingly capricious intervals (i.e., not always at the end of verses). Vocal delivery sounds conspicuously untrained, emphasizing melodramatic vocal breaks over matters such as pitch placement or controlled vibrato. Its lyrical sensibility resembles that of chicha in that it is determinedly flat, avoiding figuration in favor of direct language, and although songs are never overtly political—indeed, they are most often romantic—their tone may be even more pronouncedly marginal than those of chicha, touching frequently upon social pathologies such as alcohol abuse, teen pregnancy, and domestic violence. Onstage, performers deploy choreographed dance moves and enliven their shows with *animadores* (emcees who shout encouragement to dancing audiences), each of which is a technique borrowed from chicha. The performers who deliver these "tropical" elements usually dress in fantastic versions of traditional Andean attire, especially favoring wide, full *pollera* skirts decorated profusely and reimagined through the gaudy, eye-catching visual aesthetic raised to an art form by chicha artists such as Los Shapis.

Predictably, huayno norteño has attracted the same sorts of criticism as chicha. The mainstream press plays up lurid tales about performers, adding innuendo about illicit behavior, and decries the robust alcohol sales at live shows. Traditionalists describe the genre's aesthetic parameters not as conscious artistic choices, but as evidence of aesthetic incompetence, signs that performers lack the knowledge, originality, and emotional depth to make proper huayno music. Critiques often focus on the genre's miserabilism, finding its emphasis on hardship to be a vulgarized caricature of huayno's nuanced melancholy. Worse, given the wealth and success of its artists, the continued dominance of such themes is often read as hypocrisy, revealing their cynical concern with the commercialization of poverty and pain.

By the beginning of the twenty-first century, the earlier contrast pitting huayno's intellectual seriousness against chicha's superficiality had been redeployed within the family of huayno styles itself, such that Ayacuchano and northern huayno styles were placed in opposition as exemplars of "decent" and "lumpen" social positions. Friends and consultants often sought to impress upon me the superficial vulgarity of huayno norteño before the sophistication of the Ayacuchano style. A terse example came from one DJ who broadcast Ayacuchano music and who framed his description of huayno norteño by saying that its musicians "aren't very creative, which is very different from Ayacuchano musicians." From a purely technical point of view, it is hard to deny that such critiques hit their mark. Contemporary northern huayno is extremely repetitive, and controlled vocal production is not a prized aspect of performance. The success of a show is measured by the amount of beer sold, and these events primarily cater to dancing concertgoers who seek escape from their workaday lives rather than edification. However, over time I gleaned other possible interpretations of the style from its fans, and most memorably from Dina Paucar, its foremost exponent.

After days of phone tag, I finally arranged to meet with Paucar on a warm summer day in January. By then she was Andean Peru's most famous performer, the subject of two television miniseries, a local UNICEF spokeswoman, and the celebrity face of Telefónica's latest calling plan. In high demand throughout the country, she had little time and less motivation to see me. But she was unfailingly gracious, and after many miscues she finally managed to slot me in during an appointment at her nail salon in Lima's solidly middle-class district of Pueblo Libre. Alarmed upon arriving to find an entire mall full of nail salons, I peered into one plate glass window after another, drawing hilarity from startled ladies with outstretched hands, until finally I was hailed by a woman in understatedly elegant clothes. In the reception area, Paucar gave me the story of her rise to fame, narrating her account in a way that bespoke much practice. She began with her youth in the northern Andes, where she came to admire the stripped-down huayno style, featuring only voice and harp, that was then in vogue locally. She told me about paying her artistic dues by touring on retainer with more famous musicians, a process by which she learned showmanship, stage presence, and the art of writing songs that moved listeners. Her story culminated with her massive success in 1990s-era Lima, with songs such as "Madre," a lament for her mother based on an old huayno tune, and "Qué lindos son tus ojitos," a yearning romantic song in the *santiago* genre.[44]

Later, at my prompting, Paucar addressed the contempt that her stylistic choices have attracted. Drum machines, electric bass, and onstage *animadores*, she told me, had been a part of the style as she inherited it, and the themes of love gone wrong and proletarian life had long been established as topics that resonated with fans. It was what drew them to weekend shows, where their concerns were given an empathetic public airing. She could hardly be blamed for serving her audience by catering to their expectations. It was true that she had borrowed psychedelic chicha fashion, but she was careful to avoid the taint of impropriety that often accrued to their female dancers, insisting that her outfits remain demure enough to avoid charges of exhibitionism.

I had often been uncomfortable with the stridency of critics such as the Ayacuchano singer Ernesto Camassi, who has railed in print against the "outlandish [*estrafalaria*]" attire and inferior musicianship of Paucar and her peers (Camassi Pizarro 2007). After speaking with her, I found it especially difficult to square such critiques with her quiet integrity, and I left convinced that the critiques of traditionalists were beside the point. Where artists such as Camassi talked about their mission to preserve and educate, Paucar talked instead about the shrewd business decisions that had allowed a humble singer to master the music business. She took for granted her obligation to serve her listeners, and she seemed most intent on describing her music and her celebrity persona as a performance of selfhood, a way of refracting the struggles for progress that her audience faces on a daily basis. To frame northern huayno as an aesthetic failure, then, is to misapprehend its artistic logic. What its artists provide is an understanding of their audience's life world and the role of their romantic desires within it. They sing its daily pressures in a way that allows listeners to unburden themselves before sympathetic ears. Artistic legitimacy revolves around experiential authenticity rather than musical involution, and success is judged not by edificatory potential, but rather by the extent to which audiences are moved physically and emotionally, alleviating the stress of an existence that is draining and precarious. The continual use of familiar tropes facilitates this, meaning that huayno norteño songs are indeed repetitive; furthermore, paths to release are smoothed by the consumption of alcohol, and attendance at a single huayno norteño concert is enough to determine that reports of drunken excess are minimally exaggerated. Rather than pathologies, these choices are best interpreted as emotional shortcuts of great importance to audiences.

I know that these distinctions in musical use value would be dismissed by my acquaintances in the Ayacuchano music scene, who treated huayno norteño as little more than the ground against which their own sophisticated efforts stood out in rich variety. But huayno norteño fans were not entirely silent about the relative superiority of their chosen style either, and informal commentary often revealed a self-conscious contestation between distinct musical aesthetics, articulated to different class fractions. For instance, Fernando Cruz, director of the Ayacucho radio station La Voz de Huamanga, dismissed my interest in researching Ayacuchano music the first time that I spoke with him, describing huayno norteño as "the people's music" and affirming its loftier social importance.

The point was made more clearly on an evening when my compadres Lucy and Jorge invited me to play with Lucy's brother, an accomplished Ayacuchano guitarist. Dragging an obligatory case of beer from Lucy's corner store to her house, we arrived only to find that her brother had misplaced his guitar. Everyone was interested to hear me, though, and while I tuned up, Lucy, Jorge, her brother, and a schoolteacher friend discussed the recession of Ayacuchano music before other sounds. My compadres regretted these changes, but their guest thought that it was a sign of aesthetic democratization. He praised huayno norteño for its communicative, plainspoken lyrics and its danceable nature, qualities that set it apart from Ayacucho's affected, stilted, and snobbish style, and he chose to underline the point after I began to play. Listening to the thumping, off-beat bass lines and the lightly ornamented melody that I produced in interpreting "Adiós pueblo de Ayacucho," Lucy turned to her brother and exclaimed, "It's just like García Zárate!"[45] Any pride I might have taken in the comparison, however, was dutifully allayed by the visiting schoolteacher, who lowered his head, his eyes heavy-lidded in melodramatic boredom. He capped his act by emitting loud snoring sounds, leading to raucous laughter and rueful discussion about Ayacucho's formal and sedate huayno tradition.

Conclusion

Far from homogeneous, the Andean music scene in contemporary Peru is a dynamic space for the manufacture of social distinction. By the turn of the twenty-first century, huayno (with all its subvariants), chicha, and pan-Andean music stood in productive tension, continually reworking themselves into new configurations as broader structural changes created new kinds of listening communities. These developments rarely pit traditionalists against modernists in any simple sense. Rather, most actors are united in the assumption that artists should seek to make Andean music "modern," a handle that is irreducibly tied to foreign pop, rock, and tropical styles. Debates center upon the proper ways in which musical evolution should occur, and different actors cobble together representations of modernity from distinct sounds and images, essaying strategies to render Andean heritage in terms recognizable to those raised upon the products of the global entertainment industries.

Andean musical constituencies, then, can be distinguished in part by the way in which they align local styles with different international musics. In this sense, all of the musicians involved might be seen as participants in the process of cultural grayout that a certain vein of commentary has long predicted for such places as Peru.[46] There is no question that they displace more aesthetically challenging and hence vulnerable musics that are difficult to reconcile with the sonic parameters of the international culture industries. Nevertheless, understanding contemporary sociomusical life means studying the way that the drive for sonic modernization fosters new kinds of public distinctions even as it extinguishes others. Often these operations engage older patterns of distinction, and in contemporary Peru the opposition between contemporary Ayacuchano huayno and huayno norteño represents a modern remapping of old binaries, understandings of Ayacuchano musicality that developed much earlier.

THREE

Bohemians, Poets, and Troubadours: Ayacucho's Enlightened Aristocracy and the Foundations of Huamanguinismo

> If La Paz and Arequipa are modern *mestizas*, trying to pass for Europeans; and Cusco an impoverished, abandoned Inca princess, who keeps among her rags some tattered, precious pieces of her ancient imperial tunic; then Ayacucho is the decrepit, Hispanized *mestiza* of the Colony, ageless among her mountain peaks, faithful to the customs and beliefs learned from her fathers, the Conquistadores.
>
> —José de la Riva-Agüero, *Paisajes peruanos* (1955)

The vision of Ayacucho laid out in the epigraph above was penned by the criollo aristocrat José de la Riva-Agüero, who passed through the city on his 1912–14 journey of exploration through the southern Andes. Defying the social conventions of Lima's great families, who typically vacationed in more cosmopolitan climes, the young writer had come to explore a region that was almost unimaginably alien to his class, "isolated and separate from the [Peruvian] nation-concept (*nacionalidad*), unknown to the spoiled children of the elite" (Webb 2009). Ambivalent at best in tone, Riva-Agüero's words nevertheless echo the vision of Ayacucho held by its most passionately devoted residents over the early twentieth century. Between his visit and the 1959 reopening of the Universidad Nacional San Cristóbal de Huamanga, local artists and intellectuals strove to define the city's essential character. Like their peers throughout the Andes, they debated the legacies of colonialism, cultural contact, and race mixture. But Ayacucho's intelligentsia was unique in forging "an interpretation of *mestizaje* that privileged Spanish heritage" (Millones 2005: 202).

Accounts of Andean intellectual life during this period usually stress developments in Cusco, Puno, and Lima, all centers of indigenista activity.[1] Ayacucho's commentators also sought to bring themselves into the national ecumene, but in arguing their city's neo-Hispanic essence, they differentiated themselves from the indigenous majority rather than drawing themselves closer to it. Emphasizing their belletristic sensibilities and incurable romanticism, they fashioned an elitist discourse of urban-mestizo cultural identity, often under the rubric of *huamanguinismo*.[2] And even as they claimed for themselves a kind of Andean autochthony, their emergent cultural ideology separated the nonindigenous *señores* of Ayacucho from local Indians, making it difficult to describe huamanguinismo simply as a local version of indigenismo.[3]

In this chapter, I describe the sounds, images, and ideas that separated true huamanguinos from those who were not. In the early twentieth century, Ayacucho's middle and upper classes were undergoing rapid reformation, and changing social conditions loosened the historic meanings of such categories as mestizo, criollo, and Andean. Seeking to control the terms by which their emergent society would be described, and perhaps to escape being racialized by those who were not a part of it, the city's intelligentsia forged a self-image as an Andean elite comparable to Lima's criollo elite. Their notions of social distinction drew them away from the taint of Indianness, and musical performance became a key way of remaking inherited modes of cultural and racial distinction, particularly through the agency of an organization called the Centro Cultural Ayacuchano. The ties between sound and society promoted by this group and affiliated organizations continue to inform the work of Ayacuchano artists and mediators to this day, even as explicitly race- and class-based languages have dwindled in significance.

Ayacucho Otherwise: Race, Class, and Status

Riva-Agüero's brief description succinctly captured Ayacucho's state of decline in the early twentieth century. During the colonial period, the city was a hub of industry, sending finished cloth, leather goods, and household wares along the royal roads linking Buenos Aires to Quito. Thanks to its temperate climate, it housed mansions where nearby Huancavelica's mercury barons sought relief from that city's alpine cold. But these trade patterns were disrupted over the eighteenth century as mines ran dry and growing port cities provided cheaper conduits for the flow of goods. The final battle of Peruvian independence stamped Ayacucho's name with glory, but it also dealt a fatal blow to local commerce, as boundaries and tariffs emerged with the new states of South America. Bad land and broken terrain made extractive industry and agriculture prohibitively unprofitable, and nothing arose to replace Ayacucho's lost enterprises. Its stately houses moldered along empty boulevards, themselves choked with mud or dust according to the season. Heirs to the city's storied lineages, including its four marquises, ceded their lands and fled to the developing coast. In the Watatas valley east of town, wheat mills idled along the river, rendered useless by technological obsolescence. A weak power substation barely lit the streets of the city center, and no highway arrived until the 1924 independence centennial—and even then, travelers reached the city only after a long journey over washboard roads and through frigid mountain passes. Worst of all, the UNSCH, the second-oldest university in the hemisphere and symbol of local pride, was closed in 1886, bankrupted by Peru's humiliating defeat at Chilean hands in the War of the Pacific.[4]

Ayacucho's stagnation did not result in total insularity, though, and Riva-Agüero was not the only traveler to pass through. A different portrait appears in the 1917 travel narrative *Vagabonding Down the Andes*, by the New York adventurer Harry Franck, a commentator who was bigoted to a degree common in his era. Nevertheless, among his descriptions of crude Indians and ignorant *señores* lie some rich observations. Over several pages of invective, he amplified Riva-Agüero's pithy description of Ayacucho's decay. He described the city as a filthy, impoverished, conservative disappointment, rank with religion and weighed down by inertia. The services at the dank city hotel disappointed his already low expectations, the leisure activities of its residents were neither picturesque nor elevating, and its educated class appeared to have lost all contact with international arts and letters.

However, his account of Ayacucho and its environs was enlivened by an unexpected meeting. Clambering by donkey along treacherous mountain paths, Franck encountered a German piano. Under the eye of a lawyer and landowner named Anchorena, the upright was en route from the railway terminus in Huancavelica to his mansion in Ayacucho. This meant a three-week haul across high deserts and canyons, and Franck met the company near the journey's close. He watched in amazement as a gang of Indian peons from Anchorena's *hacienda*, hired with the promise of coca, food, alcohol, and a pitiful bonus, bore the load across the Warpa River using ropes and "home-made tackle" (Franck 1917: 376), slipping on the smooth stones of the riverbed. The incident affords some entertaining narration, but Franck's engaging tone derives mainly from the incongruousness with which he viewed the whole project. Ever derisive, he lists the journey's prohibitive costs: $500 for the piano itself, plus $250 incurred in transport—all without reckoning the labor lost at the plantation. What, it is implied, could someone like Anchorena, an acquisitive provincial in search of more ostentatious "playthings," such as his "cream-colored coast horse" (1917: 374), possibly need a piano for?

Anchorena left no rebuttal, but the very expense involved might have led Franck toward a richer vision of Ayacuchano society. The city was a backwater, but it was also the site of a vibrant intellectual life. The Anchorena in question was probably the magistrate Carlos Alberto Anchorena, and he may have been a wealthy showoff, but he was also a respected scholar and composer. Pianos were not altogether rare within the intellectual salons where Ayacucho's aristocracy met to exchange ideas and entertain one another.[5] In 1934 Anchorena and his fellows founded the Centro Cultural Ayacuchano (CCA) to advocate the importance of Andean society by promoting the dissemination of local art and scholarship. Active until 1965, it was not the only Ayacuchano site of intellectual endeavor over the early twentieth century, but its membership gave it uncommon prestige, its longevity gave it great public influence, and its journal, *Revista Huamanga*, has left the fullest record of intellectual currents over this formative period.

Franck's vision of Ayacuchano society was hardly his alone, and his evaluations of Andean elites were substantially similar to those of the Lima-based aristocracy against which Andean citizens struggled to assert their worth. Inveighing against "the tiresome 'polish' of the Latin American city-dweller" (Franck 1917: 377), he found them unbearably pretentious, their self-opinion out of proportion with their actual station. Indeed, having distinguished Anchorena, a "white man of some education" (1917: 374), from the Indians whom he found so repulsive, Franck later undercut the epithet by calling into question the "whiteness" of Ayacuchanos generally. Stating that the minds of local elites "differ only in slight degree from the *gente del pueblo* [commoners]" (1917: 385), he noted the dominance of "diluted Indians" and stated that "genuinely white persons are decidedly rare, certainly not ten percent, though there are many more than that, strutting about in what Ayacucho fancies faultless dress, who consider themselves such, and who would be astonished at the set-back their pretensions would receive in more exacting communities" (1917: 383).

In dismissing the claims of unnamed Ayacuchano notables to whiteness, Franck brought an outsider's racial understanding to bear in a context where it did not quite fit. For the New Yorker, status derived from whiteness, whiteness derived from ancestry, and faultless dressing, when practiced by people with indigenous ancestors, was a risible attempt at racial passing. But race and status were less thoroughly biologized in the Andes. Ancestry mattered, and the local social hierarchy certainly placed Indians at the bottom of the heap, but standing depended upon more than descent. Non-Indian status could be claimed by adopting behaviors, such as speaking Spanish or indulging in conspicuous consumption, that were correlated with the "civilized" culture of the modern nation-state, or by acquiring wealth and education, thereby moving away from the Indian markers of rural residence and manual labor.

Of course, hierarchized racial terms lived and still live in Ayacuchano social discourse, but they are rarely used as endonyms (Romero 2001). The term "mestizo," for instance, is readily applied to culture, but it smacks of denigration when applied to individuals, its hint of indigenous blood impugning one's claim to be treated as a non-Indian.[6] Rather, interaction relies upon a coterie of euphemisms that avoid overt references to race or ancestry. Instead, these euphemisms encompass achievable attributes such as wealth, power, education, and "civilization," that are difficult for Indians to achieve—and thereby rest irreducibly upon a racist foundation (Weismantel 2001).[7] Landowners such as Anchorena may have "considered themselves to be white (no matter what their skin color was), as superior members of the civilized race" (Mayer 2009: 88), but they more often called themselves *gente decente* (decent folk), *con apellido* (with a [good] family name), members of the *clase señorial* (gentlemanly class) or *clase media* (middle class). And though the term *blanco* ("white") might occasionally crop up, as it did in Anchorena's case, it did not rely as heavily upon his appearance as upon his wealth, his land, his maintenance of a residence in Ayacucho's city center, and his education.

Still, Franck was right that such distinctions were rarely observed in Lima, and not for nothing did the members of Ayacucho's "great families" resent the dominance of a capital where they were transformed into "highlanders and Indians" (Koc Menard 2001: 131). In the early twentieth century they were permanently haunted by the specter of Andean subalternity, which could be brought to life at the invocation of superior Limeño whiteness, and their anxieties may have been exacerbated by the recent reconstitution of the city's middle classes (Gamarra Carrillo 1996). After the War of the Pacific (1879–83) left Peru's national economy in shreds, the remnants of Ayacucho's ancestral, landholding aristocracy had left for Lima and the north, seeking means to maintain their fortunes. Their flight left a social vacuum, members of the city's petty bourgeoisie began to convert themselves into aristocratic *señores*, and the impression derived from examining regional history at this time is one of a class in continual reformation.

Through a haze of irritation, then, Franck's observations captured a dilemma faced by Ayacucho's new elites. Conscious of their precarious claims to status, they also saw themselves as legitimate participants in national life and thought of their local aristocracy as forming a social continuum with Lima's. In fact, they sometimes claimed the label "criollo," nowadays associated with the capital and its elite culture.[8] Anchorena himself stated that Andean music was "no longer only autochthonous but also *criollo*, product of the mixture of indigenous and Spanish music" (1939: 14), and a colleague's publication described Ayacuchanos as *criollo y tunante* (criollo and bohemian; M. Bustamante 1935: 29). Indeed, the term was not always so firmly affixed to Europeanized Limeños, and this alternate usage points to unconsidered registers of Andean elite experience.[9] For Andean elites, too, considered their version of *criollismo* to be an elitist form of national culture, and in Ayacucho they made its defense a centerpiece of intellectual life. The cultural narrative that arose to name this lifeworld went by the name "huamanguinismo."

Bohemian Troubadours and Quechua Poets: The Foundations of Huamanguinismo

The CCA and their like-minded peers in Ayacucho resembled their indigenista contemporaries in Cusco and Puno. There, too, gentleman scholars scoured the Indian countryside, writing up their observations in local journals, and CCA figures dialogued with them. However, indigenismo aimed to put Andean elites in touch with their "inner Indian" (Tarica 2008: 193), while the Ayacuchano circle focused on the city, defined a priori as a nonindigenous space. Their vision of Ayacuchano culture privileged Spanish heritage, promoting "an ideological distance from the indigenous population" (Millones 2005: 202), and feeding a "a purist *huamangunismo*" (Gamarra Carrillo 2007: 170–71), a hierarchized sense of local identity that rested upon identification with the Hispanic past.

The term "huamanguino" and its variants appear more often in the writings of later analysts than in those of the CCA, but in their colonial derivation they nicely capture the tenets of the urban identity that the group helped to codify. The city was called Huamanga for hundreds of years, before Simón Bolívar renamed it after the 1824 Battle of Ayacucho. However, locals still call it Huamanga, often reserving the term "Ayacucho" for the department of which it is the capital, and the demonym "huamanguino" lives on as a term for all that which bears deep ties to the city's history and its unique culture. Applied to individuals, families, or cultural practices, it suggests direct lineal contact with the storied residents of centuries past and distinguishes them from the indigenous migrants who permanently altered the city's face after the 1950s. More than anything, it suggests a colonial

Spanish pedigree, a deep connection with the noble Iberian traditions that over centuries shaped this most Spanish of Andean cities.

Ayacuchano intellectuals insistently applied this scheme of interpretation to local history and culture, breathing past into present so as to highlight the city's colonial legacies. Music was particularly central to huamanguinismo, both as a source of narrative imagery and as a performative mode of identification. In local stories, the truest huamanguinos appear as poets and troubadours in the Iberian lineage. They are bohemian minstrels who wake silent streets beneath shuttered balconies, filling the wee hours with huaynos and *yaravíes*, colonial genres that bend indigenous elements to prosodic and musical structures inherited from Spain. They enliven aristocratic salons with their verbal and instrumental dexterity, singing in a refined Quechua peculiar to this Hispanophile elite, accompanied by Spanish guitars and mandolins. And they can be found lounging in parks and cantinas, ever ready to engage in an instrumental duel or to join in the fraternal performance of melancholy and picaresque songs.

This was not merely a past ideal, but a living mode of leisure for Ayacuchano men throughout most of the twentieth century, and the narrative figures favored by the CCA were more than fictive evocations of a lost and splendid colonial milieu. However, they were selective truths, and their success foreclosed other possible repertoires of identarian imagery. Ayacucho had housed a substantial indigenous population since colonial times, as well as a proletarian mestizo majority that may or may not have shared the elite's interpretations. Further, the city's essential nature might have been interpreted in other ways—as a hotbed of revolutionary activity, for instance, prone to outbreaks such as the 1934 uprising of youths affiliated with the leftist APRA party, or as an indigenista stronghold, owing to the presence of several explicitly indigenista publications. Ayacucho, in other words, offered other avenues of collective identity, but the CCA and like organizations ensured that a determinedly Hispanist series of practices and images became the distinguishing marks of the city and its residents.

By midcentury, musical performance was not just a discursive marker of huamanguinismo, but a key mode of inhabiting one's identity as such. The success of the CCA and their allies in tying music to Ayacucho's aristocratic image may be seen most clearly in an oft-cited piece by Arguedas entitled "Basic Notes on the Popular Religious Art and the Mestizo Culture of Huamanga" ([1958] 1977). Often taken as a foundational statement on the subject, Arguedas's piece actually follows twenty years or more of local intellectual work. Echoing CCA ideas, Arguedas described colonial conflict and synthesis between Spanish and Indian elements, while asserting that the end result was a distinct mode of Andean Hispanism. And he defined the Ayacuchano elite in part through its musical affinity:

> the aristocracy of Huamanga was famous not only for its virtuosity on the guitar but also for its talent in composing *huayno* music and lyrics. This art showed, with extraordinary eloquence, the degree of influence that Quechua music and language had acquired over the centuries, in the culture of the aristocracy. The serenades and the style of *huaynos* . . . were justly celebrated for their beauty and the admirable genius with which Quechua and Spanish were blended. These arts of the dominant class, during the colony and the first hundred years of the Republic, lent prestige to Quechua and to *mestizo* music. (Arguedas [1958] 1977: 170)

Arguedas would later, after becoming Peru's foremost interpreter of Andean society, mediate past and future interpretations, so it is well worth asking about the local antecedents to his ideas. Before approaching the work of the CCA and its allies, however, it is pertinent to review what can be known about the history of Ayacuchano music.

Musical Practice in Early Twentieth-Century Ayacucho

Written records about Ayacuchano music before the 1930s are predictably thin. Commentators often registered the prominence of musical activity, but their descriptions are vague, inflected either by local romanticism or an outsider's distaste for Andean life.[10] Nevertheless, it is possible to reconstruct the tenor of musical life by tacking between such narratives and the words of residents who remember their youth and their parents' stories. Moreover, certain musicians and institutions are widely recognized by elderly locals as keepers of tradition, and while such opinions may reveal contemporary desires to reconstruct a past that never was, corroboration with other sources just as often suggests that they stand as faithful descriptions.

By any standard, it is clear that vernacular music was long a prominent everyday pastime of Ayacucho's elites and middle classes. Local residents unanimously recalled house parties as festive occasions enlivened by song and dance, and as a relief from the tedium of daily life in the drowsy city. Birthdays, *despedidas* (going-away parties), and other life-cycle celebrations were often multiple-day affairs, and they became venues where songs were exchanged, composed, or recomposed, key nodes in the interfamily circulation of favorite tunes, which might thereby become the "property" of the family itself.[11]

The decline in these celebrations and the replacement of live performance by recorded music were both regular laments of interviewees and friends. Only twice was I privileged to attend events that were described by nostalgic participants as echoes of these earlier times. One was an octogenarian's birthday, celebrated in an old house in Ayacucho's Magdalena district. I went there as the guest of Otoniel Ccayanchira, then the last professional harpist performing in Ayacucho's distinct urban style.[12] Perching his large-bellied harp on the roof of a taxi, we drove to the site of the celebration, where he was eagerly ushered into a small sitting room. While he tuned his instrument, a small coterie of elderly ladies and gentlemen struck up a commentary on the harp's decline, exchanging tales of the great performers of times past, such half-forgotten names as "Opa" (Dummy) Román, Qori Maki (Golden Hand), and the ailing Antonio "Sunqu Suwa" (Heart Thief) Sullca.[13] Avid for the music of better days, they were also severe in their judgments, unhesitant to critique Ccayanchira's playing. The birthday celebrant, in particular, listened to the harpist's renditions of huaynos, *pasacalles*, and marineras with an aficionado's ear, and though I found his comments ungracious, Ccayanchira performed classics such as "Utku pankillay," and "Almendras, ciruelas" unperturbed—perhaps owing to his faith in his traditionalist credentials, which in the end were declared to be robust.

The second occasion was the despedida that my wife and I arranged upon our 2003 departure from Ayacucho. We had tried to replicate the conditions that regulated such parties, clearing the center of our large living room, placing as many chairs and couches along the perimeter as we could manage to find, and arranging an order with a local restaurant for dozens of chicken legs and salad on the side. Most important, we purchased several cases of beer, in the huge liter bottles that lubricate social interaction at Andean social events. Our invitees ranged from members of the urban middle class to rural migrants, from our teenaged godchildren to the elderly mother of our landlady—herself the ex-wife of the guitarist Alberto "Raktaku" (Big Lips) Juscamayta, another half-forgotten local legend. They included several artists of local and national renown, including Ccayanchira, the *chimaycha* performer and luthier Marco Tucno Rocha, a migrant from the indigenous town of Chuschi, and Ernesto Camassi, the lead voice of famed huayno group Trio Ayacucho. Since I had neither asked nor expected them to perform, I was surprised when Ccayanchira arrived with his harp and Tucno with a *manolacha*, a small, obscure lute resembling a charango that is typically played in indigenous communities.

Guests trickled in and friends took charge in the kitchen, dividing up and serving the food, accurately anticipating that we would be busy elsewhere.

Before long, Camassi seized a guitar that hung on the wall, tuned up, and began to sing. He, Ccayanchira, and Tucno formed an unusual instrumental trio, and during the course of the evening they ran through an extensive selection of traditional Ayacuchano tunes. Another guest, who had sung huaynos on the radio in her youth, joined the performers for at least one song, and Camassi's voice was accompanied throughout by those of the older attendees, who not only sang along with near-forgotten classics, but also danced in the center of the room. Dragged out time and again by older huamanguinas, whose elegant steps betrayed neither exertion or exhaustion, I saw a subtlety of footwork, syncopated twists of the ankle and brushes of the heel, that I had never before witnessed in long hours of huayno dancing, typically performed as a simple alternating double-stomp. At the time this facet of the evening's experience suggested to me a studied elegance that had once attended the musical milieu of Ayacucho's respectable citizens. And while this impression may perhaps be chalked up to romanticism or credulity, the typicality of the event was confirmed over and over again by our older guests, many of whom asserted, albeit in tipsy candor, that they had not seen this kind of party in many years.[14]

If these two occasions captured the atmosphere, in attenuated form, of an earlier musical age, they also suggest the way that vernacular musical performance was organized in that era. The ensembles that were heard on such occasions can be divided into two categories: hired professionals and ad hoc ensembles assembled from among the invitees. Harpists were the most prominent class of performers for hire, and they were a pillar of musical life, working across boundaries of class, geography, and style, at elegant parties and ritual occasions in city and countryside alike.[15] Their repertoire included favorite huaynos of the urban elite, dance music of rural indigenous communities, and the cycles specific to Christmas, Easter, and Epiphany festivals. Overall the ambit of the Andean harp was once much greater that it is today, and it is no coincidence that the first Ayacuchano recording features a rendition of "Adios pueblo de Ayacucho" by the harpist Tani Medina.

Also common were informal groups such as the improvised trio from our despedida. Well-regarded players might be invited to serve as ringers at a house party, but performers were usually drawn from among family and friends, a fact that attests to the musical prowess of ordinary residents. Instrumental forces depended upon the attendance, and the choice of repertoire upon the life experience of those willing to sing. However, guitars were de rigeur for their strummed accompaniment, the off-beat accents that drive huayno dancing, and they might be enriched by tinny, chattering charangos. If attendees had access to melodic instruments, such as mandolins, kenas, or the *laúdes* and bandurrias that have fallen out of general use, these would double the vocal line and perform the *intermedios* that filled melodic dead air between sung verses—in thirds, if the players were capable. This format also typifies the estudiantina ensembles of the early twentieth century, and in this sense it is likely that the estudiantina depended upon a set of musical dispositions that had matured earlier.

In the dominance of huaynos and other genres for dancing, such as the pasacalle and marinera, the music at these two parties is also faithful to that which would have been heard decades earlier. Only the yaraví stands out for its absence. Specific to mestizo society, written in literary Spanish, often in ancient Iberian verse forms such as the *cuarteta* or *redondilla*, the yaraví is the most aristocratic of local musical genres. Designed for listening, these romantic songs, delivered with smoldering intensity and punctuated by dramatic pauses, are widely attested before the 1980s. Once treasured musical symbols of elegance, today they have largely fallen out of favor, the victim of changing tastes and social structures.

Unlike the yaraví, huayno music was shared across boundaries in the Andes (Romero 1999). These sung poems of love, lust, poverty, and abandonment circulated easily from city to countryside and back, facilitated by the bilingual fluency of Ayacucho's middle and upper classes. Traveling performers for hire were one vector, but everyday citizens, circulating throughout the region for work, education, or leisure, also traded verses and melodies. When Carlos Falconí described to me his bifurcated childhood, split between Lima, Ayacucho, and the tiny rural town of San Miguel, he insisted that familiarity with urban and rural styles had enriched him as a musician.[16] But his large stock of archaic huaynos and yaravíes was also his father's legacy. Roberto Falconí's job had taken him all over the north of Ayacucho and neighboring departments between the 1910s and 1930s. Upon returning home he habitually met with friends to drink and make music, showing off new songs collected during his journeys. Carlos learned these tunes at his father's knee, and, as second voice to his father's lead, he also learned a style of accompanimental singing that would be responsible for much of Trio Ayacucho's success.

Naturally, the home was not the only context for performance. Its urban core surrounded by larger, rowdier neighborhoods of rural migrants and proletarians, Ayacucho itself afforded many opportunities for the boundary-crossing circulation that gave vitality to the genre. Its many cantinas and *tiendas*, stores that also served as bars (or vice versa), were important sites of homosocial interaction, where drink mixed easily with song, and many kept instruments on hand. A striking evocation of this scenario came from Oriol Chuchón, a huamanguino and music aficionado who moved to the city from the town of Umaru in the early 1940s. Discussing Ayacucho's musical history, he reminisced about Taca Alvarado, a legendary guitarist who was already an old man at that time, and who is often treated as a fountainhead of the huamanguino guitar style—indeed, before hearing Chuchón's comments, I was unsure whether Alvarado had really existed. The context in which people met to share huayno music, and the style of guitar playing that made the music truly huamanguino, remained vivid for Chuchón seventy years later:

> Well, I had the occasion to hear Taca in this way. [*To Falconí*] Remember the Sunday fairs in San Juan Bautista [a working-class district]? Well, that Señor Martínez, the husband of the lady that lived by the church, he had a store there. I think he was the governor of San Juan Bautista. And in his store, every Sunday, you know who played? Opa Román on the harp, and Taca Alvarado. Well, at 8:00 A.M., every Sunday, there was Taca, playing guitar, eating cheese, and whoa, he made that guitar talk, the bass lines especially. The bass lines are what distinguish the huamanguino huayno from other kinds, the bass lines like the harp played. He played effortlessly; you could hear his guitar everywhere. And Opa Román accompanied him. And I was there religiously, sitting on a bench and listening.

Chuchón's musical background is unusual in that he learned the huamanguino guitar style from both his father and his mother, who in turn had learned to play guitar during their studies in the city. Women instrumentalists are decidedly rare in this conservative Catholic society, and even female vocal performance was often frowned upon outside the home. This gender divide is underlined by the tradition of the *serenata*, or nighttime serenade, which popular memory may hold in higher esteem than any other historical venue for musical activity. Every traveler to Ayacucho seems to have heard or participated in one of these occasions, though reports come with a heavy patina of idealization. Riva-Agüero, for instance, recalled how "one can often see, by the light of the moon, in doorways and on corners, old men cloaked in noble Castilian capes; and by the fragrant gardens, before the carved balconies and barred windows, murmur yaravíes and vihuelas" ([1955] 2004: 182). Those who remember an Ayacucho before automobiles and electricity offer similar accounts, though they are less given to Iberian romanticism. Serafina Chuchón, the younger sister of Oriol, was herself an accomplished musician, inheritor of her grandmother's varied repertoire, but she recalled the way that her gender inflected her musical experience:

> Most of all I remember the serenatas. Ladies in those days couldn't go out in the street, walk, be at meetings, parties. So, when a man was after a woman, he would put together a group and give her a serenade. And I heard those, surely all Ayacuchano men have given a serenade. And the lady could go out on the balcony, throw down a flower, but that's all. And all the serenades were done with huaynos and yaravíes, salon music, not popular songs [for dancing], but salon songs, for listening.[17]

The intellectual salon is another important link in the musical chain of huayno circulation. Huamanguino intellectual life before the 1930s was "very active, despite the economic circumstances . . . it was as if, given physical and economic isolation, *mestizo* pride survived on vanguardist ideas and attention to culture" (Glave and Urrutia 2000: 11).[18] As in much of Latin America, the "enlightened landlords" looked to France as an intellectual model, going so far as to open a French school in 1907 (Gamarra Carrillo 2007), and an enthusiasm for intellectual salons after the French tradition had been consolidated by the 1920s. In his study of these informal circles, which "brought together men and women of the directing class to discuss such diverse topics as literature, regional history, and politics" (Gamarra Carrillo 2007: 160), Gamarra shows how their events gradually assumed the form of literary-musical soirees. Here Ayacucho's elite, self-consciously erudite huayno tradition took root, a local version of Europe's art song traditions, never separate from the broader huayno tradition, but more formal, its words more stylized, its instrumental resources more exalted than those of the huaynos that accompanied dancing and drinking. Anchorena's piano was probably destined for this sort of thing, and though a salon huayno tradition may have predated the existence of these soirees, here they began to be described as crucial aspects of local culture. Gamarra, for instance, cites a 1930 article in the local weekly *La Opinión*, asserting the necessity of the literary-musical soiree "now, more than ever, when the tango and the jazz band [*yazbán*] try to impose themselves upon our spiritual world" (Gamarra Carrillo 2007: 171).

By the 1940s, the city's schools too were part of the circle through which huamanguino music traveled. Falconí learned to perform huayno not only at his father's knee, but also from his schoolteacher, the priest Ernesto Navarro del Águila, who sought to reinforce the talents of his young charge:

In those years I worked as secretary in Mariscal [a local high school], when he was a teacher. And *maqta* [Quechua: kid], he'd say to me, *hamuy* [Quechua: c'mere], *qaparinki* [Quechua: grab this], he'd say. And he sat at an untuned piano to play. I would say he is the best Ayacuchano pianist of all time. The profundity of feeling, that singular ornamentation of Ayacuchano music, he achieved it on the piano despite the fact that it's a difficult instrument. And when I would make a mistake he would say, "No, not that way, this way." Really, he's one of the teachers who shaped me, in the art, the feeling, the profundity of our music.[19]

Such intimate exchanges hint at a broader context, in which intellectual life outside the school precincts began to influence activities within—no doubt owing to participation by schoolteachers in the city's intellectual circles. By the 1930s several schools had launched estudiantinas, antedating by several years the founding of the city's storied Estudiantina Municipal, and all of these activities interpenetrated in the life of Ayacuchano boys from the middle and upper classes. A thorough portrait of a young man's musical formation in this period comes from the biography of Alejandro Vivanco, a famous kena player and one of Peru's leading Andean artists (Vilcapoma 1999: 38). According to his narrative, he and his cousin Moisés, who would become world famous as the husband of the soprano Yma Sumac and leader of her band, began their careers by surreptitiously testing their relatives' kenas and charangos. Unable to master them, they sought instruction from local players, with Alejandro taking clandestine lessons from the renowned Francisco Rivera, "El Inkario."[20] Upon his arrival at school, he was obliged to join the institution's brass band, playing first bass drum and then cornet. But after he moved on to the prestigious Colegio San Ramón, his musical career took a more serious turn under Telésforo Felices, the composer to whom is attributed the classic huamanguino huayno "Utku pankillay" (My Cotton Ball). Shortly after Felices arrived in the city, he founded the institution's estudiantina in 1930. He moved Vivanco from the piccolo to the mandolin and forced him to read sheet music. Perhaps more important, he encouraged vernacular artists to come by the school, such as the former student Tani Medina. This environment encouraged Vivanco to begin writing down the pieces that he heard, which later entered his repertoire as *recopilaciones* (collected songs). He also began composing, writing a number of tunes for the estudiantina whose titles, such as "Lágrimas de Ñusta" (The Inca Maiden's Tears), suggest the influence of indigenismo.

All of this musical and intellectual activity was systematized and disseminated through the CCA, described by Glave and Urrutia as "the axis of cultural activity in the city until the reopening of the UNSCH" (2000: 20). The CCA took up musical tendencies that already surrounded them, promoting them within a general context of Andean cultural revitalization and lending the prestige of their members to the effort.

The Centro Cultural Ayacuchano: Salon of the Enlightened Aristocracy

The Centro Cultural Ayacuchano, "a society of a literary-artistic nature" ("Centro Cultural Ayacucho" 1934), was officially founded on the second Monday of October 1934. To mark the occasion an illustrious crowd gathered in Ayacucho's official Hall of Ceremonies to enjoy an evening of music and elevated discourse. Filing into a second-story room, its windows open to the city's darkened plaza, a mixed crowd of women and men, adolescents and respected elders, probably filled benches set before a long wooden table. Presiding here, perhaps (as today) beneath portraits of politicians and generals, would have sat the society's board of directors: nine men, stiff in jackets and ties befitting the solemnities, and a lone woman, perhaps dressed in the regal embroidered blouse and skirt worn by respectable ladies of the city. The meeting almost certainly opened with words of welcome from the society's first secretary general, the mustachioed septuagenarian Manuel Jesús Pozo. It is likely that he stood before a room dominated by CCA associates and their family members, but visiting dignitaries would have been singled out for special recognition and welcome.

After the opening formalities, three of the board members gave speeches about the CCA's mission. Pozo hinted at the "superior activities that the board had planned and outlined the "elevated goals" of the society, noting that its members were motivated by the desire to "live less for our own sake and work harder for the collective interest" (cited in Galindo Vera 2000: 2). His colleague Pío Max Medina, the subsecretary, described the central role that historical research should play in their efforts, noting that "the true history of Ayacucho is still to be written, and its prehistory remains in the limbo of legend," while the society's dues collector, Magdalena Fajardo de Castro, finished with a special appeal for contributions by women, "an important factor in a society's march toward progress" (cited in Galindo Vera 2000: 2).

Leavening these weighty sentiments were musical intermezzi, whose exact nature was not recorded. However, reports of later performances, together with clues in Pozo's founding address, give indications as to what was played. Pozo had urged musicians to "consider that the Indian bears a legacy of pain and suffering that cannot be stated in words, but which is expressed via the kena, the [pan flute], and in his songs" (cited in Galindo Vera 2000: 3). In a telling phrase, he asked them to "capture the musical values that remain autochthonous in our high plains"—to seize from Indian performers the essence of their music, and domesticate it, *sans* living Indians, for use in the salon. In tune with this exhortation, the evening probably showcased pieces resembling those of notable indigenista composers based in Cusco or Lima, which "captured" an outsider's notion of Indian life via titles, lyrics, scale types, tempos, and rhythmic cells that were erroneously understood to typify Indian art. The audience may have heard something like the harvest song (*ccachua saratipiy*) featured at the CCA's next musical event, apparently based on a tune from a Quechua-speaking community. Or they may have enjoyed an original piece by a local composer, an indigenista fantasy such as "Plegaria al sol" (Oath to the Sun) "Canción indígena" (Indian Song), or Vivanco's "Lágrimas de Ñusta," all printed at the expense of none other than Carlos Anchorena—perhaps after a hearing upon his piano, last witnessed crossing the Warpa River on Indian backs.[21]

Indigenista stereotypes, however, were only one of the CCA's musical interests. Later commentaries, beginning with a 1935 essay by Manuel Bustamante (the CCA's secretary of finance), set out to rectify a perceived waning of the city's popular music. The association soon made the huayno "Helme," a sung tale of amorous betrayal, into a fixture of their activities, and affiliates such as José Jáuregui, known for the "native Ayacuchano flavor" (Fajardo 1940: 51) of compositions such as the huayno "Maywa maywachallay verde," were hailed as examples for Ayacuchano citizens. In fact, insofar as the society was mandated to "preferentially study *only* that which concerns the city" (Pozo 1934: 2; emphasis added), a focus on the "autochthonous musical values" of indigenes may have contravened their mission. Alongside indigenista fare, then, the CCA's inaugural audience may have heard the huaynos and yaravíes that enlivened their house parties and serenatas. They may even have joined in the singing of well-known songs such as the huayno "Para todos hay mañana," cited by Bustamante as an exemplar of vernacular music. In any case, the performance was probably entrusted to Francisco González, the CCA's subsecretary of finance, who took charge of most musical events in the society's early years. He may have performed solo, upon the piano, but records show that he usually played with an estudiantina. So listeners probably heard huayno arrangements and/or indigenista compositions, performed with rehearsed polish by a mixed ensemble and perhaps the voices of young ladies.[22]

Overall the evening was deemed—by the CCA, anyway—to have been an epochal episode. Using an epithet that became standard in their reports, a later account described the attendees as "numerous and select" ("Centro Cultural Ayacucho" 1934). They could just as well be described as the local *crème de la crème*. Present were the bishop of Huamanga, the city's mayor, and the provincial prefect, representing the region's highest ecclesiastical and governmental authorities. Also in attendance were teachers from the Colegio San Ramón, including the CCA's planning secretary, Alfredo Parra Carreño, the driving force behind the establishment of the society itself. He went on to become San Ramón's principal and later a representative for Ayacucho in the national congress. Pozo had also been a congressman and was only slightly less distinguished than Medina, who was a former senator, a cabinet minister, and the second vice president of the Republic—though perhaps Pozo's descent from the marquis of Mozobamba compensated for his lesser political achievements. All three were alumnae of the jurisprudence program at Lima's San Marcos University, and the society was thick with titled professionals, graduates of San Marcos, of Cusco's San Antonio Abad University, and of Lima's Normal School. Even a cursory survey of its affiliates, over its three decades of existence, shows a high representation of the lawyers, educators, priests, and politicians who dominated Peru's Andean aristocracy, and whose numbers overlapped significantly with the landowning class.[23]

This description conveys much of what the CCA was and was not. Though it was a society of arts and letters, officially mandated to avoid political issues per se, its social politics were clear: it was meant to consolidate a vision of Ayacuchano identity that responded to the interests of its elite members. The soiree format of the founding ceremony was familiar to the CCA's audience, but as Gamarra Carrillo (1996, 2007) has argued, the shift from semiprivate salon to the public hall was a striking departure, marking a fundamental change in Ayacuchano intellectual life. Two key aspects of this officialization can be inferred from the manner in which the event was situated in time and space. Falling on the second Monday in October, it coincided with El Día de la Raza, the holiday commemorating Columbus's landing in the New World and dedicated to Hispanic achievement. And by meeting in the local government's Hall of Ceremonies, overlooking the central plaza of the departmental capital, the attendees were situated at the symbolic center of government power. Addressing this refined crowd from within the very site of surveillance from which the ruling class governed the national territory, the CCA bore from its inception the imprimatur of nobility.

But a potent irony serves as an effective metaphor for the situation in which these intellectuals found themselves. Ayacucho's town hall had been built in 1924 with funds the state had allocated to spruce up the city in time for the Battle of Ayacucho's centennial (Gamarra Carrillo 2007); it therefore stood as a reminder of the city's dependent, beggarly status. The intellectual dignitaries gathered there to celebrate their distinctive culture were local elites, but they were also keenly aware of their marginality on the national stage. And this is perhaps what lends their work an air of defensiveness and provincial desperation. Their efforts at cultural revalorization were efforts to shore up their own influence (Gamarra Carrillo 1996), but consolidating their elite status meant ensuring that regional culture reflected their self-image, as people who were something more than the Indians that faraway criollo society imagined them to be. Indeed, the signs of Ayacuchano identity that were sanctioned here are noteworthy for the way that they tack between local particularity and national inclusion, between a warm feeling for the city's mestizo culture and an ambivalent rejection of its indigenous heritage.

"Incaismo, andinismo, serranismo, folklorismo": The CCA's Intellectual Agenda

The CCA's founding board meant not only to invigorate Ayacucho's scholarly life, but also by doing so to revive their derelict hometown. Though they agitated for changes in economic and political policy, the establishment of a collective consciousness was paramount. A society ignorant of its own qualities could not hope to persuade others of its worth, and from the beginning Pozo advocated "a labor of *insiding* [*adentramiento*]" (1934: 2; emphasis in original), a process of self-discovery that would teach Ayacuchanos about the sources of their common identity.[24] He underlined these goals in his first editorial as president, noting their collective desire "for progress, and to serve the city" (Pozo 1934: 1), and swearing that the CCA would, "by tenacious effort, transmit something of the intellectual and artistic greatness that our capital enjoys. In this way, we will try to decentralize culture, to make sure that . . . it has a provincial flavor" (1934: 2).

Behind Pozo's words stood a diagnosis of the relationship between Andean stagnation and national identity. If Ayacucho languished, it could not be due to lack of economic and cultural resources: these the region had in abundance.[25] It was because its residents were considered to be less than full citizens, unworthy of the nation-state's devotion—and if this was so, then it was due to the suspicion that the Indian taint made the Andes an unfit scenario of national life. As it turned out, then, there was but a single solution to Ayacucho's cultural and economic marginality: local scholars would use historical and social research to demonstrate Ayacucho's high cultural level and to "make known its varied riches so that, if possible, capital holders may exploit them" (Pozo 1934: 2). Ultimately, the CCA aimed not only to make the country aware of the riches that lay hidden in this earnest, learned backwater, but also to promote a rewriting of the Peruvian narrative, one that would fully acknowledge the worth of its Andean citizens and recognize their claims upon the nation-state.

In this the CCA resembled their indigenista peers.[26] There were concrete links between Ayacucho's intelligentsia and the indigenista circles of Cusco and Lima, where many went to study, and the CCA strengthened them by centralizing exchanges of scholarly research and providing a forum for publication.[27] The nine articles treating indigenous issues that *Revista Huamanga* published between 1935 and 1938 demonstrate the influence of indigenismo, even as they hint at the CCA's distinct agenda. Notable among them is the 1935 article "El neoindianismo en Ayacucho" (Neo-Indianism in Ayacucho), by Lúcio Alvizuri, a CCA board member. It took its title from José Uriel García's essay "El nuevo indio" (The New Indian, 1929; see García 1973), which had countered earlier, purist indigenista writings by characterizing *mestizaje* (mixture) as the site of Andean cultural authenticity. Significantly, "the *neoindianistas* defined race as culture" (de la Cadena 2000: 133), arguing that behaviors determined one's social category, and making race an achieved attribute rather than an immutable biological fact. Alvizuri applied these ideas to the communities around Ayacucho, debating the proper semantics that should surround them. He asserted that the label "neo-Indian" was most adequate to local uneducated peasants who lived according to ancestral Indian patterns, speaking Quechua and using a "singular mode of dress," because they had also experienced cross-cultural influence and shared traits with the national mainstream. He characterized Ayacucho's neoindian as "aspiring" (*aspirante*), and, "fortunately for the nation," avid for the education and cultural capital (*instrucción y educación en general*) that, "save for his color," would render him indistinguishable from the "civilized masses" (Alvizuri 1935: 87).

Alvizuri and his fellows were clearly not neo-Indians, but rather part of the "civilized masses" to which a neo-Indian might aspire. The author did not state as much, but of course he did not have to: unlike outsiders from Lima or New York, he was secure in the knowledge that wealth, background, and education made him and his peers non-Indians. Like much of the work published in *Revista Huamanga*, Alvizuri's article produces the distinct sensation that the writer is a distant observer and not an embodied participant in Indian society (Millones 2005). This does not really distinguish the CCA's work from that of well-known indigenista intellectuals, also written from a position above and outside Indian life, but the sense of distinction is arguably drawn more firmly here than in works from Cusco, Puno, or even Lima, which often reached toward spiritual intimacy with an idealized Indian subject. Even when they touched upon indigenous affairs, CCA writers tended to emphasize the sharp distinctions between the educated, sophisticated, and nationally integrated citizens of the city and the rural Indians who were as yet, lamentably, none of those things.

Indeed, Pozo's founding injunction to preferentially study the city and its aristocratic culture remained relevant throughout the life of the society, though it was never followed to the letter. Its sentiments were echoed in a speech eleven years later, when the outgoing president, Parra Carreño, reiterated that the CCA's mission was "to discover and disseminate to all four winds the essential personality of our city" (1945: 37). This profound sense of disidentification with the rural indigenous majority heavily inflected the CCA, and it highlights the limitations of describing them merely as a local branch of the indigenista movement. Gamarra Carrillo (1996, 2007) provides the best theory of the reasons for this quality of Ayacucho's intellectual work, arguing that the city's scholars were motivated by the same frustrations with centralized state authority as the indigenistas, but also by an upswing in indigenous rebelliousness and its consequences. Media reports on recent revolts in the Ayacuchano provinces, many influenced by indigenista terms of discourse, had often pitted virtuous, oppressed Indians against brutish, inhumane *gamonales* (corrupt landowners-*cum*-political bosses).[28] Alert to this hardening public stereotype and stung by its contrast with their cherished self-image as a bookish, enlightened aristocracy, Ayacucho's intelligentsia was moved to counter it. In other words, despised both because they were Andean and because they were not Indian enough to be romanticized, they sought to defend both their unique highland culture and to demonstrate their intellectual enlightenment.

This account may explain why some commentators have struggled to define the CCA's intellectual orientation. Discussing the career of the sometime CCA participant Moisés Cavero, his two sons assert that he "appreciated occidental culture . . . giving his indigenismo a character distinct from that which abhorred and condemned the conquistadores" (Cavero Carrasco and Cavero Carrasco 2007: 106). For them, this "Hispanist indigenismo" was "a provincial movement . . . [that] did not oppose itself to Spain," and which sought to "'dilute the Indian through mixture'" (2007: 124). Yet an indigenismo defined by its Hispanism stands very far from indigenismo as it is commonly understood. It is perhaps for this reason that the authors define indigenismo itself as an -ism tied to other, unheard-of movements, such as *incasimo* (Incaism), *andinismo* (Andeanism), *serranismo* (highlandism), and *folklorismo* (folklorism). These terms avoid identification with contemporary Indians, and their use raises once more the question of whether Cavero and his fellows should properly be considered indigenistas at all.[29]

Spanish Heritage and Fictional Autochthony

The relationship between Ayacucho's early intellectuals and the idea of autochthony was always shifting, and they would eventually go so far as to adopt a fictional indigenous group as figurative ancestors. However, their emphasis lay with the Spanish colonial culture and its living legacies. Alvizuri's article had asserted that even Ayacucho's rural neo-Indians were "much more predominantly Iberian than Indian" (1935: 85), and this premise runs like a background hum throughout CCA publications and those of their intellectual descendants. It periodically comes to the fore, as it did at a musical soiree in 1939, when Parra Carreño noted that the music to be heard came from the "streets of Huamanga, the serenades inherited from Spanish troubadours" (Parra Carreño, Cabrera, and Pozo 1939: 24–25). Sixteen years later, an anonymous article entitled "Pride in Tradition" described Ayacucho as a city that had always been more Spanish than Indian, stating that not even independence could modify the traditional culture (*manifestaciones costumbristas*) inherited from the mother country ("Por los fueros de la tradición" 1955: 1). The pages of *Revista Huamanga* were filled with writings about the colonial period, such as Juan José del Pino's series on Spanish architecture entitled "Momumentos coloniales de Huamanga" (Huamanga's Colonial Landmarks), and with debates such as the one over whether the plaza's commemorative statue ought to depict its Spanish founders or Pizarro, conqueror of the Inca.[30] The cumulative tone of these writings may best be indicated by a florid letter from a visiting Spaniard, which praised Ayacucho as a "heroic and legendary city, brave and indomitable, [a] piece of Spain lost among the deep Andean canyons" (Sitjar Terre 1939: 7–8).

One of the key narrative technologies through which the Spanish heritage was brought into the present was the *tradición*. Invented in the nineteenth century by the Limeño writer Ricardo Palma, this uniquely Peruvian literary genre took the form of a short narrative on a colonial theme, often purportedly folkloric in nature. Palma's tradiciones had brought to life a noble and picaresque Lima past for the delectation of its fin-de-siècle residents. A pillar of criollo cultural identity, his oeuvre constituted a self-consciously nostalgic invocation of a better, more romantic age: tales of dueling gentlemen, winsome ladies, crimes of passion, wits, ghosts, thieves, and similar fodder. Palma had even prefigured their adoption in Ayacucho by composing a tradición about colonial Huamanga, a yarn in which some drunken prelates are caught dancing to the music of local performers, "the fiercest *charanguistas* in all of Peru" (Palma [1893] 2009: 215).

The form was put to work in 1938 by the CCA affiliate Néstor Cabrera, who published a tradición in *Revista Huamanga* called "Los tunantes" ("The Bohemians"). At once a ghost story, an invocation of Ayacuchano musical skill, and a textual suturing of the colonial past to Cabrera's present, it revolved around the probably apocryphal figure of Juan Alatrista. A colonial-era guitarist and "prize of the salons" (*niño bonito de los salones*) who was "capable of making a miser cry when he sung a *yaraví*" (Cabrera 1938: 12), Alatrista is a platonic ideal of the huamanguino bohemian. The piece is a tale of terror in which the rakish Alatrista comes face to face with his own funeral while returning from a night of revels, but it is more than that. Opening with Palma's words on Ayacucho's charanguistas, it asks those readers over the age of thirty if they do not find them reflected in the great bohemians of the recent past (naming the musicians "Carrera, Olano, Gomez, and Felipe Parra"), before evoking Alatrista as the model of their type (Cabrera 1938: 11). Setting the huamanguino Alatrista, Palma's criollismo, Cabrera's readership, and their musical contemporaries in dialogue with one another, this short narrative succinctly articulates all those links between Hispanism, elitism, and music that were dear to his generation of intellectuals. And these ties were bound even more tightly when "Los tunantes" was reprinted alongside other stories in the *Tradiciones de Huamanga*, a series of short pieces published by the priest Juan de Mata Peralta Ramírez between 1969 and 1986, and later gathered together into a collection with the same title (see de Mata Peralta Ramírez 1995). Here Alatrista was joined as "the huamanguino prototype" by Taca Alvarado, the guitarist that Oriol Chuchón observed on Sunday mornings during his youth, remembered by de Mata Peralta Ramírez as "a great conversationalist, linguistically clever like Sancho Panza" (1995: 70). Between them, Cabrera and de Mata Peralta Ramírez brought the colonial ideal almost into the present, establishing a lineage that connected the idealized past to a figure remembered by much of their audience.

This discourse of Hispanism, however, coexisted with a countervailing ethnic discourse that, on first examination, seems to belie it. Soon after the CCA's foundation, scholars began to speculate in *Revista Huamanga* about an indigenous group called the Pokras, which had occupied the site of the city in precolonial times. They had been vanquished by the Inca, but those scholars who dealt with them were sure that their spirit had remained, and CCA intellectuals described them as spiritual ancestors, the progenitors of huamanguinismo itself:

> I find myself curious to ascertain what our race was, that which gave birth to true huamanguinismo, a character unmistakable among Peru's Andean cities, with something of nobility and gentlemanliness, with doses of intelligence and imagination, with a sweetness and refinement in language that makes of Quechua the filigree of sentiment. To ask what our racial origin is, in order to discover our collective psychology. (Parra Carreño 1938: 4)

This passage could be understood as a thoroughgoing endorsement of indigenous inheritance. And yet the Pokras were a figment, resting upon a single colonial reference of dubious validity and some later speculations by the nineteenth-century writer Luis Carranza.[31] Most scholars agree that this fiction served a specifically political agenda, giving Ayacucho's aristocratic intelligentsia an ethnohistorical basis on which to resist the economic dismemberment of the department of Ayacucho by the central government (Gamarra Carrillo 1996). The myth also gave locals an idiom for differentiating themselves from Cusco, the former Inca capital where contemporary indigenistas had made the ancient lords of empire into symbolic ancestors. In this sense, the Pokras provided a deep historical basis for the contemporary differences between Ayacucho and its sister cities.

Such explanations may grant too much intentionality to supporters of the Pokra myth. However, it certainly functioned in a more general way to establish the Ayacuchano elite's claim to regional representativity, granting them a surrogated autochthony without requiring a link to the living Indian population around them.[32] Indeed, within the pages of *Revista Huamanga* the evocation of the Pokras contrasts starkly with a paucity of reference to the indigenous people who actually lived within Ayacucho's precincts. The creation of a fictitious ancestral people, upon whom could be projected all those qualities of nobility, elegance, strength, and intellect that Ayacucho's aristocracy held as differentiating them from contemporary Indians, allowed them room to maneuver before charges that they had illegitimately usurped these Indians' rights over their own territory. It even explained their identification with the Quechua language and could be adduced as a source for the grace of local huayno music.

Sentimental Sounds: Defining and Performing Musical Huamanguinismo

It was an early article of faith among CCA members that vernacular music was an important locus of huamanguinismo. Live performance received equal billing with lectures and literary recitations at their events, and CCA patronage granted a sense of sophistication to the sounds heard at their soirees. Moreover, the different ways in which the society dealt with indigenista compositions and vernacular music of the city established key distinctions between the two repertoires and their users.

Contemporaneous indigenista efforts are widely interpreted as a sudden change in the nature of Andean cultural interaction, formerly characterized by a sort of cultural apartheid separating elites from masses (de la Cadena 2000; Turino 1993).[33] Yet not all of the CCA's musical activities can be regarded in this light. The scant records available suggest that local elites had long brought huayno music into their salons, and CCA writings are full of indications that members and their forebears were familiar with the tradition. Salon huaynos appeared at CCA events alongside the works of indigenista composers, and it was precisely by bringing local huayno music alongside highly stylized compositions that the vernacular musical culture of the elite, comparable in tone and effect to the criollo music of the coast, stood out against the surrogated "Indian" music of indigenismo.

An interest in music saturates the pages of *Revista Huamanga*. References crop up in tradiciones, in articles thematizing society and history, in short notes on musical doings within the city, and in reports on the national or international deeds of local musicians. Short pieces on festive traditional dance allude to instrumental or choreographic details, but only a handful of publications specifically focused on local music. Appearing between 1935 and 1949, they were all written by prominent associates, including the teachers Bustamante and Parra Carreño and the jurists Pozo, Anchorena, and del Pino, many of whom were also amateur musicians.[34] Though slightly different in emphasis, they are strikingly similar in their structure, their lines of argument, and their view of huamanguino musical aesthetics. The later authors often draw heavily upon earlier essays, and together their work shows the coalescence of an interpretive tradition that remains current today.

This analysis is incipient in the 1935 piece "Breves referencias sobre la música vernacular" (Brief Notes on Vernacular Music), where Bustamante highlighted Ayacucho's "criollo and bohemian" nature and called for the preservation of local music.[35] Originally delivered at a CCA soiree, the piece is descriptive and historical, recounting what is known about music in colonial Huamanga and listing the elements that typify the city's contemporary musical culture. He lists virtuosi on many popular instruments, as well as eccentric ones such as the harmonium, and reminds readers that there every young man sought to master the guitar. He reminisces about the serenata, where young musicians developed their skills, and, unusually, he cites in full several vernacular verses, all drawn from huaynos and yaravíes, suggesting that these genres were already seen as the foundation of Ayacucho's musical culture.

Bustamante established three aspects of musical research that were important for later writers. First, he mustered names in order to demonstrate continuity. The essay includes a genealogy headed by Juan Alatrista, who is described as a token of musical memory since 1887, when the writer Benjamín Sáez read a poem in his honor to the distinguished indigenista Clorinda Matta de Turner.[36] Bustamante's list brings a long roll of forebears into iterative contact with their purported descendants, contemporary instrumentalists who are thereby sanctioned as carriers of tradition. He provided no details as to their performance style, perhaps relying upon the evening's musical portion to exemplify the traditions in question. Indeed, the fact that Francisco González, who directed the band that night, appears on his list might suggest that this was the case.[37] The article ends with an appeal to support a diverse slate of vernacular artists, mostly guitarists, including González, the harpists "Opa" Roman and Tani Medina, who appear as estudiantina directors, and CCA favorites such as the composers Jáuregui, Anchorena, and Víctor Modesto Villanueva, "the ace of Ayacuchano musicians," whose seventeen pieces for piano, guitar, estudiantina, and orquesta include a one-step, a tango, a polka, some "serenatas," and several yaraví transcriptions, all unpublished and heard only by "the best elements of the city" at Villanueva's home (M. Bustamante 1935: 32).[38]

Bustamante's exploration of emotional aesthetics in huayno and yaraví music would also resonate with later aficionados. Though he began by describing the repertoire as "immense and varied, with an unmistakable character: sad or happy, satirical or witty, poetic or ingenuous, deep red or pink in hue, sometimes moralizing, sometimes traditional or historic" (M. Bustamante 1935: 30), the pieces he chose as examples were uniform in tone. A verse from the huayno "Para todos hay mañana" is "a well-written quatrain of jealous complaint," while another, unnamed Quechua-language song contains "a verse of self-reproach, of the lover who would abandon his beloved but cannot." The yaraví "Yo te busqué con mis ojos" describes "disappointment with reality once illusion has passed," and a piece of "serenade poetry," not specified as to genre, is a piece of "invocation and lament, capable of reconciling two hearts separated by social barriers" (1935: 30–31). This would become a trope in later accounts: an initial assertion of variety, accompanied by relentless enumeration of those varieties of experience, centering on impossible love, loss, and nostalgia, that are captured in the term "sentimental."

Finally, Bustamante set contemporary huayno and yaraví in dialogue with erudite musical practices. Beginning with an account of sacred musicians in early republican times, he memorialized José Santos Montero, who performed Palestrina, Pergolesi, composed church music, and left successors responsible for some of Ayacucho's "typical melodies" (M. Bustamante 1935: 26). Moving on to secular music, he highlighted the later musician Felipe Torres, who not only played Bach, Handel, Beethoven, and Mozart, but also taught piano in an era when playing the instrument was "the best adornment for a society lady"—among them the wife of the CCA-affiliated composer José María Jáuregui (1935: 28). Bustamante did not connect the distinct repertoires, making only the opaque assertion that "today, everyone runs from classical music and seeks a huayno or a yaraví" (1935: 28), but other pieces in the journal did suggest a direct link, including an unsigned piece on the death of the composer Villanueva in 1938, which described his house as a place where musical cultivation ranged from the indigenous huayno to Old World classics.

Later scholars would take up these elements and bring scientific or pseudo-scientific approaches to bear as well, drawing upon academic trends ranging from folklorics to psychoanalysis in order to formalize the analysis of sound and social life. The author of a 1945 article on the *araskaska* dance, for instance, began from premises like those of early social scientists, theorizing that a people's "level of development" and psychological character were reflected in their dances (Gálvez Carrillo 1945: 34). He notes that the araskaska's function is to mark marriage as a rite of passage and reads its choreography, where massed celebrants march forward in lockstep while holding hands, as a symbol for the "chains of love" (1945: 35).

Iconicity and functionalism, however, exercised these writers far less than the idea that musical expression was a window onto natural and social history. Many Andean intellectuals were influenced by *telurismo*, a doctrinal outgrowth of positivism popular at many Peruvian universities, which held that cultural groups and their expressions are fundamentally shaped by the landscape in which they develop (Pereyra Chávez 2007). Anchorena, for example, began his 1939 "Disertación sobre música peruana" (Study of Peruvian Music) by theorizing that different sounds arose initially as primitive peoples' reactions to their own diverse experiences of the natural world.[39] Later writers, including Arguedas, further adapted such ideas in arguing for a sort of climactic determinism, linking the sadness of huamanguino songs to the barrenness of the landscape and the region's consequent poverty.[40]

Telurismo was one way to ground theories of music's social power. However, articles in *Revista Huamanga* more often resembled folklore studies in reading musical style as a product of social history. The Ayacuchano intellectual Luis Carranza made just this argument in 1872 when he linked the perceived lethargy of indigenous music to Inca hegemony, which had robbed their Indian subjects of independence, vitality, and hence musical vigor. His ideas were naive and ahistorical, but they were also an attempt to theorize sound in light of sociopolitical factors. His later compatriots came to take this style of analysis for granted, and by 1946, when del Pino published the first in his series of six articles entitled "Cual es el sentido psicológico de la música ayacuchana? (What Is the Psychological Sense of Folkloric Ayacuchano Music?), the link between the two was taken for granted to such an extent that the author could state baldly that "the study of a people's social psychology is incomplete without the musical factor" (del Pino 1946: 23).

The most focused treatment of huamanguino aesthetics came in Parra Carreño's article "Cantos de Huamanga" (Songs of Huamanga, 1940), which defined huayno as "the true huamanguino song." He argued that folkloric materials, anonymous and collectively composed, "express the social consciousness of a given moment" (Parra Carreño 1940: 27), and that a thorough study might identify distinct sociohistorical layers within the local repertoire, sorting ancient, indigenous, and colonial from modern songs. However, his main object was to describe huayno as a manifestation of the huamanguino soul, which "tortures itself in pursuit of an impossible love, but never gives up" (1940: 22).[41] The essay is astute in emphasizing two typical properties of huayno lyrics above all: their emotional immediacy and their literary figuration. Noting that they primarily explore not stories, but internal states that derive from external challenges, Parra Carreño accurately captures the way that huayno music signifies: "it captures a life in one aspect [only], allowing one to determine its advantage or disadvantage, its happy or sad nature . . . [it] brings a life into view" (1940: 23). And praising the local talent for "tropes and figures," he links the metaphorical nature of huayno music to the Quechua language, which "God has made especially for hearts to speak with" (1940: 22). Stating the best huayno music is rendered graceful via "a certain indirectness, and abundant figures of speech" (1940: 23) he objects to earlier dismissals, which described "the songs of the highlands" as "mere *palomitas* and *culíes*" (doves and turtledoves, two common figures for female objects of affection; 1940: 24). Indeed, Parra Carreño's description is more apt: "[a huayno composer or singer] seeks mountains, trees, rivers, clouds, chasms, and animals in order to express, in magnificent personifications, sentiments that can render ecstasy" (1940: 22). Overall, Parra Carreño's essay describes that web of emotional and literary devices that, together with elements of performance style, grants traditional Ayacuchano huayno its beloved quality of sentiment.

Parra Carreño called for a defense of Ayacucho's distinct musical identity and stated that "our songs are becoming confused with those of Cusco and Huancayo," where they "sing and play many huamanguino huaynos as if they were from Cusco or Huancayo" (1940: 27).[42] This was an intermittent priority of the CCA and its affiliated intellectuals, with a particularly ambitious proposal appearing on the society's fourth anniversary, when its president announced a project to preserve local musical folklore (Escarcena 1938). Under CCA auspices, a commission of experts would select, catalog, and print the best of Ayacucho's native artistic production and later create a "philharmonic band" (*conjunto filarmónico*) for its performance. If these initiatives bore any fruit, they are forgotten today, and only the collection of huayno music edited independently by the CCA affiliate and estudiantina director Saturnino Almonacid made it to press.

In any case, this defense of local distinctiveness was directly related to Pozo's imperative to decentralize culture. Nearly every essay bemoaned elite indifference toward Andean music and implied that an effective nation-state would recognize the sentimental life of all its inhabitants. Observing that nationalism, "which has bloomed all over the world," is partly an artistic concern, Anchorena framed the task of highland intellectuals as "[awakening] the love of all Peruvians for national music," by which he meant the vernacular music of its Andean citizens (Anchorena 1939: 14). And while del Pino hesitated to "[raise] the issue of physical mixture," he thought that true community required "a kind of moral mixture" (del Pino 1949: 21), and that research into "popular indigenous music" furthered an understanding of the "Peruvian race" (1949: 21).

These words show the double bind that afflicted CCA intellectuals. Painfully aware of their national marginality, they sought recognition for the best of Andean culture; but, shaped by the racial ideologies of their day, they were also wary of identifying too closely with indigenous Andeans.[43] This dichotomy gives their work the curious feeling that the writers are simultaneously describing an existing musical tradition and seeking to found one where none exists. Parra Carreño declared that it was "in search of its technique" but also that in ancient Greece and Egypt, the arts had "converted the multitude into a public, and the public into a people" (Parra Carreño, Cabrera, and Pozo 1939: 24), thereby hinting at the awesome consequences that might follow its formalization. Promising that the CCA would direct efforts to understand and dignify local arts and letters, he neatly encapsulated a common attitude toward huamanguino music: though rich in potential, it was also too varied to entirely qualify as an object of identification.

Parra Carreño's comments were delivered at one of the CCA's literary-musical soirees, which is where their beliefs about huamanguino music were put into practice. Their publications give only occasional indications of the music that was heard, but they do provide a clear portrait of the genres and performing groups that were favored, revealing two main categories of performance: indigenista-style pieces and the huaynos that were dear to Bustamante and Parra Carreño.[44] Without further material for analysis, it is difficult to know whether local indigenista performances differed from those of neighboring regions, but there is no reason to believe that they did. A 1940 blurb in *Revista Huamanga* entitled "Jáuregui's Works" indicates that this composer's pieces were, at least, perceived to function in a manner similar to the way those of his peers did. He was praised for the extent to which his piano arrangements "wisely [ennobled] aboriginal music" without "absurdly twisting [it]" (*retorcimiento absurdo*; Fajardo 1940: 51–52).[45] His Quechua songs are described as an Inca inheritance, but also as art objects that had performed a "deep modification . . . in essence and structure" upon indigenous art (1940: 51). Here as elsewhere, indigenista folklore was an intellectual technology that regulated otherwise perilous identifications: it allowed urban elites to perform their respect for subaltern Others, even as it reinscribed the social hierarchy upon which their self-identity depended.

But Jáuregui's "authentically Ayacuchano huaynos" were also singled out for special attention. Along with indigenista compositions, CCA soirees thematized the music that was already identified with the urban elite culture of the huamanguinos who gathered there, and which was prioritized in their written investigations. In reports on their activities, the two genres appear to be distinguished both by performance ensemble and by terminology. "Compositions" by figures such as Anchorena or Vivanco, whose works bear traces of the indigenista imagination, are performed by "orquestras" of unstated format, usually directed by Francisco González. But there are an equal number of references to "vernacular music," usually rendered by Ayacucho's Estudiantina Municipal. These evenings are likely to have featured the well-known huaynos and yaravíes hailed by Bustamante and Parra Carreño, genres that still form the core of that ensemble's repertoire. Though rehearsed and polished, the style of playing that dominates estudiantina performances was not radically different from that heard elsewhere in Ayacuchano life. If the CCA's soirees promoted the consumption of art music based on indigenous musical materials, they also promoted the value of the vernacular music that surrounded listeners in their everyday lives. The message was undoubtedly clear: the urban elite already had an acceptably sophisticated musical culture, while rural Indians did not.

The CCA's soirees, then, were performative in more ways than one. They not only featured different kinds of music making, but they also made sound a public method of reinforcing social hierarchy. There are frustratingly few indications about the huamanguino "vernacular songs" that were heard, but the lone exception speaks volumes about the kind of music that was singled out as such. A 1939 soiree saw the first recorded performance of the song "Helme," under the direction of the ever present González. Destined to become a centerpiece of huamanguinismo, the song is unique both for its narrative form and for its purported historical veracity. A story of infidelity and its consequences, it describes the love triangle between Santos the muleteer, his wife, Rosa, and the huamanguino student Hermenegildo, or Helme, who woos Rosa during Santos's trading journeys. Informed by an anonymous note of his wife's philandering, Santos pretends to leave town, and when he circles back, he catches the lovers together in his house. Enraged, he murders the unfortunate student and loses his mind. On this evening, the song itself, which narrates the events in a loose and elliptical way, was prefaced by a lecture from Cabrera invoking Palma and his tradiciones once again to frame the story of Helme, dating the events to 1831 and describing how he learned the tale from city elders in his youth.

This is the only recorded instance in which the CCA brought vernacular music into direct contact with colonial history and criollo cultural genres. However, the act of patronizing local huayno music in their select meetings, and their arguments for its intimate relation with huamanguino identity, gave the genre a pedigree unlike any other. As a mode of musical huamanguinismo, local huayno became an expression of Ayacuchano elitism, a product of and evidence for the refined, sentimental sensibility unique to the city's educated classes. And in its implied opposition to indigenous musics, it transmuted local distinctions of class and race into the musical realm, where they remained available for uptake by later artists and scholars.

Epilogue: Huamanguinismo's Legacy

According to the Cavero brothers, the CCA's "Hispanist indigenismo" was an "academic version that never became an organic indigenismo like that of Cusco" (Cavero Carrasco and Cavero Carrasco 2007: 50). It remained elitist in orientation, its events were infrequent, and overall the CCA probably did little to alter the everyday existence of average citizens.[46] Nevertheless, it was influential among those sectors of Ayacuchano society that were best positioned to shape public discourse about the city, and later commentators have echoed Límaco's assertion that the CCA provided the only cultural events during the 73 years that the UNSCH was closed (Límaco 1959: 33). This statement depends upon a patrician view of culture, but it does hint at the organization's stature. It shaped not only the self-image of the local elite, but also the expectations of those who visited the city and those who imagined it from afar.[47] In fact, the CCA's influence is best reflected in the reports of outsiders, which often use the very images that fill the pages of *Revista Huamanga*. Visiting in the mid-1930s, a scion of Lima's wealthy Miró Quesada family was escorted by members of the city's elect. He gives no names, but his account of an evening devoted to conversation and musical entertainment recalls the events of the CCA, and the performance he witnessed, clearly staged for his benefit by a local folkloric ensemble, brought together the genres that entertained CCA audiences. Writing later, he prefaced his recollections with some words about the colonial-era fame of Huamanga's intellectual class, only afterward describing the evening in language that could be drawn from the pages of *Revista Huamanga*:

> All this I remember when, on my first night in Ayacucho, I go to the Alameda [a riverside park] with some enthusiasts. On a terrace atop an ostentatious arch, before a double row of trees set between superb gardens, the conversation begins, the pleasant recitation of the historic city's legends. Before long, the enchanting music: the nostalgic notes and upbeat rhythms of "huaynos" [*sic*], played on charango, guitar, flute, violin, and harp: or, alternately, the strange steps of the scissors dancers, their costume covered with glittering beads. (Miró Quesada [1938] 2004: 207)

Whether or not the CCA furnished Miró Quesada with this living tableau, his writing suggests the success of their identity work. CCA writings and activities stabilized a repertoire of ideas, images, and sounds that came to identify the city and its people. They brought to contemporary self-awareness a Spanish colonial city with a fiercely intellectual class, its nights and its salons animated by a unique musical sensibility, one that had made huayno music into a poetic vehicle for delicate and refined sentiment. They made the aesthetics and interests of the elite synonymous with the space of the city and wrote others out of the huamanguino narrative, constructing "an image of distinction based on a Hispanist discourse" (Urrutia 2001: 122), even as they claimed to gesture toward social inclusion.[48]

But this evaluation acknowledges only one side of the double bind in which Ayacucho's elites found themselves, a double bind that they grappled with as average people caught in hegemonic structures of racial inequality. Faced with a system that hierarchized a white coast above the Indian highlands, these scholars refused the image of indigenous contamination thrust upon them. Proud of their erudition, confident that their aristocratic highland culture was continuous with the Europhilic criollismo of Lima, Ayacuchano elites articulated a claim against racialization by arguing their Spanish inheritance and their intellectual progress. In other words, they sought to escape Peru's racial double bind not by defending Indian legitimacy, but rather by drawing themselves more closely to whiteness; and in seeking a modicum of dignity for themselves, they became victims and perpetuators of an exclusive racial system.

FOUR

The Commercial Huayno Business: Making Music and Producing Publics at Dolby JR

In 2008 I sat in the back of a pickup truck carrying students from one of Lima's universities to conduct research in the Andes. A search for cassettes within the cab led to talk about music, an exchange of views about Andean music between two seatmates. They agreed that Ayacuchano music stood out for its superior lyrics and musicianship, with the elder interlocutor lecturing his young charge about the superb "testimonial" songs of the violence era. They also agreed upon the tawdriness of huayno norteño, poking fun at its subject matter and parodying its extensive electronic drum fills. Aesthetic rapport established, their conversation turned to contemporary Ayacuchano artists such as the Hermanos Gaitán Castro, two brothers who began by performing in the traditional Ayacuchano style but achieved mass popularity after incorporating foreign elements. They agreed that the Ayacuchanos were incomparably superior to northern artists, having maintained the core markers of the huayno genre—that is, up until their album *Son del Sol*, when electric guitars and drum kits moved their music beyond the pale of thoughtful musicianship into crass commercialism.

Between 2000 and 2008 I participated in dozens of similar conversations. By then the huayno styles of Ayacucho and the north had each been transformed and taken up by performers throughout Peru. They also became articulated to new musical values and different listening communities, with Ayacucho's "select" style standing opposed to the populist fare of the north. The Gaitáns were early leaders in reworking their home city's huayno style, and such conversations always reminded me of my first experience with live Ayacuchano performance, when in 2001 I paid an exorbitant sixty *soles* (around $17)—six times the usual admission charge—to attend the duo's fifteenth-anniversary concert at the exclusive club La Estación, in Lima's Barranco district.

Over the 1990s, Ayacuchano musicians sought to rework traditional huayno music into a pop genre while retaining its old signifiers of social distinction, and artists such as the Gaitáns gave weekly concerts, drawing thousands of listeners to open-air venues in Lima's downtown and smaller stages throughout its periphery. Close attention to these events, to points of sale, and to the radio broadcasts that promoted Ayacuchano music would have revealed the pervasive involvement of the record label Dolby JR (later renamed Dolly JR). It was here that contemporary Ayacuchano huayno was consolidated between the 1980s and the twenty-first century, as Dolby employees fused old aesthetic discourses with new emblems of cosmopolitanism and moved them toward emergent markets likely to find such hybrids appealing. They and the musicians they worked with did not make the Andean middle class, but they made it newly visible, by providing public sites of articulation and recognition where it could be named as such and where its members might forge a sense of intersubjectivity.

Much of their success can be traced to traditional Ayacuchano huayno's reputation as an erudite form, and before exploring the contemporary style I review the recorded work of a prior generation, showing how those values were circulated in the first place. However, the style also appealed because of its conspicuous cosmopolitanism, and the pairing of these qualities attracted many young, upwardly mobile Andean listeners, those who sought evidence "that their 'ethnic' sensibilities can be made intelligible to a modern subjectivity" (Greene 2005: 153). In creating music that catered to these concerns, Dolby helped to rework the lines of distinction that had once placed huayno on the lesser side of binaries such as modernity/tradition, global/local, and hip/square. But this process also reinforced the notion that modern subjectivity requires the successful mastery of foreign and/or elitist cultural standards. Insofar as the Ayacuchano synthesis of local and global was counterpoised to huayno norteño's misguided aesthetics, Andean musical circulation remapped age-old binaries between discerning citizens in tune with the categories of respectable society and a subaltern sector whose ignorance of those categories proved its poor preparation.

Recording Music and Representing Markets

Studios and labels are corporate institutions that mediate the dynamic relationship between musicians, listeners, and the broader social field in which both are suspended.[1] However, they are staffed by real human beings whose sociocultural, economic, and artistic interests influence the musical choices that they advocate. The collaborative, sometimes conflictive nature of studio work makes any given recording a negotiated compromise between the different priorities of all parties. The products of the process may affirm existing sociomusical values or recast sounds and sonic relationships. In either case, the social career of a given recording is powerfully prefigured by the ideas wielded during its creation, making the studio into a site where "sound engineering becomes cultural engineering" (Grandin 2005: 224).[2]

Genre, meanwhile, is a key tool that employees use to structure recording and the marketing process that follows, allowing people who are "desperately seeking the audience" (Ang 1991) to envision and, at best, to reify a volatile consuming public as a series of manageable, sharply distinguished taste communities with relatively settled parameters of purchasing behavior.[3] Targeting a new record toward those most likely to buy it reduces the risk involved in launching it and minimizes the laborious process of developing new artists by narrowing the field of musical conventions that will surround their work. Nevertheless, "production does not take place simply 'within' a corporate environment . . . but [also] in relation to broader culture formations and practices that are within neither the control nor the understanding of the company" (Negus 1999: 19), and record companies can never completely determine the overall direction of popular musical development. Instead, the discursive markers that identify a particular genre are "first constructed and then articulated through a complex interplay of musicians, listeners and mediating ideologues, [a] process [that] is much more confused than the marketing process that follows, as the wider industry begins to make sense of the new sounds and markets and to exploit [them] in the orderly routines of mass marketing" (Frith 1996: 88).

Building on these insights, we might ask how the construction of a new genre discourse, and the consequent projection of a new target market, together create the very social categories that are ostensibly served in these processes. Industry personnel may view their actions primarily as a way of ensuring sales, but commercial acts can also be socially creative acts when the give-and-take of generic evolution stabilizes a new coalition of sound, ideology, and listenership. At Dolby JR, the signifying sounds that filled Peru's public sphere were sorted, reworked, and stabilized in a new relation to one another, suggesting new understandings of huayno music and its audience. But it would be ingenuous to say that Dolby products "expressed" that audience's identity. Instead, it is more useful to ask how the label's sound emerged in the normal course of production and marketing, and how it drove the emergence of common values and points of reference among listeners. Ayacucho's contemporary huayno style initially represented little more than a contingent solution to a commercial problem: however, once it entered the everyday spaces of conversation and consumption where social relations are made, it became a trope through which its public figured ongoing social changes.

Technological change played a role here, and Dolby's influence depended in the first instance upon the appearance of cassette technology. It gave recordists cheap access to the tools of reproduction, breaking Peru's large record companies and making independents such as Dolby the primary producers of Andean popular music. But the success of Ayacuchano music also depended upon the initiative of Dolby's first director, Julián Fernández, who capitalized upon artistic and social trends, beginning with the Ayacuchano protest huaynos that emerged during the 1980s. As the first to commercialize this music on a large scale, Fernández helped to launch the careers of many influential musicians and earned the social capital required to succeed in Lima over the 1990s. These factors became decisive once he began to encourage musical products that combined the integrity and prestige of traditional music with pan-Andean music from Bolivia and Chile. A boom in the latter style over the early 1990s revealed that Lima's young, affluent listeners imagined and embodied Andean heritage in new ways, connecting with it through sounds that struck a balance between ethnic pride and metropolitan urbanity, and Dolby responded by drawing its sound into the ambit of Ayacuchano's elegant huayno, creating a contemporary style that combined the appeal of each.

As such, Dolby's work illuminates the practical workings of cultural globalization, which are often experienced as anonymous, inevitable, and capricious, even though they are mediated by local agents. In this case, Dolby's employees walked the line of an artistic dilemma, one derived from their audience's belief in the "twin reifications" of tradition and modernity—a clichéd dichotomy that nevertheless continues to operate powerfully for everyday listeners (Wallach 2005: 153). The impact of this ideological binary demands to be understood in local terms, and not only because its dichotomizing effects resist easy systematization. The very emblems of modernity and globalism also vary from place to place, and many of the new sounds that Dolby drew into huayno's orbit do not bear such overtones outside Peru: balada music, for instance, is regarded elsewhere as kitschy and dowdy, while pan-Andean music bears "folk" connotations within the world marketplace.

Dolby's position recalls Greene's description of Nepali *lok pop* musicians, "caught up in a mutually-constituting tension between desires for something authentic and traditional on the one hand; and drives toward a new, cosmopolitan, commercially-empowered society on the other" (2002: 44);

further, their determination to "produce music that is accessible to and enjoyable for all, and that also preserves the crucial, distinctive elements of the folksongs" (2002: 48), parallels the compromise that was forged at the Peruvian label. Indeed, accounts such as Greene's seem to characterize the operations of musical globalization better than many competing formulations, which often imply either that cultural hybrids are callow attempts to gain the aesthetic high ground before competing cultural manifestations, or that those who create them are unambivalent about their impact on local lifeways. These are real possibilities, but such hybrids often emerge in a messy and unselfconscious way, and some people who act as vectors of globalization are committed traditionalists trying to mitigate the effects of a globalizing culture industry. Like them, Dolby's recordists strove to control contemporary Ayacuchano music's evolutionary direction, developing new ways to gauge their own evolving standards of cultural authenticity and using a discourse of "commercialism" to distinguish the reasonable use of "modern" sounds from crass attempts to capture the cosmopolitan audience.

Finally, the increasingly decentralized nature of Dolby's recording process signaled an important shift in the Andean music business. The contemporary Ayacuchano huayno style that took shape there demanded new kinds of expertise from engineers, arrangers, and studio players and devolved authority from featured artists to these kinds of music workers. By the early twenty-first century huayno production had become a complex process that stood in stark contrast to its humble beginnings fifty years beforehand as a studiously faithful translation of received highland tradition.

The Golden Age of Commercial Huayno

Peru's IEMPSA label pioneered domestic record production in 1949 and soon afterward began to produce huayno music. By the mid-1960s Virrey, Discos Smith, and Sono Radio all ran successful rival operations in Lima.[4] In these early years the huayno industry capitalized upon, and helped to drive, a broader shift in Andean performance. Previously, Andean concerts had catered to provincial elites and Limeño intellectuals, largely via performances by estudiantina ensembles and mostly featuring indigenista fare. After midcentury, Lima accumulated an Andean public of increasingly humble origin, and the artists who performed in the city's coliseos changed their commercial strategy, recreating their vernacular idioms with greater fidelity.[5] Singers abandoned the exoticist trappings of indigenista performance and adopted regionally-specific stage names and attire, with Jilguero del Huascarán (The Goldfinch of Huascarán), Pastorita Huaracina (The Little Shepherdess from Huaraz), Flor Pucarina (The Little Flower of Pucará), and others taking the stage in pollera skirts, ponchos, broad-brimmed hats, and other sartorial emblems of their provincial homes.[6] Because the labels favored releases by performers with established audiences, the musicians who drew migrants into Lima's coliseos quickly moved to the center of the commercial huayno business as well. Soon industry personnel began to recruit directly from the highlands, with Gilberto Cuevas, IEMPSA's artistic director, leading "artistic caravans" of IEMPSA performers to venues around the country and using them as scouting expeditions.

In the studio, control over content was substantially given over to artists, and although the promotional apparatus of the record industry intensified a star system that already operated through radio and coliseo advertising, there is little reason to believe that the music on disc differed greatly from that performed at home.[7] Indeed, since the labels recruited performers who had already proven successful, the records produced by the labels seem to have tracked contemporaneous developments in performance.[8] Demands for efficiency did drive some standardization in musical accompaniment as studios came to maintain in-house backing bands and rosters of studio players, famously including the guitarists Víctor Angulo and Antonio Gutiérrez (Land Vásquez 1992). These professional accompanists studied existing recordings to develop a mastery of local styles, a recursiveness that made for greater homogeneity across different recordings. Overall, however, the business of huayno recording was governed by the assumption that audiences sought recognizably traditional idioms. For this reason, the 1950s and 1960s are usually described as huayno music's true "Golden Age," though today's performers treat recordings from the broader era between 1949 and the early 1980s as canonical benchmarks of authenticity.[9]

When Ayacuchano performers began recording in the mid-1960s, their "stylized music [sought] to reproduce the gentlemanly and noble 'airs'" of earlier generations (García Miranda 1991: 22). Their fidelity to the erudite, sentimental salon performances of Ayacucho's old elite might be expected, given the background and the preservationist goals of the musicians themselves. Extraordinarily, the city's first wave of recording artists was drawn entirely from its urban middle class, and all were university graduates.[10] Their work departed from the politicized discourse of cultural authenticity that suffused the folkloric scholarship of the age.[11] Liner notes and public commentary insistently characterized these albums as something more than vehicles for entertainment, pitching them as instructive documents that safeguarded an imperiled inheritance. As these artists translated into the national sphere the evaluative conceits inherited from their predecessors, they created an unbreakable link between Ayacuchano music, intellectual rigor, and social distinction, setting the city's huayno style apart from that of other urban centers.

The building of this musical reputation began in earnest in 1966, when the guitarist Raúl García Zárate released an LP on the Sono Radio label entitled *Ayacucho*. He quickly followed this up with *Más música de Ayacucho* (More Music from Ayacucho), an album featuring him and with his older brother, Nery, as the Duo Hermanos García Zárate.[12] Within months Trio Ayacucho released *Con el mayor cariño* (With All My Love) on the IEMPSA label, and these two pioneering groups became the leading arbiters of Ayacuchano tradition, a position they retained some four decades later.[13] They were not alone for long; rather, they initiated a boom in Ayacuchano record production that lasted until the early 1980s. During that time Trio Voces de Huamanga, Edwin Montoya, and the Tuna Universitaria de la UNSCH, an estudiantina-style ensemble sponsored by the city's university, also established themselves as exemplars of the Ayacuchano style. None of these figures ever achieved the general popularity of artists from the north or central Andes, but they placed the city's unique style in the national ear and established the body of work that later performers have treated as the bedrock of musical authenticity.[14]

It is difficult to account for the record industry's sudden interest in Ayacuchano music in the mid-1960s. However, some Ayacuchanos attributed the surge to the recent reopening of the Universidad Nacional San Cristóbal de Huamanga. The 1959 reestablishment of the shuttered institution was a major national event, driving countrywide curiosity about the forgotten city. It created a demand for reportage about local life and customs and also rekindled city residents' interest in Ayacuchano culture and history. Most important, the renowned scholars who were attracted to teach at the university came with a mission of development, and their efforts to spur local investigation had repercussions beyond the classroom. María Luísa Bustamante, a noted professional who entered the UNSCH in 1959, remembered both the dramatic change in the tenor of city life and the role of the university in promoting local culture:

> People began to revalue Ayacuchano music, the reopening of the university uncorked everything, music, everything. That was when [music groups] emerged. They were motivated by the [university's] Cultural Center, and local institutions, too, began to focus on everything that was part of our culture. The professors came and said that [the university's developmental mission]

should be cultural as well. They and the intellectuals, via the university, they tried to promote [our culture] in every way. So, [in] a city that was asleep . . . this gave intellectuals an incentive, it created enthusiasm.

Burga and Gamarra echo Bustamante's comments, describing the generation that came of age in this climate as one newly "passionate to learn, to know the region, [and] their own culture" (Burga 2010; see also Gamarra Carrillo 2010). Students and faculty applied scientific and literary methods to the interpretation of local society, defending Andean cultural complexity and distinctiveness before a dismissive coastal elite.[15] Steeped in a vision of shared folkways as the location of a precious authenticity that was threatened by the growing influence of mass society and by the prejudices of a neocolonial state, many adopted the task of documenting, preserving, and promoting the region's unique cultural manifestations. Local institutions such as the CCA had long advocated similar ideas among a limited social circle; now they moved to the center of a broader intellectual life. Moreover, their influence was felt beyond the classroom, as people associated with the university created spaces and organizations for cultural outreach.

Music became a prominent part of these activities via institutions such as the university's Cultural Center, which promoted public lectures, music and dance performances, and eventually artistic competitions as well. University *verbenas*, or evening soirees, gave fledgling performers the opportunity to play before their peers. And the Tuna Universitaria, founded in 1963 after a visit by the *tuna* of the University of Madrid, became dedicated to cultivating local music, though it also performed a repertoire shared by *tuna* groups across the Ibero-American world. Besides becoming a fixture of city life and recording albums at the institution's expense, it also became something of a training ground for folkloric performers, and by the 1990s most of Ayacucho's outstanding artists had passed through its ranks.[16] Finally, even as the UNSCH fostered musical activity, local businesses began catering to students' developing tastes in leisure, and complementary spaces emerged outside the university precincts, such as the *peña* (live music club) where the singer Mario Laurente, lead voice of the *tuna* ensemble, launched a solo career by imitating Lima's commercial recordings:

> In 1968 or '69 a peña appeared on 28 de Julio Street, the first peña in Ayacucho. I played there with one of Ayacucho's best guitarists, a guy named Cotrado, who was ex-director of the Tuna Universitaria. With him and the Zárates, we put together a group, and every weekend we performed there. And people went—it was packed. At that time Don Edwin Montoya appeared, his

records appeared, and we liked them a lot. We sang his songs here in Ayacucho, I learned all his *huaynos* . . . very beautiful, old songs.

The formation of Trio Ayacucho also suggests the university's influence on Ayacuchano musical activity. The lead vocalist, Ernesto Camassi; the second vocalist, Carlos Falconí; and the lead guitarist, Amílcar Gamarra, all had informal musical experience before studying there. Gamarra and Camassi had even played music together before entering the university.[17] But according to Gamarra, in their youth they had preferred to play coastal valses, Mexican boleros, Caribbean music, and other commercial popular genres. He told me that only upon beginning his studies "did Ernesto turn to [huayno]. When he entered the UNSCH, that's when he became more *huaynero*," eventually inviting Gamarra to join a group dedicated to performing local songs instead of tropical numbers. By 1964, when the trio came together to play at a university verbena, all three members were titled teachers. In words later penned by Camassi, they were "united by [their] love for art and [their] vocation as educators," determined to promote "traditional songs miraculously rescued from oblivion" (Trio Ayacucho n.d.).

Combing through a repertoire that was mostly solicited from the older relatives of Camassi and Falconí, the trio particularly chose to "rescue" huaynos that bore documentary traces of the region's social and affective history, songs that expressed, in words that would appear on their album *Juntos como siempre* (Together Again), "the emotionality of a city and its people. Songs of yesterday, today, and forever . . . each with its own history . . . and each history its own romantic structure" (Orozco and Trio Ayacucho 1982). The group was also keen to record huaynos whose formal rigor and literary sophistication flattered their own superlative evaluation of Ayacucho's "outstanding poets and singers, who . . . maintained in all its purity that refined style, that mode of singing and speaking verses that is like nothing else in Peru" (Camassi and Trio Ayacucho n.d.).[18] Balancing these historical and literary concerns, the group arranged and played songs such as "Vapor brillante" (Bright Steamship), a chronicle of outmigration addressed to a vessel that bears away the speaker's beloved, and sung poems such as "Con el mayor cariño" (With All My Love; see fig. 8), a restrained and genteel plea for attention from a female love object.[19] The trio quickly attained a level of professionalism that led to appearances in Lima and eventually, in 1966, to a contract with IEMPSA, which released a single pairing those two songs, each of which has been considered emblematically Ayacuchano ever since.

8. Huayno "Con el mayor cariño"

The style of interpretation heard on records by Trio Ayacucho shows how artists of the era balanced fidelity to the past with commercial novelty. The trio restricted their accompanimental resources to the Spanish guitar, the most Ayacuchano of instruments, with each member taking a different role: Falconí played the strummed huayno rhythm, Gamarra played solo leads, walking bass lines, or ornamented melodic fills, and Camassi alternated between support for one or the other (see fig. 9). Camassi and Falconí harmonized in parallel thirds, singing with the "strange mix of happiness and nostalgia" that defined Ayacuchano sentiment (Camassi and Trio Ayacucho n.d.). Together with their focus on venerable classics, their conservative choices led such observers as Vivanco to single them out as "the group that [had] most faithfully preserved the salon huayno style" that he heard during the 1920s and 1930s (Vilcapoma 1999: 80). And yet their interpretations were novel in important ways. If sentimental, their vocal technique was also idiosyncratically brash, its power and heavy vibrato recalling the Mexican bolero artists that Camassi admired, rather than the restrained delivery of their local peers.[20] Gamarra's playing was innovative too, and became more so over time. In introductions and solo passages, he often departed from the traditional practice of merely reiterating a song's main tune, instead creating new melodies that drew upon his experience with various non-Andean musical sources (fig. 9).[21] But insofar as guitaristic virtuosity was associated with local huayno performance, and insofar as the group's dramatic vocalizations served the emotional tenor of song texts, these modifications were understood as extensions of traditional technique.

The Hermanos García Zárate present an instructive set of parallels and contrasts. Firstly, it cannot be argued that their careers were entirely motivated by a new sense of cultural identity discovered at Ayacucho's university. They were slightly older when they began to record and had been degree-holding professionals for some time: the younger Raúl (b. 1932) was a lawyer, and the older Nery (1926–1982) a schoolteacher, graduates respectively of the Universidad San Marcos and the Pontificia Universidad Católica del

Perú, the country's foremost universities. Their musical background was extensive, and both had been members of the Estudiantina Municipal de Ayacucho, Raúl playing guitar and *laúd*, while Nery provided the lead voice. More important, Raúl's solo guitar skills, already evident at age twelve when he debuted in concert at Ayacucho's San Juan Bosco elementary school and honed over an adolescence spent playing Andean and criollo music, had allowed him to triumph at a folkloric competition in the city of Cusco. This, in turn, led to a radio show in that city called *Raúl García y su guitarra* (Raúl García and His Guitar), as well as a later show on the Lima broadcaster Radio Nacional, and eventually to a position as Andean music director at the record label Sono Radio. The brothers had worked with scholars of the

9A. Opening section of huayno "Jarana," as performed by Trio Ayacucho

9B. Opening section of huayno "Jarana," as performed by Trio Ayacucho

Centro Cultural Ayacuchano, figures such as Saturnino Almonacid and Telésforo Felices (see chapter 2), both of whose original and collected huaynos they included on early albums. Finally, Raúl's solo work focused on stylized arrangements of huaynos and indigenous tunes, recalling the interests of earlier indigenista performers and marking a continuity between the indigenista and commercial huayno eras that is often downplayed. Overall, the García Zárates acted as a bridge between the recording era and an earlier musical period.

Despite the differences in their trajectories, the recordings of the Duo Hermanos García Zárate responded to the same intellectual and commercial climate as Trio Ayacucho's. The two groups sought to differentiate themselves, but the same notions of authenticity and Andean revindication framed their work.[22] Like the trio's, the García Zárates' performing idiom was a refined version of the old salon huayno, arranged for two guitars and two voices and occasionally reinforced on later albums by estudiantina-style instrumentation, including mandolins and kenas. However, if Trio Ayacucho was beloved for its unique vocal interpretations, the García Zárate reputation rested largely upon Raúl's masterful playing. The lead voice of Nery, whose gentle, melancholy style led to the nickname "El Pajarito" (The Little Bird), was certainly well regarded, but Ayacucho's reputation for musical refinement has been figured most insistently in relation to Raúl García

10. Huayno "Umpa rosas," as performed by Los Hermanos García Zárate

Zárate's guitar. His solo efforts set a new standard in virtuosity, and though the duo's recordings featured sung duets, his playing greatly enriched them, weaving lively bass lines and delicately ornamented melodic solos around the harmonized vocals (see fig. 10). Beginning with his first album, commentary has drawn together his class background, his education, and his polished technique, taking him to have "demonstrated that folkloric music, executed with skill, sensitivity, and quality, can stand on the same level as classical and erudite music" (Perlacios Campos n.d: 235).

Arguedas penned an early commentary of this kind, mobilizing tropes of class, technique, and authenticity to describe García Zárate and his instrumental idiom upon the release of his first solo album, *Ayacucho* (1966). Beginning with a disquisition on Andean musical syncretism, Arguedas argued that colonized Indians rarely attained a mastery of elite music, while by contrast the "gentleman musician could and did descend, whether for artistic interest or because of cultural contamination, to interpret Indian music." Calling García Zárate "the clearest example of a gentlemanly guitarist who has mastered the entire repertoire of an Andean city, in which are represented all classes and social strata of Andean Peru." Arguedas lauded his balance of cultural authenticity with stylized elegance, famously noting that García Zárate's "virtuosity [had] not disturbed the purity of the folkloric music that has been his life" (Arguedas 1966)—no small concession from a scholar who had derided the "mixtifications" of indigenista music. Later commentators picked up Arguedas's ideas, creating around García Zárate a singular aura of discernment and folkloric wisdom and making him the vessel for a superior version of huayno music. The record jacket of his album *Recital de guitarra* argued that "because of [his interpretations] the huayno, [once] libeled as monotonous and repetitive, begins to attract disciples, no longer among its old constituency alone, but also in the spheres of those who consider themselves cultured . . . it is leaving behind its shoddy air and entering a stage of technical refinement, without losing its deep autochthonous roots" (Velarde and García Zárate 1970). And this opinion was ratified within the world of classical music, "fully backed by the opinion of prestigious international concert guitarists who, passing through [Lima], have had the chance to discover his exceptional virtues" (García Zárate 1973).

The sophistication of García Zárate's music is emphasized in more subtle ways as well, via sartorial and other cues that appear on album covers and promotional materials. Since his second solo album he has been listed as "Dr. Raúl García Zárate" in recognition of his professional background—though the notes for *Recital de guitarra* acknowledged that he might be thought of as "more properly doctor of guitar and huayno music." He is often pictured in the tuxedo of a classical soloist, and in the notes to his 1979 album *Recital folklórico*, where he is accompanied by a chamber orchestra, he insisted that "Andean music does not need to disguise itself, but to dress in coat and tails." Following a classicizing strategy that is familiar from other contexts, he has sought to place his style within the discursive space of the concert hall, harnessing its prestige to raise Andean music's social profile. Besides concertizing in the venues and apparel, and according to the performance conventions, of classical soloists, he has advocated the transcription of Andean music into staff notation and published his own arrangements in collaboration with the classical guitarist Javier Echecopar (García Zárate and Echecopar 1988). Finally, he has supported the development of a parallel pedagogy, teaching privately and at Peru's National

School of Folklore and inspiring programs of instruction elsewhere, including Ayacucho's own Conservatorio Musical Condorcunca.

Like Trio Ayacucho, the García Zárates distinguished their playing from that of earlier musicians, and though it quickly became the Ayacuchano standard, at the time it represented something new. García Zárate's achievement was to study and master Ayacucho's panoply of traditional guitar techniques, amalgamating them into a synthetic whole. According to his peers, he gathered all of Ayacucho's ornaments, introductory figures, accompanimental patterns, and alternate guitar tunings, many of which had been jealously defended by particular regions, social groups, towns, families, or individuals, in order to craft a guitar idiom that lent itself to virtuosic reelaboration. In this sense, the recordings of the García Zárates were unique even though they hewed closely to traditional practice. Laurente, a distant cousin, told me that he attended family parties in his youth just to watch the young Raúl play. He confirmed that the duo's initial records featured music like that heard at the family's birthday, baptism, and holiday parties.[23] Nevertheless, García Zárate's stylistic breadth was unprecedented, and it caused problems for other performers. Falconí expostulated admiringly that the diminutive guitarist had "taken all of the music there was to take, and left the rest of us with nothing," no musical tools with which to forge a distinct sound and commercial identity. And Camassi concurred, telling me that the trio had been forced to adapt harp figures and other unusual idioms for the guitar, creating new resources that might stand out from those that García Zárate had captured for himself.

These records fostered a selective vision of Ayacuchano tradition, bringing forward the notions of genteel bearing and musical refinement that had permeated the salons of Ayacucho's early twentieth century. Alongside peers from other regions, they ruled the public space of Andean music until changes in the marketplace altered patterns of recording and distribution. Indications of such change began to appear in the late 1960s, with the emergence of independent labels such as DINSA, Tupac Amaru, and Ollanta, which often specialized in local musics overlooked by the more powerful enterprises.[24] In helping to diversify the recorded music scene, these smaller labels laid the groundwork for changes that would come with the 1980s advent of cassette technology, when a boom in piracy destroyed the large companies, their prices undercut by inexpensive copies sold on street corners and in markets throughout the country. The ability to reproduce masters cheaply and the ever lower prices of recording equipment made costs less prohibitive and potential rewards higher, leading adventurous if inexperienced entrepreneurs into the field. Learning from their predecessors, they exploited markets previously overlooked by record companies and offered materials at prices within the grasp of humble buyers. They became the primary producers of Andean commercial music, and Ayacucho's Dolby JR was emblematic of them.

Dolby JR: New Huayno, Small Scale

Julián Fernández founded Dolby JR in Ayacucho in 1987. After a long period of decline, local huayno's revival as a means of protest was well under way, and Fernández hoped to capitalize on it by filling a gap in the existing system of circulation. Established labels had released a handful of protest songs, interpreted by such artists as Martina Portocarrero and Nelly Munguía.[25] However, inflation and cassette piracy were decimating sales, executives willing to take a risk on untested sounds were few and far between, and it was difficult for younger musicians to break into the business. Fernández was a student of obstetrics at the UNSCH, but he ran a small business selling cassettes in and around the city of Ayacucho, and at school he had fallen in with the intellectuals who were "renewing" Ayacucho's huayno style. Sensing a business proposition and motivated by his admiration for their music, he took upon himself the low-risk venture of recording for local distribution, hopeful that his familiarity with the trade would allow him to his recoup initial investment.[26]

Record studios existed in the highland cities of Cusco, Huancayo, and Arequipa, but there were none in Ayacucho, and Dolby JR's early productions were somewhat homespun. Recorded using a home stereo onto a standard chromium dioxide cassette tape with the cheap microphones Fernández was able to scrounge, they sometimes featured audible birdsong or street noise. Recognizing these limitations, Fernández boosted sales by undercutting competitors' prices and renting local radio airtime to promote his releases. He was right that a demand existed for the artists who lay untapped by major studios, and soon his tapes sold sufficiently well to tax the company's meager reproduction capabilities. With chained dual-cassette machines running off dubbed copies for hours on end, Dolby set up shop as a bona fide music label, and as capital accrued, Fernández invested above all in professionalization, renting time slots at Lima-based independent studios such as JAFE and sending artists there to take advantage of their superior equipment and know-how.

By 1992 the company had produced dozens of recordings featuring most of the artists who would later become outstanding interpreters of contemporary Ayacuchano huayno, including Ángel Bedrillana, Max Castro, the

Gaitán Castro brothers, Trudy Palomino, and Kiko Revatta.[27] Following long-standing practice, matters of style and repertoire were typically left to the musicians themselves, with the label assuming all production costs and retaining in exchange the masters and most of the profits.[28] Recordings usually included a mix of huaynos, featuring traditional songs alongside the new, socially conscious tunes that excited Fernández's generation. They also included recent compositions that drew upon the melodic, harmonic, and structural techniques of protest-song composers while avoiding their political tone. Often they featured one or two songs in another traditional highland genre for the sake of variety, an uptempo *carnaval*, pasacalle, or araskaska, but huaynos were the mainstay. Arrangements and performance style hewed close to the traditional manner, with introspective, emotive vocal lines delivered over the accompaniment of paired guitars.

The label's initial audience base was composed largely of locals and Ayacuchano migrants residing in Lima, but interest in the city's novel sounds and fiery politics spread as fast as cassettes circulated throughout Peru. Indeed, during the violence Ayacucho, as the epicenter of the conflict, came to stand alongside Cusco, the ancient Inca capital and lodestar of indigenismo, as a national referent of Andean authenticity. Dolby began to receive orders from around the country, and Fernández, recognizing the benefits offered by Lima's centralized services and its large Andean population, moved the label there in late 1992. He acquired sound equipment and a rented space in the industrial district of La Victoria, opened a studio of his own, and acquired a stand at Mesa Redonda, a building in Lima's central market where music dealers from all over the country come to buy merchandise at wholesale prices. By establishing a space at Peru's national music clearinghouse, Dolby JR effectively announced its wares as something more than a parochial concern of Ayacuchano listeners and consolidated its cultural credentials as Ayacucho's only record label dedicated to the city's distinctive music.

Their public profiles raised by their recordings, Dolby's artists found growing performance opportunities in Lima. Many moved to the capital, and soon Ayacucho's contemporary huayno scene was anchored not in the highland city, but in the capital. As it grew and diversified, however, many performers changed their musical idiom and deemphasized political themes. This was partly influenced by the changing political landscape. The 1993 capture of Shining Path's leader, Abimael Guzmán, rapidly mitigated the worst excesses of the violence and tempered the urgency felt by audiences and performers to express political outrage. More important, under the arbitrary, authoritarian regime of Alberto Fujimori (1990–2000), the threat of prosecution for *apología* (the crime of justifying terrorism), was a real concern for protest singers, whose songs might easily be read as antimilitary and antigovernment (as indeed many were), rather than antiwar.[29] In the interest of professional survival, most Ayacuchanos continued to record and perform innovative huaynos, but they refocused their lyrics on the timeless themes of love and loss.

Ayacuchano artists also began to adopt elements from pan-Andean music and international pop styles. This is more difficult to explain in a systematic way. It is possible that the move to Lima in the 1990s freed musicians from critical oversight by elders, who largely viewed the pan-Andean style as an insult.[30] It is more likely, though, that this shift was driven by a sudden surge in the popularity of pan-Andean music, which came into vogue just as young Ayacuchanos sought to establish more durable careers. The early 1990s saw a boom in pan-Andean performance all over Peru, largely driven by the rising popularity of saya, a genre based on a festive music and dance tradition of the altiplano region. It, in turn, is inspired by the *tundiki* music of Afro-Bolivian communities, and both versions traded heavily in stereotypes of African exoticism, virility, and sexuality.[31] In performances by Bolivian groups such as Los Kjarkas, these stereotypes were coded through polyrhythmic accompaniment and titillating lyrics, while the erotics of the dance paired women in tiny skirts, showing off their legs and underwear, with young men executing athletic, masculine leaps and kicks. This was a far cry from the conservative dancing that typifies highland Peru, and it also eased the cerebral seriousness of earlier pan-Andean music, reframing it as something self-evidently Andean, and yet also accessible, trendy, and fun. Most important, it attuned young Andeans to a pan-continental media environment where pop musical legitimacy was tied to tropical, Afro-Latin sensibilities rather than stale Andean folklore. Mendoza has described how this "Andean tropical" idiom allowed young Cuzqueños to imagine themselves as participants in a cosmopolitan formation, "[uniting] them with the rest of the urban 'modern' youth of the southern Andes" (2000: 212). More generally, saya opened the door to a new, pop-oriented version of the pan-Andean style, featuring catchy, upbeat dance genres such as the tinku or the (Ecuadorian) *sanjuanito*, which was immeasurably more popular in Peru than its highbrow, anti-imperialist predecessor.[32]

Ayacuchano performers faced the same kind of Andean public that Mendoza observed in Cusco, but, given the derisiveness of chicha's reception in polite society, they knew that experiments in modernizing huayno music often came to a bad end. Pan-Andean music's aura of artistry, its indisputable highland roots, and its growing trendiness, however, made it a promising source for emblems of metropolitan cool. Recent Ayacuchano records had already "estheticized the ears" (Neuenfeldt 2005: 95) of the Andean public, inflecting the regional style's long-standing prestige with the idea that it was also a dynamic and evolving tradition. Together these trends gave musicians some leeway to work more freely across the boundaries of Peru's Andean popular music scene.

A New Proposal: Los Hermanos Gaitán Castro

The Gaitán Castro brothers made the next important step in the transformation of contemporary Ayacuchano huayno. By 1993 they had released two albums on the Dolby label but then they decided to depart from the traditional mold. They recorded their third at their own expense in an independent studio. Released in 1994 as *Amor, amor* (My Love, My Love), the record included five huaynos from Ayacucho and four from the Northern or Central Andes. Producers and musicians believed that this geographic variety facilitated its uptake by a broad swath of listeners, and later albums featured a similarly diverse set of songs. But the Gaitáns colored all of them using a pan-Andean instrumental palette, and this had a more significant impact on the Andean music scene. With little experience in the international style, the duo had hired the musicians José Meza and Arturo Flores, who played charango and winds respectively, to help them graft pan-Andean timbral resources onto the two-guitar base of Ayacuchano huayno. All songs, in other words, were united by a new aesthetic paradigm, one that might be heard as an updated version of Ayacuchano huayno or a local variant of the pan-Andean style.

The title track, "Amor, Amor," was a lament for a romance gone wrong that recalled classic huaynos on the theme of unhappy love. It became the Gaitáns' outstanding hit, and its opening moments concisely illustrate their new style. Written by the Ayacuchano composer César Romero in the 1980s and originally entitled "Mi propuesta" (My Proposal), the song had already been recorded several times in traditional versions, including one by the Gaitáns themselves. For the new recording, the duo augmented the spare, guitar-based accompaniment of the earlier version by using pan-Andean instrumentation to color spaces in the musical texture. Thus the track's opening, according to Ayacuchano precedent, features a solo guitar playing the song's melody in parallel thirds over a basic huayno guitar strum, but it is surrounded with sparkling, high-pitched arpeggios performed on the charango (see fig. 11). During the third phrase, a kena flute weaves a countermelody under and around the solo guitar, filling gaps in the original

11. Opening section of huayno "Amor, amor," as performed by Duo Hermanos Gaitán Castro

tune. Throughout, the recording foregrounds vocal and guitar lines in this manner, leaving the instrumental markers of pan-Andean music to provide a subordinate, coloristic role.

Other tracks adapted the markers of other regional huayno styles to this instrumental combination. The Central Andean tune "Pasajero en el camino," for example, transferred the distinctive melodies and rhythms of the region's saxophone and harp orchestras to harmonized kenas and guitar, sometimes copying passages from the original 1960s-era recording by Picaflor de los Andes. And while the kenas, pan flutes, charangos, and rhythmic patterns of pan-Andean music were foregrounded, the duo also drew upon the conventions of other popular musics. Their new rendition of "Amor, amor," for example, rejected the delicate emotionalism of Ayacucho's traditional vocal style for the melodramatic inflections of balada music, Latin America's musical vehicle par excellence for expression of yearning romanticism.[33] By contrast, the record's two northern huaynos, "Corazón mío" and "Otra vez me equivoqué," featured driving rhythms in the strummed charango part, bluesy fills in both charango and flutes, and a propulsive bass line that suggested the aesthetics of hard rock.[34] In this way, the Gaitáns translated certain characteristics of regional huayno styles into their nearest pop music equivalents: sentimental Ayacuchano huaynos came to occupy the role of the romantic ballad, while the more extroverted styles of the Central or Northern Andes occupied the slot of rock or metal.

The Gaitáns' worldliness was also communicated sartorially: the duo grew to reject the traditional attire of earlier performers in favor of casual clothes or rock-star paraphernalia. Their disavowal of regional authenticity was clearly designed to capture a broad swath of the Andean public, but it rankled many observers. The guitarist-turned-producer Óscar Figueroa told me that "they haven't 'sectorized' their music. It's not directed to any one group, but to the market at large. They try to reach the people who like [pan-Andean music], that's why they include the instruments that attract that audience," and later went on to tell me that musical choices "have to do with education, with self-esteem, with the way that you show you're from [the Andes], and the way you show your cultural affiliation," interpreting the duo's music as a rejection rather than an extension of highland tradition. Indeed, *Amor, amor* was condemned as a betrayal, and in an epithetic dismissal that was in wide currency, the Gaitáns were accused of "Bolivianizing" Peruvian music, diluting it with fashionable images of Andean identity bearing greater international cachet than local huayno music. Ten years after the fact these changes were a raw issue for such performers as Ernesto Camassi, of Trio Ayacucho, who told me that César Romero's song "Mi propuesta" "was completely Bolivianized. We recorded it, but I changed the music, because it was totally Bolivian . . . at this point, I'm not interested. I don't pay attention. I know [younger artists are] ruining the huayno, but I don't want to make noise about it."[35]

Responding to these statements in a 2003 interview with me, Diosdado Gaitán Castro nodded in recognition and added, "Yes, they also say that we're just a product of marketing." He countered by describing their music as a creative reelaboration of the huayno tradition, saying that "[Andean music] is as alive today as five hundred, six hundred years ago. It's like a stream, which flows, passing through stages, and we have to live according to our time. The artists of today, we're the owners of our age, and we have to say the things that correspond to our age." In their own view, the Gaitáns' music responded to a way of being in the world where international circuits of musical exchange do not stand in opposition to a highland inheritance defined by its radical locality. And undoubtedly the Gaitáns' fusion mitigated divisions that had divided Andean listeners into antagonistic factions. In 2003 Pedro Arriola, a former member of Yawar, Peru's most widely recognized pan-Andean group, contrasted the contemporaneous atmosphere to the attitude taken some two or three decades prior:

[Back then] we played the classic [pan-Andean] repertoire, Chilean, Argentinean, mostly Bolivian, and erroneously we didn't look to Peru. We did learn some songs, but filtered through versions by pan-Andean groups. For example, one of our first Peruvian songs was [the Central Andean tune] "Hermanochay," but we didn't go to the source, we covered [the Chilean supergroup] Inti-Illimani's version. Ridiculous, right? But that was because we had no connection with huayno, and we felt rejected by those who sang huayno, because they considered us "Chilenized," "Bolivianized." We felt closer to this *so-called* "Andean" music. We thought the lyrics had more content, that the music was more developed in literary, harmonic, and melodic terms. For us, it was more interesting. There was a mutual rejection, between the young generation of so-called Andean musicians like us, and Andean musicians properly speaking. A reciprocal critique.

Arriola went on to praise the fusion between Ayacuchano and pan-Andean music as an index of "integration, one that's moving slowly . . . now, people speak much less of styles, now we try to speak only of Andean music." But of course, this musical triumph might be read as something of a pyrrhic victory for huayno music. It meant bending the aesthetic specificity of Peruvian song to fit parameters perceived as more metropolitan, an action intended, in another of Arriola's phrases, to make it "sound more universal, without destroying the Andean sound altogether." And Diosdado Gaitán Castro's response to criticism, premised upon the idea that global pop elements are tied to the "time" of modernity, depends upon a notion of traditional huayno as music outside that time, insufficiently contemporary to survive without adjustment. In this sense, the Gaitáns' work both ensured the greater popularity of songs from Ayacucho and reinscribed huayno's reputation as a parochial throwback.

Consolidating Style and Market: Dolby in the 1990s

After the Gaitáns' success other artists moved to copy their style, but most had little experience with pan-Andean performance, and soon arrangers and studio players became central to Ayacuchano production. Arriola was one of them, and shortly after the release of *Amor, Amor*, the singer Kiko Revatta asked him to help with a forthcoming release. Arriola fleshed out Revatta's finished recording of Ángel Bedrillana's contemporary huayno "Para un viejo corazón" by following the Gaitáns' model, dubbing a continuous charango part over the existing guitar accompaniment and adding flute solos to fill melodic gaps in the existing guitar line. The track was warmly received, and in Arriola's words, "If the Gaitáns gave the first indication of this style's potential, then this song, which was a national hit, made it clear."

"Para un viejo corazón" was recorded at Dolby JR, where Fernández once again sensed a business opportunity, and when it became a hit the producer gave the emergent style a commercial home. He established connections with studio players and arrangers such as Arriola, and before long, Dolby was associated with a rotating group of pan flute, kena, guitar, charango, and bass players who appeared on nearly every release.[36] Huayno artists still came to Dolby in large numbers, hoping to further their careers through its superior distribution network. No longer, though, were performers entrusted with artistic decisions. Now the studio required that new artists place their songs at the discretion of Fernández. He took on a larger directorial role, mining the principles of earlier hits in search of further success, and the studio began to run according to a new logic of production. Typically, artists recorded vocals and guitars only, leaving studio workers to amplify the sonic palette. This system ensured constant and efficient production, and as album after album emerged blending pan-Andean instrumentation with Ayacuchano songs, the stylistic experiment of the Gaitáns took on the air of a musical movement. If Fernández's initial role had been limited to providing a conduit for the distribution of edgy political huaynos, now the label's cachet, coveted by artists seeking an entrée into the business, and its resources, which allowed Fernández to hire the workers needed for commercial success, put the label into a position where it mediated the stylistic evolution of contemporary Ayacuchano huayno.

Fernández also expanded his promotional activities, placing the emergent style before those consumers that he expected to find it compelling. He invested in radio dissemination and live performance, channeling his wares toward an upwardly mobile sector of Lima's Andean migrant community. In 1995 he rented airtime to promote an upcoming concert featuring his artists, an event that he named "Ayacucho en el corazón de todos" (Ayacucho in All Our Hearts), and both activities moved Ayacuchano to new and unusual corners of Lima's public space. The concert was held at the band shell of the Campo de Marte, a large venue near Lima's downtown that usually catered to the city's middle classes. More important, Fernández chose to promote the concert via the FM station Radio del Pacífico. With its clearer signal and stereo broadcasting capability, the FM band was traditionally reserved for such "select" musical styles as pop, rock, salsa, and música criolla. As recently as 1987, huayno had been relegated to Lima's AM band, and even there most shows aired in the wee hours of the morning

(Lloréns Amico 1991). Fernández instead rented the 10:00 A.M. time slot, the prime hour for casual listening, ensuring that people outside huayno's existing listenership would encounter his label's fresh sounds. This was a tremendous financial gamble, at a rate of US$1500 a month, but Fernández believed that the music might appeal to a wide enough audience, and that its appearance on FM radio would create enough buzz, that he could recoup his expenses.

Its placement in mainstream spaces implied that contemporary Ayacuchano huayno was no dusty relic, parochial and suitable only for the unprofitable predawn hours. Nor was it like the chicha music of marginal migrants, proudly defiant of mainstream morals and aesthetics. Rather, it took on an air of social respectability and cosmopolitan cool. While it is difficult to establish a direct link between Fernández's efforts and the growing profile of the music he promoted, his event brought an extraordinary five thousand people to the Campo de Marte. His outlay recovered, he reinvested the profits in another event, and for the next several years Dolby JR acted as a concert promoter as well as a record label. Holding shows on a regular basis, Fernández and his associates established a tripartite nexus between recording activities, radio play, and concert appearances. Within this space listeners gathered around Ayacucho's new huayno style and became aware of themselves as members of a new kind of consuming community. They were collectively addressed via mainstream, citywide radio broadcasts and rendered visible to one another when they attended the events promoted by the programs they heard. In the process Dolby JR consolidated a panregional audience, one united not by their ancestors' province of ancestry, but rather by their identification with an Andean style that blended key indices of tradition and cosmopolitanism. At the time Arriola had recently returned to Peru after several years spent living abroad, and he described the transition in perception:

> [Before], you heard [Ayacuchano huaynos], but not so much, not like in Ayacucho. People knew songs like "El hombre," "La rosa roja," "Flor de retama," but no one related to them. Later, though, the music began to be heard everywhere. It started to capture an audience in Lima, and programs appeared, not on AM but on FM. It was via FM radio that this movement caught on, and massive concerts began to take place starting in 1995. For the first time, Dolby organized the festival called "Ayacucho en el corazón de todos," because now there was a public for it. And at these concerts, great artists like Kiko Revatta, and the Gaitán Castros, consolidated their audiences.

Once the parameters of this musical scene were established, competitors emerged, and some artists preferred to record at independent studios, hoping to retain greater control over profits. But with Dolby producing the lion's share of contemporary Ayacuchano records, other studios and performers largely acquiesced to the parameters that Dolby audiences had come to hear as the contemporary Ayacuchano sound.

The New Terms of Sophistication and Sentiment

Fernández himself believed that Dolby's success had less to do with his own savvy than with the inherent sophistication of Ayacuchano huayno. When I asked him why audiences were drawn to it, he responded with tropes inherited from earlier generations, saying that

> Ayacuchano music has always been the classiest [*más decente*] style in Peru, after música criolla: the classiest kind of huayno. It has the most [coherent] structure, content, and poetry. Performers are careful to record songs by recognized composers, with a high literary value. Poetry. And I think that it's music for people of all social levels, even the upper classes.

Guided by this belief, Fernández tried to manage the use of pop elements with an exemplary respect for tradition, taking care that the label's products retained the features that made Ayacuchano huayno a connoisseur's art. In practice, this meant that he took classic recordings as a model, asking artists to follow their example, while confining pan-Andean instrumentation to a supporting role. He tolerated no changes in melodic or lyrical structure, treating the recordings of Trio Ayacucho, Edwin Montoya, and the García Zárates as a kind of huayno urtext and enforcing adhesion to what was heard there. In his opinion, these actions constituted a fully sufficient respect for tradition:

> Look, Ayacuchano huayno has a musical structure, a spinal column, a vertebra. So, some things have been added, some instruments. But it will always be huayno, because it's got a structure. There have been some changes . . . there have been certain combinations between Ayacuchano music and Bolivian music. So, there's a little bit of fusion, combining of repertoires, maybe in order to make it more marketable, but not structurally, OK? It's still Ayacuchano huayno, you understand?

This balance between innovation and tradition became an especially self-conscious part of the label's artistic discourse as competitors pursued further stylistic experiments. Most listeners and musicians drew the distinction via the Gaitáns' 1999 album *Son del Sol*. Here the duo buried huayno's subtleties under the sounds of a drum kit and distorted rock guitars, and they also recorded a greater diversity of song types, including the pan-Andean rock-fusion classic "Todos juntos," by the Chilean group Los Jaivas. The album was widely dismissed as evidence that the Gaitáns were no longer serious about thoughtfully "modernizing" the huayno tradition, insofar as its loud, aggressive sounds directly traduced the key qualities of the Ayacuchano tradition. By the time I began fieldwork in 2000, the duo was widely derided within the contemporary Ayacuchano huayno scene as a group that had become thoroughly *comercial*, a term whose full significance I explore below, but which can be taken to signify "commercially adventitious" and lacking in any commitment to artistic worth.

Dolby's dominance and reputation gave the label substantial leeway in shaping perceptions of the musically normative, and Fernández used its discursive authority to temper musical experiments such as those of the Gaitáns. He refused to incorporate innovations that offended his sense of musical propriety, and over the late 1990s Dolby came to be seen as a studio with a studied commitment to tradition within a rapidly evolving Andean music scene. This did not mean that the label eschewed artistic and commercial innovation, however. One way to explore how Fernández enacted a balance between Ayacuchano tradition and stylistic fusion is by considering the label's next major success, which reinterpreted the amorous tone of huayno music via the musical resources of balada. Fernández deplored the Gaitáns' departure from the restrained sentimentalism of traditional huayno, and in 1998 a record by the new group Duo Ayacucho presented him with a vehicle for remedying this stylistic drift. According to Fernández, he designed the album's musical idiom in pursuit of this goal:

> After the Gaitáns began to take a new musical path, I looked for another duo. I tried to find someone who would continue to do things in the traditional style, but who would also take suggestions from me. For example, take the way that we recorded "Paloma torcaza." You could play it uptempo [*bailable*]. But one day I started to think about the words, and they seemed really romantic. I said to myself, why should it be played uptempo if it's romantic? So I arranged the song in a better way. I loved balada, I've always been a fan of that music, and I tried to combine the romance of both genres. I proposed that [various artists] record the song, and whenever we'd get together I'd sing it.

Finally, I sang it for Duo Ayacucho, and it piqued their curiosity, so they put it on their CD. I gave them the style, because they wanted to do something like the Gaitáns, but I wanted them to do it in a more traditional way, with more sentiment, that sort of thing.

"Paloma torcaza" (Dove, Turtledove), an old huayno recorded by the Hermanos García Zárate in the 1960s, was Duo Ayacucho's biggest hit, and it set the tone for their entire album. Their version respected the original structure of the song, keeping Ayacuchano guitars high in the instrumental mix and leaving the arranger, Fredy Gómez, to add a routine layer of kena and charango fills (see fig. 12). Fernández also added a new kind of introduction, a narrated passage addressing an absent lover and spoken over a free guitar part, that framed the song as a kind of romantic daydream.[37] Most important, however, the singer, Carlos Prado, delivered the song in the crooning, melodramatic manner of balada singers, filling the track with sighing vocal breaks and sudden changes of intensity. A departure from the original version, the interpretation nevertheless refigured Ayacucho's

12. Huayno "Paloma, torcaza," as performed by Duo Ayacucho

romantic sentimentalism in a parallel pop idiom. Detractors deplored it as "light," "digestible" fluff, but it was hugely successful, generating a "romantic" movement within the contemporary huayno scene that was widely interpreted as an appropriate modernization. Óscar Figueroa, for example, singled out Duo Ayacucho for praise, saying that they "keep the songs the way they used to be. They just add a kind of modern sound that makes it more attractive, and it works, you know?"

By 2000 these discourses and practices of production had been informally codified into a series of tropes that appeared constantly in studio work at Dolby—which, owing to concerns over its trademark, was at that time renamed Dolly Producciones. Recordists at Dolly used these tropes to distinguish their recordings from those of rivals and to explain the choices they made in the studio. Insofar as these discursive figures involved descrying audience preferences, they recall the process that Negus describes as "'defining music in its market' and 'the market in its music'" (1999: 28). However, the phantom entity glossed as "the market" exists only as a hypothesis about potentially shared dispositions, until the moment that it becomes incarnated in the acts of particular consumers. It determines real musical choices during studio work, and in the moment that the resulting musical objects are adopted by consumers, human subjects and the objects of their desires may appear to "fit" one another. But the basis of this market, the very parameters by which it comes to recognize itself, arises from the recordists' educated guesses about what might be made to appeal to an as yet unformed group of consumers. For this reason, it is critical to examine the way that they imagine their audience and the way that they encode their imaginings in figures of speech and musical sound, for it is here that musical distinctions and social distinctions come to stand for one another.

Dolly employees might be regarded as creative subjects, similar to the public television producers considered by Dornfeld (1998), who, in fashioning a media product, also produce a notion of their selves in relation to the work they produce. In this case, the pursuit of a judicious balance between cosmopolitan and traditional materials allowed recordists to present themselves as thoughtful mediators with a respect for heritage. In this sense, the musical standards used within Dolby's studio environs might best be seen as a series of strategies for managing the conflict between a felt commitment to tradition, on one hand, and the need to cater to popular tastes, on the other. In practice, though, these principles were often expressed using distinctions inherited from earlier generations, and because such distinctions were used to separate contemporary Dolly products and workers from their rivals, they created new ways to define relations between different

Andean popular musics and their respective listenerships. By figuring their working practices against those of less conscientious producers, Dolby's studio workers both performed a meaningful sense of self and inscribed new kinds of difference in Peru's Andean music scene.

The Discourse of Recording

Alongside releases of contemporary Ayacuchano huayno, Dolly produced albums in the older Ayacuchano style as well. Such recordings rarely generated a profit, but precisely for this reason they helped the label to preserve a certain intellectual cachet, a reputation as a business with enough commitment to folkloric tradition that an important product would be marketed at a loss. During the late 1990s and early 2000s Dolly released albums by such classic performers as Edwin Montoya, Trio Ayacucho, Trio Voces de Huamanga, Los Sureños, Los Tres de Huamanga, and Julia Illanes, all musicians who had flourished between the 1960s and 1980s and who sought to capitalize on Ayacuchano huayno's resurgence.

This commitment to tradition is what drew the engineer Eladio Díaz to work there. He explained the long hours that he was willing to put in, as Dolly's only regular sound man, by telling me, "I've worked in other studios, but here I feel more invested, because their ideas are like mine. I don't notice the time passing. Unfortunately for me, I love huayno more than anything." A graduate of the National Engineering University, a native of Ayacucho, and a music aficionado, Díaz had taken some private courses in sound engineering, and, unlike many workers at Peru's bootstrapping independent studios, he was conversant with the language, technique, and routine of studio work. Thanks to his deep knowledge of traditional music and his ear for detail, he was entrusted with substantial artistic control over the recordings he oversaw, and he intervened in solo albums by more learned performers. When I began to observe studio sessions, he was working on a CD by Walter Mendieta, a teacher of traditional Ayacuchano guitar at the National School of Folklore, and even Mendieta ended up refining his interpretation of the huayno "Adios pueblo de Ayacucho" at the engineer's request. After the first take, Díaz observed that Mendieta's introduction was too harmonically innovative for the centerpiece of the classic Ayacuchano repertoire and asked the guitarist to change it. Mendieta pieced together a new introduction modeled upon García Zárate's classic version, and after numerous alternate takes it was eventually released according to Díaz's vision.

In this sense Díaz often acted more as a cocreator than a facilitator for the musical vision of the performers he recorded. But his role as the label's stylistic custodian emerged more clearly in interactions with certain session players. Many groups had begun working regularly with arrangers and musicians, and some of the professionals were in high demand. They began to receive credit in liner notes, indicating the esteem with which their work was regarded and the extent of their contribution. Even so, many of them entered the huayno scene from outside, and their lack of familiarity with it presented occasional challenges for a label invested in mitigating the dilution of the classic Ayacuchano style. On another occasion, a vocalist named Rosario Hernández laughingly described her recording sessions as a constant and heated discussion between Díaz and her arranger. A young graduate of the National School of Folklore, he had already found commercial success with an artist named Hamylton Fernández, loading his hit record *A la hora exacta* (Right on Time) so heavily with rock, pop, and balada music that its Andean qualities were widely held to be barely recognizable. He hoped to repeat the process with this new singer, who found herself largely sidelined in the debates between the two men. When I asked Díaz about the case, he described how the recording process pitted him, the recordist charged with reining in stylistic excess, against the arranger and his emerging class of professionals, who often pressed for the full deployment of their talents:

DÍAZ: Sometimes they resent it, but I try to correct them, because these arrangers are usually young. The old guys work by ear. The kids of today have studied [music], but they haven't traveled much. By contrast, I've heard a lot of music, and because of that, sometimes they listen to me. Sometimes they don't. I try anyway. Often you can reach an agreement with the principal artist.
JT: So, it's your job to watch over regional specificity?
DÍAZ: Yes. Sometimes you can fix it in the final mix, when they're usually not there.

Dolly's productions were nevertheless shaped by the recognition that mass audiences had moved away from the traditional music that its employees found compelling. Even the older artists who recorded there made expedient stylistic compromises; describing his work on Trio Ayacucho's 2002 recording, Díaz explained that "they have a particular instrumentation, voices and guitars, that they're known for. But now the public knows [huayno music with] other instruments, and it sounded empty, so we put in a few arrangements, violin, kena, so young people would listen to it." Concerns about tempering innovation with reverence always remained close to the surface, and they shaped most conversations about recording practice. Such discussions were often organized around the term *comercial*, whose utterance constituted a critical judgment about the artistic value of a song, artist, recording, or even another record studio. Fernández himself used it to distinguish the seriousness of his enterprise from its peers. "I've got my politics, my way of working," he told me, "but it depends on one's cultural level. In Peru a lot of people start businesses [just] because they . . . come into some money. But they haven't got the know-how to run it, and they don't take care of the product's quality. They're more interested in the commercial aspect, they just want to recuperate their costs."

At first I found the term contradictory and confusing, since recordists and musicians used it in two different but related senses, distinguished by vocal inflection. Uttered neutrally, it described production choices that made a record widely salable—for instance, concessions to mass taste such as the use of kenas on Trio Ayacucho's CD. When uttered with a deprecatory inflection, signaled via a descending vocal contour and a distasteful facial expression, the word connoted something else, which might be glossed as "merely commercial." Huayno records that were "merely commercial" grafted trendy sounds onto traditional idioms with little regard for their compatibility, marking their creators as profiteers seeking to capitalize on the fashion of the moment rather than committed aficionados invested in creating a durable, culturally authentic, and artistically satisfying product. In this sense, although the label's own "commercial" recordings were admittedly distinct from their traditional releases, the care that label employees took to design appropriate arrangements safeguarded the value of the recordings as serious contributions to the ongoing development of huayno music.

The line between these two ideal types was variably situated, and one observer's judicious musical innovation stood as another's threat to the integrity of the huayno tradition. Precisely for this reason, though, distinguishing the commercial from the merely commercial was central to the evolving discourse of huayno production. It enabled the continual reinvention, amidst ongoing stylistic change, of the distinctions that marked true connoisseurship. The very act of making the distinction was a performance of good taste, a way to reestablish the limits of musical propriety and to perform the superior connoisseurship that made Ayacuchano musicians and listeners different from their peers. In the studio, it was enacted when mediators exerted control over instrumentation and interpretive style, and a concern to avoid commercial excess in these choices shaped much of the music produced in Ayacuchano record studios.

Nevertheless, the criteria used to judge the suitability of a given musical idiom were flexible, and they changed constantly to allow the justification of new nontraditional elements. One rhetorical strategy used to rule in new instrumentation, for examples, was analogy to traditional practice. Particularly emblematic is the case of the electric bass, which has become a standard feature of huayno recordings since the 1980s.[38] I often asked about the bass and was repeatedly told that it was acceptable because it approximated the role of the guitar's *bordón* (walking bass line) in traditional Ayacuchano music. But this explanation went against the grain of its actual role in contemporary recordings, which feature nothing resembling the classic bordón style. Instead of an active countermelody at the bottom of the musical texture, the electric bass was typically limited to playing the chordal roots of the accompanying harmony. And Arriola, for one, seemed to indicate that the instrument's uptake was more a matter of accommodation to the evolving aural expectations of a mass audience when he told me that contemporary huayno had a "more universal" sound, because of its "full range of highs and lows."[39] This discursive mechanism might be viewed as a post hoc justification for bending traditional music in a more profitable direction. But it might also be seen as a way for musicians and mediators, who were thoroughly invested in their own respect for folkloric authenticity, to exert some control over stylistic evolution and their own identities as huayno aficionados even as they conceded to market pressures. In other words, these methods of distinguishing proper commercial concessions from improper ones allowed them to maintain the sense of connoisseurship and to resolve their own hesitancy about the tension between their commercial and personal goals.

A discourse of propriety, however, requires alters against which to figure itself—in this case, recordings that did not show a proper response to commercial pressures. When I asked Díaz about the differences between contemporary huayno styles, he began by attributing Ayacucho's success to Dolby's efforts. However, drawing upon his experience at a number of different studios around Lima, he went on to characterize the dominant huayno norteño music of the era as less sophisticated, elegant, and thoughtful:

> The producers have worked a lot. Dolby, Dolly, they have been [Ayacucho's] producers, for fifteen, twenty years now, and have been supporting artists for a long time. There are producers from other places, but they just do it for money, and here they take care of the musical aspect too.... I think that music from Ayacucho makes more sense, it's more logical [*ordenado*], musically, it fits the text better, it's a little more rational than music from other regions, that's what I like.... Besides, with respect to Ayacuchano music, the audience likes it more because they make good arrangements, they include

non-Ayacuchano instruments, but it's done correctly, carefully; they work a lot on their arrangements. By comparison, in [huayno norteño] there's no pattern of arrangements. Ayacuchano music is more classy [*decente*] in that sense—it's not too chicha.

It was primarily in opposition to chicha and northern huayno music that people involved with contemporary Ayacuchano huayno figured their own notions of musical legitimacy and sincerity, drawing upon and extending older distinctions between the intellectual aficionados of Ayacuchano music and the poorer, less educated listenership for its stylistic alters. Ayacuchano aficionados characterized chicha and huayno norteño as less intellectually demanding, less musically variegated, and less refined than Ayacuchano music. The songs were considered to be lyrically insipid, neither aiming at nor achieving the richness of Ayacuchano huayno's sung poetry. And the artists drew indiscriminately upon dance music and electronic instrumentation rather than carefully planning their stylistic incorporation. But above all, it was the fact that these decisions were seen as self-evidently motivated by profit rather than by a concern for artistry, as merely commercial production choices, that drove the discourse of Ayacuchano superiority. In making the distinction, Ayacuchano musicians and mediators did not merely engage in social and stylistic chauvinism. They figured themselves as subjects who, alone among their peers, preserved the values of folkloric tradition that in an earlier age had lent huayno music and Andean peoples in general a hard-won measure of respectability.

Of course, the very speakers of these ideas relied upon a foreign style in their own work. However, the pan-Andean style arguably presented a lesser degree of dissonance. The highland origin of its instruments made the logic of their incorporation less strained, and even the traditionalist Díaz answered my questions about proper instrumentation by saying that "normally, in the arrangements, you respect a musical style. For example in an Ayacuchano song . . . minimally, there should be two guitars, rhythm and lead . . . old songs, they might stay like this, but with new music, you can include other instruments, like sax, [pan flutes], and [other Andean flutes]." By 2001 pan-Andean music and contemporary Ayacuchano huayno recordings stood for one another to a substantial degree, sometimes leading artists, mediators, and fans to treat them as equivalents. Indeed, the convergence between the two styles, unified by their elective stylistic affinities and by a common listenership, was considerable. As Dolby's framework gained a national listenership, fewer and fewer of the artists who took it up were Ayacuchanos. Meanwhile, artists recorded an ever greater diversity of song types from across the Andean region, and mediators regularly argued the need to find a new term for this stylistic hodgepodge, one more adequate than "huayno." Overall, it seemed poised to become a local, distinctly Peruvian take on the pan-Andean style, with all its attendant connotations.

Conclusion

Images of sophistication, careful technique, and sonic perfection circulated constantly in the milieu of contemporary Ayacuchano huayno. They shaped the decisions that producers and engineers made as they sought to live up to a musically superlative reputation, while reframing their products for a changing listenership. Such talk may sometimes have arisen from chauvinism, but it was also a discursive means through which such workers aspired to control the direction of Andean subjectivity. In a context where listener expectations of musical relevance were increasingly driven by transnational sounds, these mediators fashioned themselves and their audience into particular kinds of people, full of respect for their heritage and yet open to ongoing developments. They sought to profit from musical activity, but they were more than callous agents of commerce seeking to cash in on international trends or victims of a homogenizing global culture industry. Rather, they were everyday subjects who grappled with the forces of globalization, seeking to mitigate its transformative power.

Such mediators were also were key agents of sociomusical creation, forging new relations among emergent coalitions of people, sound, and affect, and codifying the musical distinctions that would separate their audience from those gathered by their rivals. By encouraging a certain class of the Andean community to inhabit their terms of musical discourse, they did not merely satisfy a market, because there is no market for products that do not yet exist. Instead, when mediators at Dolby created an image of the listenership for their new, hybrid products within the studio walls, imagining what listeners were like and what kinds of products would appeal to them, the mediators moved toward making this potential subject real. And when individual constituents of this market showed up at the Campo de Marte, purchased CDs, called in to radio shows, and named themselves as fans with a shared interest in a musical product, they proved Dolby employees' skill at sociomusical engineering.

Nevertheless, the means used to sell contemporary Ayacuchano music rely upon modes of distinction that are indebted to Peru's noxious inequalities of race and class. By wielding old terms of huamanguino discourse against huayno norteño and chicha music, the agents of the contemporary

Ayacuchano scene did more than name different audiences: they provided new terms with which to establish hierarchy within the Andean public sphere. And if the recording studio was an important site in which the different threads of this subject position were brought together, then it was through radio broadcasts that it was most effectively brought to the subjects who were expected to inhabit it.

FIVE

Finding the Huayno People: Music Radio, DJ Talk, and the Shape of the Andean Public

A few weeks after Lima's pirate station Radio Gigante went live in 2001, DJ Alfredo Loayza was still unsure about the extent of its listenership. He thought that it was large, since the station's broadcasts, including his own "Gente huayno" (Huayno People), took requests from all over greater Lima. But the day that the station's DJs held a live promotion on the air, announcing a giveaway of free beverages and T-shirts, they were shocked to run out of merchandise in minutes. No matter where their mobile team went—the Gamarra commercial center at the heart of downtown, the district of El Salvador in the far southern cone—they were mobbed by listeners who had found the station despite its low wattage and recent vintage, tucked away at the heart of the FM dial, next to the powerhouse rock station Radio Zeta.[1] And those who left work or home to pick up a free T-shirt or a bottle of Kola Real surely represented a fraction of the listenership. For Loayza, the promotion demonstrated the existence of a vast audience for music that was largely absent from legal broadcast spaces, controlled by consortia contractually obligated, he was sure, to disseminate more lucrative foreign styles.[2]

Loayza's story reminded me of a minor event that took place some months earlier in Ayacucho. Carlos Prado had become one of the most popular contemporary Ayacuchano huayno artists after the release of his first solo album, which featured upbeat Quechua-language songs alongside crooning songs of heartbreak. When he played Ayacucho in 2003, his concert was promoted by a local pop station, La Caribeña, and I knew that he was due there for a live interview the afternoon before the show. I listened as a DJ hyped the young man's forthcoming appearance, speaking with breathless insinuation about his good looks, charm, and romantic sensibility. Eventually I made my way to the nondescript station premises, hidden amidst garages and building supply stores on a dusty side street. Unexpectedly, the block was pullulating with young women, who so crowded the station's doorway that I had to be admitted by an employee serving as an impromptu bouncer. And as Prado inside spoke to callers on-air, the people outside screamed and jostled for a glimpse, performing a kind of fan behavior that represented a recent innovation in the huayno scene.[3]

The evanescence of radio's "communities of the air" (Squier 2003) makes it particularly difficult to grasp their character, even for radio personnel such as Loayza, whose pirate status ruled his station out of the data produced by ratings agencies. Dispersed among the population in range of the signal, radio audiences materialize only sporadically, when they respond to particular broadcast events. They need never meet any of their fellows, and they may never act publicly upon their membership. Since much radio listening happens in private, it is hard to tell which, if any, radio communities an individual belongs to. But anyone with a receiver soon discovers that the medium traverses many subcultures, simply by tuning in and hearing different forms of address aimed at distinct groups of listeners. The medium's power to align musical habits with particular categories of personhood is no less impressive for becoming visible only in the rare moments when subjects act in concert. Even if listeners identify with nothing they hear, they glean the content of the categories in play and the markers by which members are recognized.

In this chapter I explore how radio broadcasting shaped the public image and the listenership of contemporary Ayacuchano huayno. The style emerged at a time when Peru's airwaves were largely divided between foreign pop, on one hand, and Andean music from regions outside Ayacucho, on the other. In order to capture potential listeners, DJs manipulated the contextual and discursive features of their own programs in ways that resonated with the broadcasting tropes of rival genres, taking advantage of existing listening dispositions to frame public experience of the newer style. More specifically, these DJs made it stand for a consumerist yet thoroughly "Andean" subject position that could be inhabited by cosmopolitan, economically ascendant listeners.

This would not have been possible without radio's prior centrality to life in urban Peru.[4] Emanating from ubiquitous transistors as well as more modern technologies, radio sound accompanies work and leisure, eases the solitude of time spent alone, and provides a context for socializing; it is rare for a household to pass an entire day without tuning in.[5] Loayza neatly captured its place in Lima, describing the ebb and flow of the broadcast day and calling attention to the different categories in play over its course:

People get up at 6:00 or 7:00, and they're doing something else. If they listen to radio, usually they want to hear a station where you hear a lot of time checks, or news. While they're making breakfast, or getting ready for work. In that slot, you get few listeners: or rather, lots of people listen, but not attentively. Then it's rush hour; traffic is terrible at 8:00 A.M. At 8:00 or 9:00, they get to work, and at 9:00 people start to listen to the radio. Listenership goes up, because people are working and have their radios by their side. They keep the volume low, [but] whatever they're doing, they're listening. At work, or at home, cooking, it's easy, because no one else is around. In workshops, factories, on the bus, wherever you go, people are working. But they have a radio—wherever you go, at work, there's a radio. At 1:00 the listenership decreases, because at lunch people watch TV. But 2:00, 3:00, 4:00 P.M., after lunch, they rest or snooze, whatever, and lots of people listen. And at 4:00 it goes up again, because people go back to work, until 6:00, 7:00, people are on their way home. It's rush hour in traffic, but they listen at home, and in the bus. Not after 8:00, because in Peru, a house with no TV on after 8:00 is pretty rare.

Some of this listening is involuntary, much of it is distracted, and not all broadcasts feature music. But radio's day-to-day redundancy and its wide reach encourage shared frames of interpretation to find purchase. Above all other media forms, it structures aesthetic dispositions, creates common histories of consumption, and links users into like-minded social groups. It was central to the consolidation of a listenership for contemporary Ayacuchano huayno artists even before the program *Ayacucho en el corazón de todos* aired in mid-1990s Lima, and in fact that show drew upon broadcasting techniques that had been honed in Ayacucho, where the station Frecuencia A Record was recognized as the style's bellwether institution.[6] Many prominent DJs, including Loayza, had worked there, and though it had fallen from the peak of its popularity, its influence was disproportionate to the scope of its operations. Here I focus mainly on activities at Frecuencia A, and particularly on the program of its leading DJ, Miguel Ángel Huamán; but by 2001 contemporary Ayacuchano music appeared on most of Ayacucho's radio stations, as well as a handful of pirate broadcasters in Lima, and I amplify my account with observations from these competitors.[7]

Agency on the Airwaves: Theorizing Radio and DJ Work

Given its ubiquity and its central role in the music business, radio broadcasting has received surprisingly little attention from scholars.[8] This is partly because music radio does not lend itself to the kind of rich textual analysis that enlivens writings on media forms such as television, cinema, video games, or internet technology (Hilmes and Loviglio 2002a), and partly because radio's relationship to the promotional activities of the North American record industry meant that it "seemed completely captured by capitalism to a greater extent even than most other media" (Hilmes 2002: 7).[9] Organized in a nonlinear fashion to deliver content-poor goods to intermittently attentive consumers and guided by "the specific requirement to maximize audiences" (Hendy 2000: 743), music broadcasting seemed suited for little beyond delivering demographically calculated slices of listenership to advertisers (Berland 1993a, 1993b; cf. Barnes 1988).

However, if the relationship between commercial radio, audience maximization, and monetary profit is axiomatic, less certain is the notion that radio's ancillary effects are socially negligible. As with other kinds of commodities, users of commercial radio clearly recognize themselves as members of social groups with common investments (D. Miller 1994; García Canclini 2001). Such communities may be new, previously unrecognized kinds of groups, or their membership may depend upon extrinsic ties such as ethnicity, class, gender, or age cohort, in which case their shared conception of that category is inflected by their listening experiences. In either case, the medium shapes the very bonds of which durable collectivities are made. Furthermore, the low overhead and user-friendly nature of radio have regularly allowed new or silenced voices to enter the public sphere, especially in times of social or technological change. The postwar United States, for example, saw a sudden profusion of independent stations and hence a surplus of airtime, allowing representatives of marginalized regional, class, and ethnic communities the space to essay programs that "were often crassly commercial, yet included an astonishing array of accents, expressions, and attitudes" (Rothenbuhler and McCourt 2002: 367).[10]

Approaches to radio have also been limited by their restrictive geographic focus. Critiques of commercial programming derive mainly from studies of North American and European media environments and rely on comparisons with public broadcasters such as the BBC, CBC, and NPR, or on such independent institutions as college and pirate radio (Berland 1993a, 1998). Operations in other contexts reveal that different histories of development produce different expectations and modes of media interaction; that the radio business is organized and financed in distinct, often haphazard ways; that direct corporate influence is mitigated; and that the actions of employees are thereby less overdetermined (see also Ahlkvist 2001). For instance, in Peru, as in many countries (see Hennion and Méadel 1986), the radio public is much larger than the record-buying public, and the record industry's weakness makes radio the key site for disseminating music and musical ideologies. This also means that artists' income from live performance far outweighs their meager royalties, and their need for promotional airtime leads to a different, arguably less intrusive kind of clientelism than that which drives U.S. radio.

Most important, people use commercial radio in a manner distinct from other media, and it demands analytical tools that are specific to its idiosyncrasies. Rather than attending to music radio's "message" or narrative arc, listeners mainly use it to shape the affective texture of daily life: to construct a relaxing environment, a party atmosphere, or a consoling ambience. Interaction with radio sound is often transitory and distracted, and even though hosts try to retain audiences as long as they can, programs allow listeners to drop in and out of them as needed. Its effects cannot be approached using the hermeneutic methods developed to analyze soap operas or news programs, but broadcasts are nevertheless organized via ideological categories that, in their very capacity as unremarked background assumptions, become hard to disavow to the extent that they become the common sense of local sound worlds (cf. Turino 1999: 228–29). Commercial radio, in other words, is socially efficacious "because it weaves its magic through pleasures and subliminal framings" (Abu-Lughod 2005: 9).

Commercial radio broadcasts, then, should be approached indexically, in terms of the way that musical texts are associated with or dissociated from other kinds of marked objects and discourses. In one of the few works to address radio work in this way, Spitulnik has illustrated that there are

> several implicit or ongoing levels at which "audiences" are prefigured or indexed in media practice. For example, in radio broadcasting this happens through the choice of program content, code, and stylistic nuances, as well as in the use of certain modes of address . . . [the] signaling of audiences also occurs through several metapragmatic devices which frame the communication event, such as titles for distinct programs or time periods and promotional slogans which advertise the station, exhort listeners, and define a mood. The point, then, is that listeners as collectivities (i.e. "as audiences") are signaled and constructed in broadcasting practice . . . and such linguistic processes play an important role in establishing this sense of collective address and participation. (Spitulnik 1994: 44)

Two implications of Spitulnik's words bear further extrapolation. The first is the central role of DJs and radio managers, who design the experience of listening itself.[11] Far from acting as mere gatekeepers, whose role can be assessed by enumerating the songs they allow to pass (Ahlkvist 2001), radio workers organize ideas about music by linking it to other materials over the course of a broadcast (Hennion and Méadel 1986), and it is "through their voice that . . . radio assumes authorship of the community, woven into itself through its jokes, its advertisements, its gossip, all represented, recurringly and powerfully, as the map of local life"(Berland 1993b: 116). DJs, in other words, are agents who determine the very shape of the listenership they gather, define the bonds that unite them, and map them onto local contexts. Understanding their influence means analyzing the entire inventory of their programs and showing how they use framing devices to situate music within that broader experiential field.

Of the many framing devices that are manipulated in radio work, the most mundane may be the conventions of scheduling. However, the organization of the broadcast day can acquire strong social connotations, as when pioneering American companies "differentiated the radio schedule by gender, creating a divide between daytime and prime time [separating] programming forms directed at lower- to middle-class housewives" from "serious" forms aimed at men and wealthier women (Wang 2002: 349). Once time slots are inflected in this way, DJs and managers may use them to sort or resort songs, artists, and styles, implying that particular combinations of objects belong together. But they may also use them to hierarchize musical genres, placing songs in more or less prestigious spots over the broadcast day, or within individual programs.

The most important of framing devices, however, is the tone that DJs adopt in addressing their public. Spitulnik has described how Zambian radio's easy, bantering mode of locution, immediately familiar to pop music consumers everywhere, conveys "a mood of optimism, prosperity, having fun, and being in touch with a wider modern world . . . an imagined cosmopolitan community of affluence and excitement" (1994: 315) and attributed the global uptake of this discursive style to its ability to project the assumption that listeners are familiar with a class- and culture-specific quality of experience. DJs use it in "a very deliberate effort to signal a certain kind of audience—and more generally—*a certain kind of lifestyle*[,] one of modernity and cosmopolitanism: being up to date, listening to the latest music and lingo, and having fun—or even more precisely—having the *leisure time* and the *sensibility* to *enjoy* radio listening" (1994: 321; emphasis in original). This mode of discourse, in other words, does more than lend a metropolitan sheen to the music that it accompanies. In societies where worldly sensibilities and monetary affluence are also signs of a properly civilized subject, its uptake produces the listener's very self-recognition as a fully modern individual. It proves that he or she possesses the proper orientation to distinguish and claim the bourgeois, cosmopolitan mode of being in the world that provides social legitimacy.

This DJ style produces new kinds of consumers more efficiently than social amelioration. Like commercial radio everywhere, it "[contributes] to the familiarization of a leisure- and commodity-oriented way of life" (Lacey 2002: 23), and it helps to delegitimize those modes of being that do not revolve around cosmopolitan desires and commodities. But it can also be used to sanction new patterns of consumption for those who already live by those desires and commodities. In the case of contemporary Ayacuchano huayno, this mode of discourse, combined with the savvy manipulation of other framing mechanisms, indisputably helped to make the style into a popular success.

Most of the enterprises that broadcast Ayacuchano music during the 1990s and 2000s were by global standards tiny operations, run in a semi-improvisatory fashion and staffed largely by "hobbyist" DJs with little or no training. Nevertheless, they had a power over public musical space far greater than that of foreign peers. Working at the center of Peru's privileged musical medium, their actions organized the sense of "groupness" that grew among the genre's fan base. Seeking to tap emergent markets, they drew middle-class Andean listeners into a mutual awareness of their shared subject position and helped them to conceptualize that subject position in relation to musical structures. This, in turn, depended upon shifts in the Peruvian social and technological landscape, and upon the savvy with which mediators deployed their inherited understanding of broadcasting patterns.

Early Peruvian Broadcasting: Pioneers in the Public Sphere

By the time contemporary Ayacuchano artists began their rise to prominence in the 1990s, Peru's radio business was sixty years old, but huayno broadcasting was somewhat younger.[12] The country's first radio license was granted in the mid-1920s, at a time when President Leguía was pushing to create a modern, unified nation-state.[13] Radio took its place alongside Lima's new cinemas and boulevards as an emblem of modern convenience and collective progress, but it was also conceived as a vehicle for cultivating national sentiment.[14] Operations debuted under the moniker OAX on June 20, 1925, opening, in a move that underlined the medium's status as a tool for nationalist pedagogy, with a speech by Leguía himself. Educative intentions, combined with the concentration of expensive receivers among the upper class, meant that content tended toward the highbrow in these early years. Nevertheless, amateur performances of classical or parlor music, scholarly lectures, English lessons, financial news, government speeches, and similarly edifying content were sometimes leavened by comic monologues and even performances of such foreign popular genres as "one steps, fox-trots, tangos, and *pasodobles*" (E. Bustamante 2005: 210).

The pioneering station's installations devolved to the state after it folded in 1926, and the effects of the Great Depression ensured that OAX remained alone until the mid-1930s, when nine more stations debuted against a tumultuous political background.[15] Facing worker agitation for labor rights and political representation, as well as border disputes with Colombia and Ecuador, the Benavides regime (1933–39), like its predecessor, used radio to help foster a sense of national unity. The price of receivers had already fallen to within reach of those who earned working-class wages, and in an effort to convince the masses that their leaders recognized their contributions, the government promoted populist programs devoted to sports, dramas, and, above all else, the various musical genres beloved by the capital's working classes.[16] OAX had broadcast occasional performances of valses by the Gamarra-Salerno duo in the 1920s, but now the música criolla group Los Criollos began to perform on OAX (1934) as well as Radio Goicochea (1935), and a 1944 survey about the radio habits of the Lima public would soon show that the genre had become the sentimental favorite of the mass audience.[17] Meanwhile, Radio Dusa established a house jazz band that performed "tangos, [Mexican] rancheras, swing music, and fox-trots" (E. Bustamante 2005: 213), and the 1944 inauguration of Lima's Radio Victoria featured the Caribbean dance music of the Lecuona Cuban Boys (Nabeshima 1992).

The late 1930s and 1940s saw radio become a true mass medium as dozens of stations rose and fell in Lima and many more sprang up in the provinces. Cusco's Radio Cusco led the way in 1936, and 1942 saw the establishment of the Compañía Peruana de Radiodifusión S.A., which eventually rebroadcast via repeaters throughout the country. Another national group was anchored by Radio Victoria, which emerged in 1944 and eventually became the flagship of Peru's most powerful chain. By 1958, when another boom led to the founding of new stations throughout the country, most departmental capitals in the South Andes housed one or more broadcasters on the AM or shortwave band, their signals carrying news, educational content, radio dramas, personal messages, and popular music deep into the local countryside.[18]

Amidst all of this activity, Andean music occupied a decidedly secondary place, one that was filled not by vernacular huayno, but rather by the stylizations of indigenista artists. In the 1930s, for example, Radio Nacional's resident ensemble included the Ayacuchano harpist Florencio Coronado, as well as members of Áncash's Conjunto Típico Huaracino; both would go on to become leading indigenista performers, the latter as the Conjunto Ancashino Atusparia.[19] Other stations, including Radio Dusa, Radio Goicochea, Radio Internacional, and Radio Lima, broadcast occasional performances by similar groups or individuals over the 1930s and early 1940s, including the Cuarteto de Cámara Incaico (Inca Chamber Quartet) and Moisés Vivanco, who won a talent competition with his Trio Los Estudiantes in 1938 before introducing soprano Yma Sumac to the world via Radio Nacional in 1942 (Limansky 2008).[20] Vernacular Andean music, meanwhile, dwelt on the margins until midcentury, when two bellwether institutions, with two different approaches to broadcasting, emerged in different locations within a few years of one another.

The first was Cusco's Radio Tawantinsuyo, founded in 1948 as a competitor to Radio Cusco and designed to promote Cuzqueño regional identity. Broadcasting in Spanish and Quechua to city and countryside alike, it simultaneously reflected Cusco's legacy as the indigenista musical heartland and foreshadowed the rise of vernacular huayno music, featuring indigenista performers alongside such vernacular huayno soloists as Pancho Gómez Negrón and Raúl García Zárate on programs that included *La hora del charango* (The Charango Hour) and *Raúl García y su guitarra* (Mendoza 2008). After adding a shortwave signal in 1955, Radio Tawantinsuyo reached well beyond the department of Cusco, and its programming line inspired enthusiastic imitators throughout the southern Andes.[21]

Soon Andean radio programming emerged in Lima as well, where the growing migrant population made it commercially viable, and led to a slightly different business model (Lloréns Amico 1983, 1991). Its pioneer was the entrepreneur Luis Pizarro Cerrón, whose methods were widely copied and helped drive the "Golden Age" of huayno music. A promoter of folkloric shows, Pizarro asked for a slot at Radio El Sol in the early 1950s, and was given the use of the unoccupied, ostensibly unprofitable airtime space before the official 7:00 A.M. beginning of the broadcast day. *El sol de los Andes* (Sun of the Andes) debuted at 6:00 A.M. Because of the dearth of Andean recordings, it focused on live performances by musicians known to Pizarro, who were happy to promote upcoming shows in the capital. It also reached highland settlements that lay within range of the signal, and soon migrants based in Lima began to treat it as a link to their hometowns, asking Pizarro to air messages too urgent for the post.[22] The show's profile rose as it became a cherished institution, leading station managers to charge Pizarro new kinds of fees and leading him in turn to seek sponsorship from businesses that catered to migrant consumers.

As the show's blend of community service with musical dissemination began to generate revenue, competing programs began to fill Lima's airwaves in the 4:00 to 7:00 A.M. slot.[23] Most DJs were hobbyists, aficionados, or promoters of some sort, and like Pizarro, they worked as concessionaries, thereby avoiding the management dictates faced by regular station employees. Their programming was shaped instead by a peculiarity of the early Andean broadcasting scene. Shows usually targeted listeners from a single locale, focusing on music and events pertinent to a particular town, province, or department. Sponsored by businesses, migrants' associations, or individuals linked to that area, such shows allowed migrants with common origins to locate one another across Lima's fragmented urban space and communicate with their home regions more easily. These shows also provided familiar cultural referents for isolated and lonely migrants, recreating the bases of highland identity and social organization in the capital. For this reason, they have typically been described as agents of integration, allowing newcomers to find and engage with the networks of support required to achieve success in the harsh metropolis (Doughty 1970; Vivanco 1971). However, insofar as such programs were narrowcast to a thinly delimited slice of the migrant public, they may also have preserved the regional fragmentation that characterized life in the highlands itself.

Whatever their effects, the shows were easily financed by proceeds from events organized by program hosts or by capital raised from migrant businesses. Relieved of the pressure to maximize audiences, these shows were described by Lloréns Amico not as "enterprises which yield economic gains, but rather a musical and cultural promotion device" (Lloréns Amico 1991: 187), which fell "outside the rating system and, therefore, [did] not depend directly on the amount of listenership" (Lloréns Amico 1991: 187). This made them low-risk sites for disseminating huayno music. Indeed, artists and record labels soon adopted the concessionary model, creating programs to promote new releases and upcoming performances. At the same time, the audiences for community-based shows easily blurred into one another, as listeners stayed with a particular station for the next program and thereby learned about music from beyond their immediate home region. In the aggregate, then, these radio shows promoted a sense of mutual self-awareness among Lima's Andean migrant community that transcended but did not replace more particular, microregional identifications. Second-generation migrants, whose sense of self was often less firmly rooted than that of their parents in their ancestral community of origin, increasingly consumed and recognized a variety of Andean music styles, and by the early 1980s it was possible to discern "the new phenomenon of national popularity for highland singers [which] could indicate the appearance of common referents transcending the regional diversity that has until now been maintained in Andean music" (Lloréns Amico 1983:140–41).

Early Broadcasting in Ayacucho

Before the late 1980s, Ayacucho's airwaves were dominated by AM stations Radio Ayacucho (later Radio Nacional), Radio La Voz de Huamanga, and Radio San Cristóbal. Their programming echoed tendencies established elsewhere, and among them they carved the local airwaves into two distinct zones of operation, naturalizing patterns of musical consumption that structured the operations of their successors. One zone aimed for the city's urban middle-class market with national and international pop. The other, which catered to rural peasants and migrants from the countryside, largely featured huayno music from the Central Andes, and later chicha music as well.

Radio Ayacucho, founded in 1958, operated mostly in the first of these two fields. This subsidiary of the Lima-based Radio Victoria chain brought to the highland city sounds that were trending all over Latin America. It broadcast some huayno, especially in the very early hours of the morning, but a former DJ, Isaac Argumedo, told me that programming focused mainly on "[coastal] valses, cumbias, rancheras, boleros, guarachas, [and] pop." In 1968, it became a part of the government-run Radio Nacional chain, and local programming was curtailed, though Argumedo continued to host an early-morning show called *Así cantan los pueblos andinos del Perú* (So Sing the Andean Peoples of Peru), featuring huayno from all over the Andes, until all local content was shut down in the 1990s.[24]

A second station, Radio San Cristóbal, targeted a similar but younger audience. Property of the archbishopric of Ayacucho, it featured shows such as "Éxitorama" (Hit-o-rama), which catered to university students with songs by the Beatles, the Argentinean pop star Leo Dan, and other, mostly international artists. Ayacuchanos typically recall Radio San Cristóbal less vividly than its competitors, and its eventual disappearance seems to have had few repercussions.

By contrast, Radio La Voz de Huamanga (The Voice of Huamanga) catered to the region's Quechua-speaking peasant majority. Fernando Cruz, son of and successor to its founding director, stated that the station was "entirely for the lower classes [*eminentemente popular*]," and that its original purpose was "outreach [*proyección social*] . . . rural towns lacked telephones, telegraphs, any kind of communication. Radio was a means of connecting people, and the idea was to build a bridge between the capital and the rural towns." After its 1963 inauguration, La Voz built this bridge by broadcasting in Quechua and Spanish, by acquiring a shortwave transmitter that brought its signal to the entire department, and by establishing a for-profit, on-air message delivery service. Widely used by migrants and rural visitors to send messages back home, this service drove a wide audience to the station, giving it unmatched influence over its listenership's musical habits.

Radio La Voz became the city's main huayno broadcaster, but its patronage of music from Ayacucho was thin. This situation stood out most in the station's birthday salutations, whereby patrons sent festive greetings and a dedicatory song of their choice to a listening dedicatee. Rather than music from Ayacucho, requests increasingly came in for the huayno recordings of such Central Andean artists as Picaflor de los Andes, Flor Pucarina, and Estudiantina Perú, whose long period of national dominance in the huayno industry began just as La Voz was founded.[25] Cruz, echoing an opinion widely shared among older Ayacuchanos, told me that his station "stood out because it made an alien style take root here" and attributed the growing taste for Central Andean music to his father, who had come to Ayacucho from the Central Andean city of Huancayo: "initially we played [Ayacuchano huayno], but it's depressing. So it occurred to my father to disseminate [Central Andean] music, which was for dancing, and 90 percent of the . . . birthday salutations became [Central Andean] music." Aficionados of Ayacuchano huayno listened bitterly as the influential station fostered and then satisfied local demand for the competing Central Andean style, saturating the airwaves with its distinctive harp-and-saxophones bands rather than Ayacucho's genteel guitars. Some are said to have called for fines against the station's management for activities detrimental to the city's cultural integrity.[26] Nor were their concerns about the displacement of local customs entirely unfounded, for Ayacucho's urban proletariat and rural peasantry vigorously took central Andean music into their festivals and celebrations.[27]

By the 1980s, then, Ayacucho's broadcasting space sorted established elites from rural peasants and new urban migrants, dividing them into two distinct taste communities tied to competing radio stations. Ayacucho's own music was conspicuously marginal, and many residents echoed Miguel

Ángel Huamán, who told me that "there was huayno, but never *our* huayno" on the local airwaves. This situation may have been a response to the close-knit nature of the small city, and Carlos Falconí explained Trio Ayacucho's dearth of local performing opportunities by noting that "[nobody] wanted to see us [in Ayacucho]. They saw us all the time, it wasn't a big deal." Furthermore, radio was treated largely as a conduit for escapist entertainment, and the elitist reputation of the city's huayno style may have discouraged DJs and radio managers. Argumedo seemed to indicate as much when characterizing the media presence of huayno music in this era:

> Who listened [to huayno] in the city? Migrants. The birthday salutations, they were all huayno, and mostly people preferred huayno from [the Central Andes], because it was livelier and happier. Ayacuchano music, boy, it was salon music, slow, you had to listen and understand the words . . . Ayacuchano music, it was heard in houses that were a little more high-class—for example, the family of a Raúl García Zárate didn't listen to music from Huancayo.

These words speak tellingly of the way that Ayacuchano radio helped to naturalize new patterns of musical distinction. The broadcast hours aimed at the city's elite were populated with coastal and international music, while the city's burgeoning lower classes, with little connection to or love for Ayacucho's own traditions, were targeted with the Central Andean style. Lacking both cosmopolitan cachet and earthy appeal, Ayacucho's huayno music was rendered anachronistic, the quaint and faded custom of a particular class and generation. Although it was never absent from the airwaves, it was shunted aside during the 1970s and 1980s, confined mostly to the time slots of the early morning. Even the spaces where it found a home, such as the highbrow station Radio Wari, tended to confirm its status as an elitist pursuit.

The 1985 appearance of Radio Wari, however, portended deep changes in Ayacucho's media landscape. In the late 1980s and early 1990s a decrease in the price of transmitters brought FM radio's superior signal within the reach of local investors. The city experienced a sudden broadcasting boom as several aficionados became small radio impresarios virtually overnight, working from their homes or back gardens.[28] The expansion of broadcast space gave untested actors room to essay unproved ideas, and as the dial became saturated, station managers were encouraged to accommodate such risks in pursuit of audience share. Both developments furnished the spaces within which local huayno music was reborn as a mass phenomenon over the course of the 1990s. Accomplishing this, however, meant challenging the associations between genre, time slot, radio band, and DJ style that had come to be experienced as normative expressions of distinction.

Huayno on the FM Band: *Ayacucho en el corazón de todos*

The music that initially aired on Ayacucho's new FM stations was determined by the nature and the received connotations of FM technology itself. FM radio's line-of-sight signal, interrupted when it meets a solid mass, is often limited in the broken terrain of the Andes, and in Ayacucho coverage is largely restricted to the city limits. As such, FM broadcasts excluded the rural peasantry a priori. But its superior sound, far less vulnerable to atmospheric interference than AM transmission, meant that FM radio was already identified as the elite radio band, and in practice it was understood as a medium for "a 'special' kind of programming, as having sonic and technical qualities that should only be used to satisfy middle- and upper-class audiences" (Lloréns Amico 1990: 51). Most of the FM stations that appeared in the late 1980s and early 1990s, then, were dedicated to the cosmopolitan rock, pop, and tropical music, such as salsa and cumbia, that was traditionally directed toward those social sectors. And most managers further distanced their operations from the staid image of AM broadcasting with names that conveyed dynamism or modernity, such as Cinética, Satélite, or Mélody, chosen respectively for their overtones of energetic motion, technology, and the English language.

In this era of expansion most stations took up the concessionaire business model, and promoters of various kinds gained prime slots in the city's broadcast schedules. In 1991 this model allowed contemporary Ayacuchano music to appear during off-peak morning hours, in a space financed and produced by Dolby JR's Julián Fernández. Entitled *Ayacucho en el corazón de todos*, like his later program in Lima, it was meant to promote his company's recordings of politicized huayno music. The modest success that it attained between 1991 and 1993, when Fernández moved to Lima, hinted that a listenership existed beyond its initial audience of intellectuals and musicians. But it remained marginal within the daily schedule, airing before 7:00 A.M. on Radio Cinética, and because of this it did not contribute as heavily to local musical dynamics as did later efforts by the show's host, Miguel Ángel Huamán.

Huamán had begun to work as a DJ in 1985, and although his background was in pop radio, he was also an aficionado of Ayacuchano huayno. This was slightly unusual among a generation that, according to Huamán, had "a kind of complex . . . it was degrading to listen to huayno. I don't know who made it that way, but that tendency was strong. Everyone wanted something that was more modern." In his early work he had mastered the charismatic, bantering style of a pop music DJ, and by collaborating with Fernández he developed a familiarity with the huayno repertoire, close relationships with the label and its artists, and a reputation as a leading huayno DJ. Taken together, these skills and connections were pivotal in recasting the image of local huayno music once Fernández left town.

In 1996, after a leave of absence from the airwaves, Huamán rented a space on the fledgling FM station Frecuencia A, managed by the veteran DJ Isaac Argumedo. He chose the peak hour of 10:00 A.M. and filled it with Ayacuchano music. Politicized huayno was on the wane, and he mostly dedicated his show to the more accessible love songs that were emerging from Dolby and other studios at the time. Nevertheless, even Huamán felt that "it wasn't right. Listening to Ayacuchano huayno, it wasn't the right space. I mean I thought, 'This isn't the right space.' I'd done this for many years, and I said to myself, '10:00 A.M., huayno?' It doesn't fit." His apprehensions seemed to be confirmed when friends ridiculed his new program, "saying 'Miguel Ángel, you used to do pop, contemporary music, now you do huayno?' They made fun of me, said I'd lowered my standards. They said it to my face."

The implication that contemporary Ayacuchano huayno belonged in the same space as the pop styles that filled midday FM slots clearly drove against the grain of existing practice. Since Huamán was a talented DJ, though, his program soon became the radio's standout show, expanding to fill adjacent slots when other DJs failed to appear for their shifts. With his listenership increasing, Huamán and Argumedo decided to change the station's format, narrowing it to a lineup of contemporary Ayacuchano huayno and luring pop DJs with demonstrable talent to host programs with relatively centralized playlists. According to Argumedo, an informal survey showed but a slightly favorable response to the idea of an all-huayno station—six respondents in favor, and five against. Nevertheless, on this basis Frecuencia A was launched in late 1998 as "the first folkloric station of the department," and soon it became a local media institution.[29] Other stations moved rapidly to imitate them, with the rock station Radio Mélody converting to huayno literally overnight, and in Huamán's words, "That's where the idea that [Ayacuchano] huayno should only be played in the early morning ended for good."

Frecuencia A's success rested crucially upon the way that DJs manipulated the framing devices of their programs, drawing upon new rhetorical registers and sonic cues to shift the public image of the music they played.

These moves were calculated to draw a middle-class listenership, and Huamán recalled later that

> everyone was listening to Frecuencia A. We were pretty smart with our programming; we thought about it: how can we get people in an office to listen to us? It was tough, because Ayacucho was always invaded by stations from Lima, and people liked their style. So we created a really nice programming style. We made it so that you could listen to this music in a kitchen or in an office. We made ourselves sweet.

The station's employees knew that upwardly mobile city residents who spent their days working in offices, public institutions, or the home treated radio listening as a palliative from the drudgery of labor. Such consumers were drawn in by music they enjoyed, but also by DJs who created the atmosphere of consumerist leisure that Spitulnik called "the upbeat beat" (1994: 315). Since that atmosphere was exclusively tied to broadcasts of pop, rock, and tropical music, Frecuencia A's huayno DJs drew heavily upon the tone and discursive devices of those radio genres. Intuiting that their target audience would need to be coaxed into thinking of dowdy huayno music as something comparable to other favorite genres in worldly cachet, they spoke in the slick, slangy, and melodious manner of salsa and rock DJs, interspersing broadcasts with humorous asides and joking on-air with callers. And by publicly linking this hip and raffish form of address to contemporary Ayacuchano huayno, DJs encouraged listeners to approach it on new terms as a style whose slick appeal was untroubled by its deep local roots.

Nor was this atmosphere a matter of linguistic skill and language register alone. A meeting at Frecuencia A in January 2003 made clear the extent to which sound effects, radio bumpers, prerecorded station breaks, and other metapragmatic cues were critical to making broadcasts sound appropriately modern and professional. Owing in part to competitors' adoption of their model, audiences had decreased substantially, and Argumedo called a meeting to discuss methods for recapturing Frecuencia A's flagging listenership. Convoked on a Saturday morning in a small room just outside the station's broadcast booth, it was conducted over the noise of a weekend show hosted by the DJ Coco C, who played incongruous snatches of seashore sound effects, including pounding surf and the cries of seagulls, between and often over his musical selections.[30] In a fitting echo, the meeting itself featured no debates about musical content, but instead took the form of an extended discussion about how to imitate the professional-sounding sonic cues of more successful competitors. The use of new and catchier station identifications, bumpers, *cuñas* (effects) such as the seaside sounds used by Coco C, clips signaling the opening of the broadcast day and of individual programs, and prerecorded ("pilot") CDs to use in DJ absences were all proposed as improvements that would "revive" (*realzar*) the station and ensure the return of listeners.

Huamán had by this time acquired an afternoon gig at Radio La Caribeña, the city's most popular station, and much of the conversation revolved around Frecuencia A's more successful rival. Much like an American CHR (Contemporary Hit Radio) station, La Caribeña secured its large audience by monitoring the airplay of rivals to discover trending hits and renewing its playlists accordingly. Indeed, its calculated blend of musical genres, typically a sequence of rock, pop, salsa, tropical music, and contemporary Ayacuchano huayno, testified eloquently to the last-named genre's transformation into a local pop style. Its broadcasts were interspersed with attention-grabbing sound effects and electronically processed station identifications, all designed to foreground a mood of animated entertainment. A signature cuña featuring the phrase "La Caribeña: síííí, suena!" (roughly, "La Caribeña, yeeeah, it rocks!"), followed by an energetic swooshing sound, was used most frequently, with female giggles, laser sound effects, and other noises connoting fun and excitement all coming a close second.

In the end, implementation of these changes at Frecuencia A seemed rather random and sporadic. Nevertheless, the meeting showed the extent to which radio work revolved around matters extrinsic to the music itself. And if DJ talk was left unaddressed at this particular meeting, that was not necessarily a sign of its triviality: rather, it should be taken as a sign of confidence that the station's employees needed no help in bringing off this most important aspect of radio work.

DJ Performance: Framing the Music

DJs are more than people who spin music. They are professional performers, and their work is central to the public career of the music that they spin. Their primary duty is to create an atmosphere that persuades listeners to tune in, a task that requires the development of a persuasive on-air personality as well as the mastery of supporting rhetorical and technological skills. Their talent is primarily evaluated in light of their knack for entertaining rather than their detailed musical knowledge, but a command of both is ideal. The tone that they choose determines the entire listening event, letting consumers know what kind of music it is that they are hearing, from the point of view of the DJ and the listenership that she or he stands for. DJs also perform localness, situating their broadcast within a day-to-day context familiar to listeners and ensuring that they perceive its relevance to their lives. Overall, it is their actions that connect listeners to musical categories and allow them to apply their understanding within the local milieu.

The engaging ambience of Huamán's show stood in stark contrast to the limited conditions under which it was realized. The first time that I sought him out at Frecuencia A, I was sure I had come to the wrong place. The adobe-walled building with a tiny hand-lettered sign, the creaky wooden door opening onto a large, bare courtyard, and the absence of a receptionist or any other station employee all violated my expectations of a modern, slickly professional installation. Once I located the broadcast booth, opening off the back of a dark, empty room hung with posters of Duo Ayacucho and the Gaitán Castros, I was further surprised by the station's spare setup: two dated CD players, a cassette deck, a stereo head, a minuscule mixer, and an obsolete microphone, all set atop a rickety wooden desk that was jammed into the tiny room, and all a far cry from the Macintosh G4s and glassed-in booths I had seen at local pop music stations.

These conditions notwithstanding, day in and day out Huamán and his colleagues created broadcasts whose vigor and professionalism belied their objective limitations. In motion from the moment he arrived, Huamán would enter the station at 10:00 A.M. with a stack of CDs. Easing himself into the closet-sized broadcast booth, he lowered the volume on the pilot CD spinning in the player and, bending to the microphone, announced the time of day along with the station's identifying slogan. As he energetically set the program's tone, his melodious tenor ranged over the breadth of his vocal capacity, conveying a sense of humorous diversion. As he spoke he grinned irrepressibly, relishing the role of entertainer and confidante:

> 10:03 A.M. at Frecuencia A, the first folkloric station of the region . . . I'm a little sick, as you can see, it's really too bad. I got a cold two days ago, and it doesn't want to let go. We'll have to wait four days, six days still, because a cold lasts eight days, right? They've recommended that I take [*pauses*] Vitapyrena, whatever that is. Anyway, I'll get better the natural way: drug-free [*laughs*].

Nearly meaningless on its face, such chatty banter is typically reviled by older huayno DJs, who entered the field at a time when radio workers took seriously the duty to inform and educate. But this aversion to gravity is central to Huamán's job, which is to create an atmosphere of trendy bonhomie that listeners will want to inhabit for two hours. This means deploying conversational registers and rhetorical gestures that induce a sense of rapport in disembodied listeners, making them feel that they are spending time with a particularly cool friend. It also requires the ability to seamlessly weave together the humor, intimacy, and hard facts that listeners expect from a broadcast, and "good deejaying" is judged according to "how skillfully the disc jockey blends a personalized commentary with time checks and channel identification . . . and with the musical selections themselves" (Spitulnik 1994: 340).

And so Huamán dexterously fills the space around his musical selections with apparently frivolous conversation, in-jokes, and local references, all calculated to assure his listeners that they are participating in a fun, fashionable experience that might be situated within the listener's lived environment. He weaves station identifications, time checks, song titles, artist names, and advertising into a constant patter that maintains his program's forward drive and keeps listeners waiting for the next bon mot. He imbricates these elements with a mix of urban slang and Ayacuchano references, impressing upon listeners both his program's urbanity and its localness. Using idioms and toponyms native to the city, while saluting specific listeners within range of the broadcast signal, he projects a deep familiarity with their environment and cultivates the notion that they are addressed both personally and as part of a larger public.

The various elements and functions juggled by a commercial DJ typically interanimate each another over the course of a broadcast. The sense of humor pervading Huamán's entire show, for example, is often used in conjunction with inside references in a way that recalls conversational interaction between real-life friends. Together, these techniques liven up aspects of the program that would otherwise remain dry, such as song introductions and advertisements:

> Let's go, with the Orquesta Américas, band of the quack-quack brothers, the ducks, the ducklings, Ronald and Hugo Dolorier. . . .

> Here at Frecuencia A, coming to you courtesy of the Tres Máscaras clinic, of Dr. Jorge Luis Fernández, a member of the Peruvian ophthalmologic college with a degree from the U.S. Don't trust self-trained doctors—trust a clinic where you get service from a professional, like Dr. Fernández. He's always there, not like these dudes who, you know, they come, they go, they'll be back next week . . . what a lost cause! Your eyes need quality care.

A lighthearted reference to the local musician Hugo Dolorier, nicknamed El Pato (The Duck), and a droll extrapolation upon a routine advertisement: each allows Huamán to turn the most functional aspects of his program into satisfying bits of entertaining repartee.

A second discursive artifact pervading Huamán's broadcasts is the evocation of romance, a near-constant in pop radio, where "suggestiveness, innuendo, and stimulation of the imagination are central to [its] popular appeal" (Murray 2002: 136). Huamán's innuendo frequently used the content of songs themselves as a point of departure. This might appear, for example, over an instrumental lead-in, as Huamán drops his voice to its lower range and softens his tone, ending with a recitation of the opening lyrics:

> A shout-out to Sandra, Sandrita, where are you, Sandra? Ah, there you are! A kiss for Sandra. And to *you* as well, a shout-out to *you*, so you don't get sulky. And this song for you, for you with love: "Tu eres ángel de mi vida, ángel de mis ilusiones" [roughly, "You're the love of my life, love of my dreams"].

Insinuating an anonymous romantic intrigue, Huamán draws listeners imaginatively into his personal space and suggests an intimate rapport with his public. But this passage also demonstrates another key tool in Huamán's on-air discursive repertoire: the act of addressing specific listeners. Comments such as these are sometimes directed to Huamán's personal acquaintances and sponsors, but they are also solicited by callers making requests. Saluting their requesters by name on-air publicly ties Huamán's persona to the local area and the people who inhabit it, making his public audible to itself and encouraging the perception that the program and its content are identified with the community.

The use of local idiomatic expressions achieves a similar effect, even as Huamán's translocal colloquial vocabulary contributes to the program's aura of contemporary cool. His speech is liberally peppered with expressions, drawn mostly from Lima slang, that constitute the popular register of streetwise Peruvian youths. But he also draws on phrases particular to Ayacucho, including Quechua-language cries of encouragement derived from huayno performance:

> A shout out to the *cuerazo* [hottie]!

> Yeah! Hey! Let's go ... to the Muyurina Valley, where we met, and where you *me pusiste cachos* [put horns on me, i.e., cuckolded me].

Finding the Huayno People / 167

Sapachallan warmi! Ama waqaspalla! (Quechua; Lonely woman! Don't cry now!)

Finally, the most satisfying moments of Huamán's broadcasts come when he combines several of these domains in a single segment. In the following broadcast fragment, he segues from an ad for a bullfight to a personal salutation and lets the audience know that he has made a (rather opaque) joke at the addressee's expense:

[*Recorded moos*] *Olé, olé*, Rocío Cóndor, listening at [bus company] Expreso Molina Unión! OK, OK, just a joke, don't get mad . . . don't forget, this Saturday, November 30, an afternoon of bullfighting in Huascahura, don't miss it![31]

Though Huamán was superlatively skilled in this sort of discourse, Frecuencia A's older DJs also used it to great effect. On one occasion, when Huamán failed to arrive for his program after a long period of absences, Argumedo expressed his frustration on air, needling the absent DJ with unstated references to his nickname, Conejo (Rabbit):

Looks like today, once again, Miguel Ángel Huamán is on strike, gone to harvest carrots. Hey, Frecuencia A's pet's gone missing! What's up with that guy?[32]

Technical skills were also considered to weigh heavily in a show's success and constituted a point of pride and personal one-upmanship among many DJs. Observing Huamán at work made especially clear how even the limited technology at Frecuencia A could lend nuance, flair, and continuity to a program's sound. As Huamán spun a track, he would let the opening—always instrumental in commercial huayno music—unfold beneath his improvised banter. While speaking, his hands flew around the small mixing board in front of him, frenetically raising and lowering the faders, matching mic and CD volume so as to prevent sudden clashes of intensity—no small feat, given the rapid-fire nature of his improvisations. Furthermore, he monitored the song's progress as he spoke, timing his narration flawlessly to end precisely upon the entry of the lead vocals. He took pride in his ability to nail this spot every time, and as he illustrated to me the importance of the technique, he physically underlined the point, holding up his index fingers and drawing them slowly together while imitating his own inspired babble; when they met, he leaned back in satisfaction and assured me that this crucial talent was possessed only by truly capable DJs. Techniques such as this, or the ability to crossfade evenly and gradually across song transitions, may appear mundane, but they maintain the mood and flow of a program, and they index a level of professionalism that Huamán and his colleagues were sure lent legitimacy to themselves as professionals and to the music they played.

Finally, advertisements significantly inflect the shows on which they air, their high production values or the elevated nature of the products they advertise suggesting to listeners the show's appropriate target audience. Most advertisements airing at Frecuencia A were tailored for a middle-class, relatively young listenership with some money to spend on entertainment and leisure activities.[33] In fact, a great number of the advertisements there and on other contemporary Ayacuchano huayno shows were produced and narrated by Huamán himself, in a private home studio where he did a booming business and, in the process, made his voice and his declamatory style the sound of commercial Ayacuchano radio.

The primary job of DJs is to attract listeners, not to cultivate cosmopolitan subjects per se. But by attracting young, upwardly mobile audiences with a slick DJ style laden with local references and suffused with an air of personal intimacy, agents such as Huamán placed huayno within a space that sounded incontestably "modern" and made its consumption into a means of signifying the self. Nevertheless, not everyone was favorably disposed toward the style and its public image.

The Limits of Pop: Disidentification with Huayno

Frecuencia A and its competitors upended assumptions about the links between music, modernity, and social status, but the stations' operations were aimed primarily at a listenership that was young, urban, and upwardly mobile. As such, they also reinforced existing lines of musical distinction, separating the musical habits of the city's relatively privileged classes from their subaltern fellows. This was not lost on local radio employees, who were nearly unanimous in attributing the style's success to Frecuencia A while remaining ambivalent about Ayacuchano huayno's ultimate significance. Its commercial rebirth was evaluated as a positive social change by Walter Muñoz, director of Radio Wari, a respected business devoted to serious reporting and highbrow artistic content:

For about four or five years now, almost all the stations are playing Ayacuchano huayno . . . it's been revalorized, and that's really the work of a handful of local stations. Frecuencia A has done the most, given it the most support, it's number one. The rest of us have slots for it, Cinética and Mélody have slots too. Before, the influence of other styles was really strong, but now this new current is being supported by radio stations, and artists too. Everyone's doing their part, so much so that new artists are appearing, and that didn't happen before.

But Muñóz's statement that "almost" every station broadcast contemporary Ayacuchano huayno points to an important lacuna in its public uptake. Even as the style attracted listeners among the elite and middle classes of Ayacucho and Lima, it remained conspicuously absent from the radio stations, concert venues, and CD stands catering to the rural peasants and migrant proletarians who make up Peru's majority. Those spaces instead continued to feature Northern and Central Andean huayno, and the two stylistic fields became publicly entrenched as new markers of musical distinction, standing opposed to one another in the way that rock, pop, and tropical music had stood opposed to Central Andean music in an earlier age.

For this reason, it is striking to compare Muñoz's statement with those of Fernando Cruz, director of the self-styled "peoples' station" La Voz de Huamanga. Interviewed mere days apart in 2002, each tried to quantify Ayacuchano huayno's popularity by estimating the number of live performances that took place in the city. Muñoz confidently declared that local huayno was outperforming other styles by a three-to-one ratio, while Cruz declared instead that Ayacuchano music was the loser by a factor of five to two. More generally, Cruz insisted that the local huayno style had a very limited listenership, and when I voiced skepticism about his claims, he elaborated his statement by evaluating the style's social connotations:

> We use that music as filler, but people in Ayacucho don't like it. Why? Because it's corrupted by pan-Andean music, and romantic music [i.e., balada]. I think you should examine who's going to these concerts, cultural events, what social class they're from, or where they're from, if they're coastal people or Andean people. Imagine, a foreigner like you likes this music, but I'm positive that Ayacuchanos don't. Promoters say that it's not profitable. Well, it is for a small group at other radio stations, but not here.

Cruz's estimate about the proportion of live performances in Ayacucho was far closer to the truth, as huayno norteño shows were far more numerous and far more profitable than contemporary Ayacuchano shows. Still, he underestimated the latter's popular uptake, which was made clear whenever Ayacuchano artists such as Carlos Prado, Manuelcha Prado, or Max Castro came to the city and played sold-out concert venues. This disjuncture in perception may have arisen, in part, from the terms in which Cruz evaluated musical success, which rested upon the receipts of promoters. Ayacuchano events, at which little liquor was sold and entrance fees were set high, were risky, low-yield ventures. Huayno norteño events, by contrast, were guaranteed to move significant quantities of profitable alcohol, and therefore they were far more attractive to professional promoters.

More generally, the disjuncture in perception testifies to the position that contemporary Ayacuchano music had attained by the early twenty-first century. Having become once again a popular site for bourgeois citizens to identify themselves as the inheritors of a proud Andean heritage, it remained linked to that limited social sector. Speaking as a director who served that listenership, Muñoz underestimated the considerable dominance that Northern and Central Andean music continued to hold among Ayacucho's far larger subaltern population, unconsciously demonstrating the vectors of social bias along which the style moved through the world.

Nowhere was this distinction clearer than at La Caribeña. On-air, the station's patterned format alternating Ayacuchano music, rock, pop, and tropical hits audibly demonstrated the style's subsumption by consumerist cosmopolitanism. The building that housed its studios, however, also housed the installations of Radio IncaSat, which, though under the same ownership, was exclusively devoted to chicha and huayno norteño. Their respective broadcast booths were so closely situated that DJs could gesture to one another. However, the broadcasts were resolutely aimed at distinct markets, maintaining separate CD libraries, promotions, and advertisers. Over several days I spent there, not once did I see a CD move from one side to the other, and the two broadcast booths stood as a metaphor for the wider social career of the two styles.

Choosing the Songs: Musical Values and Clientelist Pressures

The huayno artist Naranjita de Sucre became a sensation in 2006, and my compadre Adrián, like others, sang the praises of her catchy, upbeat dance tunes. However, when I asked him why she had become so popular so fast, he spoke not of her singing, her lyrics, or any other artistic matter. Instead, he highlighted the work of her publicist, explaining how the concert promoter and club owner Wallpa Waqay had driven her popularity with his huayno television program, using his national media presence to "make her big." In these years just before widespread access to online methods of distribution, huayno DJs and fans took for granted that the hosts who dominated Peru's entertainment media held unrivaled power. Word of mouth and cassette and CD trading were often locally important, but because of either their cumbersomeness or their expense, their influence was secondary to that of accessible, gratis, omnipresent broadcasts.

Many DJs entered the business inspired precisely by the idea of wielding such influence over public space, but cases like that of Wallpa Waqay and Naranjita de Sucre were hard to pinpoint. Though I followed the activities of Frecuencia A and other huayno stations over many months, the connection between airplay and Ayacucho's broader musical tendencies remained frustratingly vague. In the absence of sales figures or professional marketing surveys, everyday observation and hearsay remained the only methods for gauging how, when, or whether listeners became invested in the sounds they heard over the airwaves.[34] DJs themselves relied upon these methods, but it was unclear how effective they were at assessing the inclinations of their listeners, and the decision to turn a rising song into a certified sensation via increased airplay often seemed to rest upon scant signs of audience approval. In any case, DJs claimed that they rarely conceded to audience demand, allowing their own inclinations to be swayed only when they incurred a commercial obligation to promote a particular artist.

Indeed, although DJs rarely described themselves as linchpins in the relationship between popular music and society, their beliefs about musical value had an enormous influence on the content of the musical categories the DJs worked with. And they did characterize their work as a means of shifting the parameters of consumption pursuant to commercial or sociopolitical ends, or both. Most fit neatly into the "musicologist" paradigm outlined by Ahlkvist, seeing themselves as musical connoisseurs dissatisfied by the conditions of the radio business, their "real challenge . . . balancing their personally high standards with what the market will bear" (2001: 347). Few were so eloquent, but many characterized the music they worked with in terms such as those chosen by Keti Bedrillana, host of Radio Atlantis's *La magia del canto andino* (The Magic of Andean Song), who told me that "huayno is a medium of communication. It's not a stone, not an object: it *is* the Ayacuchano, the living Ayacuchano. The business of disseminating values and culture is not just about nostalgia for the past, it's about today, the modern times that we live in." She and her like-minded peers saw music as a way to explore emergent truths about national society, and their work as a way of rectifying Peru's reified distinction between the space of the modern and the location of highland culture. As savvy consumers, most of whom were under forty years old, they had spent their lives moving imaginatively between local and extralocal poles of identification. They believed that a notion of authenticity organized around strict traditionalism could only limit their contribution to the ongoing development of Peruvian society, as citizens came to live ever more fully through global idioms, and they meant to hasten the obsolescence of such untenable oppositions by cultivating an Andean style that reconciled them.[35]

Their success should be regarded as partial on several grounds, especially since many people continued to regard huayno music as incompatible with the very idea of modernity. This binary shaped the attitudes of people such as my neighbor's daughter in Ayacucho, who recoiled at the idea of preparing a huayno number for a local talent show and told me, "No, I want to sing something modern, maybe something by Britney Spears." For her, and for many others determined to transcend the social limitations associated with highland heritage, contemporary Ayacuchano huayno was a doomed stab at updating a musical style incapable of signifying anything but archaism. More important, insofar as DJs such as Huamán may have perpetuated the very hierarchy they sought to subvert, by pointing to the adoption of foreign elements as a mark of progress:

> Our music's more widely accepted now, because it's more, let's say, refined. I think our music has developed, as the years have passed. Young people wanted something more up to date, more slickly recorded. You've probably noticed that Ayacuchano artists today make better records—they're more detail oriented. Before, we heard all kinds of music from other countries here, and our music was embryonic, and no one listened to it. Before, it was—how can I say this—it limped; it was incomplete.

Such figures of scarcity or incipience were meant to indicate a fatal lack of variety, one that damned local huayno before the flutes, drums, electroacoustic guitars, saxophones, synthesizers, and samplers that saturated Ayacucho's airwaves. In a widely used formulation, the basic guitar-and-voice template of earlier recordings sounded "empty," shorn of the sonic panoply heard in "modern" Euro-American pop and pan-Andean music and hence unable to claim coeval status with them.

But if such statements reassert the subalternity of huayno music in one register by assuming that its "modernization" will proceed with reference to parameters set elsewhere, they also force interlocutors to recognize the complex and changing nature of highland society. They reposition local artists as active managers of emergent identity formations, rather than the passive victims of a cultural onslaught from abroad. The DJs who worked with the genre compared the contemporary situation favorably with the years before, when young people turned to rock, salsa, and pan-Andean artists in search of cultural role models, arguing that their actions had encouraged listeners to confront and overcome inherited prejudices about the proper boundaries of Andean identity. Indeed, the use of pan-Andean genres, instruments, songs, and imagery by contemporary Ayacuchano artists was often a point of pride, further evidence of Ayacucho's musical and scholarly prowess. Following those forebears who had codified the city's reputation for musical and cerebral leadership, DJs praised local artists for adopting traditional pan-Andean themes of cultural revindication, seizing the initiative from Bolivian, Chilean, and Ecuadorian artists and giving Ayacucho a leading role in shaping the pan-regional Andean identity increasingly associated with the genre.

These were the central criteria used by all of Ayacucho's contemporary huayno DJs, but such broad parameters left much room for individuation, and programs were noticeably idiosyncratic. At Radio Mélody, for example, DJ Raffo Corantes often filled *La fiesta de la música* with local recordings of sanjuanito, an Ecuadorian folk genre that Ayacucho's club bands had adapted into an upbeat dance style. Huamán, by contrast, avoided it in his concurrent slot at Frecuencia A, instead promoting the neotraditional artists with good voices that he preferred, singers such as Yolanda Pinares and Luis Ayvar, each of whom became a local sensation in 2001–2 after he put their recordings of old tunes such as "Amor herido" and "Wayanakito" into heavy rotation.

In this environment an artist's success might depend upon cordial relationships, the fleeting whims of a powerful DJ, or a combination of the two. On another occasion, Huamán borrowed my recordings of "Expreso Puquio" and "Ayla," as performed by Manuelcha Prado. A showstopping guitarist and singer-songwriter from the southern town of Puquio, Prado was recognized as a ferocious cultural advocate and a promoter of Quechua-language tunes. Sung in the simple but energetic manner of indigenous huayno performance, full of ornamental falsetto cries but devoid of expressive vibrato, and accompanied only by the driving rhythm of his guitar, these recordings were redolent of rural tradition, and unlike the city's sophisticated huayno music. Huamán found them admirably original, and, confident that he could turn them into hits, he began inserting them after more commercial songs in the course of his broadcast. Later, he asked to borrow a rare CD by the pan-Andean duo IAO. A fairly marginal group based in Paris, it was mainly recognized for "Ayacucho," a light-hearted song praising the city's friendly character. Somewhat surprised that he asked for this dated and obscure recording, I brought it to the station, where he explained that he planned to wield it against a local group's cover version of the song. The band in question had defaulted on a recent contract, playing only half their promised set. Blacklisted, it had lost some public exposure, and Huamán hoped to exacerbate the matter by "burning" the band's new single with an original that he considered far superior.

Naturally, the opportunity to wield influence in this way was crosscut by DJ obligations to sponsors and management. Such pressures are difficult to specify in a general sense because arrangements varied widely and were often informal. Many concessionaire DJs, for instance, took their programming cues from the bands, labels, or concert promoters they represented. Others were hobbyists, intellectuals, or representatives of cultural associations, and although they had near-total freedom from managerial oversight, they paid for their rented space with self-recruited advertising and sometimes faced pressures from their sponsors. Even these shows required a listenership sufficient to attract sponsors in the first place, making unusual sounds such as "Expreso Puquio" rarer than the kind of familiar material that retained a broad audience.[36]

Stations that did not operate as concessionaires, such as Frecuencia A and Radio Mélody, faced different pressures. Typically they had no centralized playlists, and DJs, employed for their perceived expertise, selected music according to their own personal tastes. But these stations sought to maintain a distinct sound, and directors might call out a DJ perceived as straying too far from their musical line.[37] Furthermore, managers and DJs were often the targets of personal pressure from friends and professional pressure from colleagues, managers, and artists, all of whom came by broadcast booths to drop off advance singles, chat up influential DJs, and use their powers of persuasion in pursuit of sympathetic airtime.

Most important, however, was the extent to which musicians and promoters acted as a major source of advertising revenue for such stations. This regularly led to business agreements that would be viewed as payola in North American radio. Andean artists typically make very few royalties, depend upon concert proceeds for their income, and spend a good deal of time touring.[38] A successful live performance requires advance hype on a scale that can only be prepared through radio broadcasts. As a result, artists or their local agents typically purchase a combined advertising and pay-for-play package in the cities of their upcoming shows. Under the terms of a standard contract, managers might agree to broadcast advertisements a specified number of times per day, but also to increase the air time dedicated to the music of the artist in question and to hype it informally in the course of regular DJ banter. All of these activities exert a noticeable effect on the content of a given program, since DJs are obliged to create an artificial buzz around a particular artist's sound.

Even in such cases, however, the exact quantity of airplay might be vaguely defined, and DJs with strong objections could plausibly play very little of the featured artist's music.[39] In general, Ayacuchano DJs' looser obligations to management and advertisers gave them more programming leeway than is usually possible for U.S.-based DJs. Notions of DJ freedom inherited from the concessionaire model remained powerful, and DJs retained significant leeway to program in accordance with their musical values. And finally, this system never precluded listener input entirely: as Berland has noted, the unity of the categories that DJs use to organize their broadcasts is provisional, and "to the extent that their purpose is to represent collective identity as a unified totality, each is a work of ideology, continuously disassembled by the creative disloyalty of listeners" (1993a: 146). Listeners, by identifying with and demanding to hear music experienced elsewhere, might force a change "from below," as it were, in the musical category tended by the media figures who controlled their sound world. And audiences clearly failed to identify with DJ tastes on some occasions: in the two cases cited above, for example, the career of Huamán's contract-breaking nemeses proceeded apace, and Manuelcha Prado's songs attracted some attention without becoming hits. Such instances belied DJs' belief in their absolute monopoly over public taste, but they were rarer than their obverse. Overall, DJs retained an unmatched power over the local soundscape and a remarkable role in coordinating music, identity, and social space.

Conclusion

Keti Bedrillana nicely characterized radio's social efficacy when she told me that it "has a magical ability to communicate. You wouldn't believe it, but when people hear music over and over, they get used to it, they identify with it, and this is a way of transmitting values and culture." She aimed to inculcate an "Andean cosmovision" through highbrow pan-Andean music and drew a contrast with programs where "values and culture" took a back seat to consumerism. However, if we are to take seriously the notion that "the dissemination of messages through mass media provides a unique potential for large numbers of otherwise different and unrelated people to orient around the same (or similar) depictions of the world" (Turow 1990: 15), then we require a more precise understanding of *all* the various ways that different kinds of media produce such sites of identification. Without losing sight of the public sphere's colonization by capital, we should ask how the implicit categories of commercial media shape both the materials they transmit and the ideas of the people they attract. For this reason Hilmes has called for analyses that reconsider "musical formats not as mere commercial formulas, but as important culture-defining and boundary-reinforcing exercises" (2002: 13).

We might go further and reconsider our assumptions about the use and purposes of radio itself. Social historians of technology such as Sterne (2003) have written eloquently about the provisional connections between technologies and uses, noting that such connections are culturally constructed and not innate to the technologies themselves. In this sense, we might consider the idea of contracted musical airtime as an intrusion upon radio's public commons, pathologized under the dismissive term "payola," as a critique with little relevance in such contexts as Peru, where music broadcasters are not assumed to be democratic entities, and radios are not used in a way consistent with such an understanding.

To understand the mechanics of media, music, and social identity means asking how social pressures, technical affordances, and economic structures determine the actions of media workers. But it also means recognizing the ways that media workers exert agency within those circumstances. As contemporary Ayacuchano huayno became a mass-mediated phenomenon, it articulated a listening public unlike that previously attached to huayno music. But this identification between music and social group was not the logical culmination of tendencies latent within a changing country, and its success did not depend, in any simple way, upon the way that the music "represented" an existing social group. Rather, its mediators recognized that the nascent Andean bourgeoisie craved social legitimacy and might be convinced to invest in a style that contested dominant discourses of Andean archaism. Invading the best slots of the FM band and framing the music with an innovative style of locution, people such as Huamán and businesses such as Frecuencia A established an enunciatory space within which a new subject position took audible form. And by placing it within local contexts, reiterating their actions day after day, they helped individual consumers to understand themselves as members of a social entity with a historicity superseding the moment of listening.

EPILOGUE

Folkloric Frames and Mass Culture: The Public Faces of Contemporary Andean Society

In 2001 one of Peru's national television networks aired a telenovela entitled *Amor Serrano*. It had already run more than once, and most of my friends were uninterested in revisiting it. I was fascinated, though, because it seemed to capture perfectly the sociocultural moment that I saw reflected in Ayacuchano musical activities. The main plot concerned the ambitions of an Andean migrant named Máximo Yunque, who had made good as a businessman in Lima. The beginning of the series found him avidly pursuing the trappings of respectability that would correlate with his upwardly mobile status, including a mansion in the wealthy barrio of Miraflores, a tutor who corrected his verbal and social malapropisms, and a marriage contract with Micaela Montes de Oca, a woman of reduced means with an aristocratic name. Like most telenovelas, the show had a message, in this instance one decrying social prejudice. By the end of the series both Yunque and those who surrounded him had learned to value his Andean heritage, and he had stopped trying to shed the signs of his highland origins.

The program seemed novel not for its rather trite message of tolerance, but for recognizing the reality of Andean mobility. It was also noteworthy for its musical semiotics, since each central character bore a kind of leitmotif, a brief snatch of melody meant to telegraph his or her social status. Micaela's upper-crust mother appeared onscreen to passages from Joaquín Rodrigo's guitar concerto *Fantasia para un gentilhombre*. Her secret boyfriend, a motorcycle-riding tough, was accompanied by the electric guitars of the Peruvian rock group Los Mojarras. And Máximo was associated with contemporary Ayacuchano huayno, performed by the Gaitán Castros and by Manuelcha Prado.

By the time I returned to Peru in 2006, the topography of the Andean public sphere was shifting dramatically, and again a telenovela spoke forcefully of the transformation under way. This time, it was *Chacalón: The Angel of the Poor* that impressed upon me the swift pace of social change, with its portrayal of the deceased chicha artist as a folk saint, his succor sought by Lima's downtrodden.[1] Cutting back and forth between different historical periods, it entwined the artist's hard-bitten life story with the challenges faced by his devotees in the present, using this narrative device to present a general history of Andean migration and a sort of origin story for contemporary Lima. The program's images of marginality and struggle in the city's tough barrios contrasted starkly with *Amor Serrano*'s tale of Andean uplift, and though both series were idealized, stereotyped takes on Peruvian life, together they tracked a palpable shift in the tone of Andean public culture.

The next day, when I visited the Mesa Redonda section of Lima's central market, its dense agglomeration of music stalls resounded with chicha music by Chacalón and his peers. It was probably the first time in over a decade that chicha dominated the area's soundscape, and indeed, the program augured a newfound interest in Peruvian cumbia that has only grown in strength. The alternative band Bareto soon released ska-inflected reinterpretations of classic cumbia and chicha tracks, performing them in centers of hipster cool such as the Lima bar Botero. Faded cumbia artists returned to the center of national attention, now saluted as vernacular poets and spokesmen for the country's popular classes. Cumbia was declared to be a pillar of national culture, joining huayno and música criolla as officially sanctioned emblems of *peruanidad*. Cumbia and the associated huayno norteño style came to stand together as the dominant sonic representations of Peru's Andean citizenry. And together these styles ensured that this social group was defined not in relation to the symbolic apparatus of bourgeois respectability, but rather by its refusal of those very terms of distinction: by its fervent dedication to humble artists who embodied proletarian values of hard work and self-improvement.[2]

These series attracted enormous ratings among Peru's viewing public, dominated by an Andean proletariat that remains far larger than its Andean bourgeoisie. They and their associated musical styles became objects of fascination for commentators who, as in the 1980s, found within musical discourse the keys to the mindset of a majority that remains opaque to Peru's established elites (Alfaro Rotondo 2006; Ferrier 2010; Tucker 2013). The shows were widely imitated as producers sought to tap the purchasing power latent within the poorest but broadest sector of the Andean community—in point of fact, *Chacalón* was itself inspired by the success of an earlier series devoted to the life of the huayno norteño artist Dina Paucar. Between 2004 and 2010 Peru's airwaves were saturated with copycat narratives, and as a musical complex that aligned cumbia with huayno norteño rose in profile, it displaced contemporary Ayacuchano music from the central place that it had recently occupied in public life. As of 2012, the "modernized" Ayacuchano style appeared to be a fad that had been overcome, and some of those invested in the cumbia–huayno norteño complex dismissed it as the last gasp of a shopworn musical ideology, based on elitist notions of folkloric authenticity and picture-postcard traditionalism, irrelevant to the bustling urban milieu occupied by most Andean citizens (Bailón 2004). From this point of view, Ayacuchano artists' attempt to preserve folkloric principles within the frame of pop aesthetics was worse than an unconvincing musical strategy. It had alienated a mass listenership moved by different notions of aesthetic worth, and insofar as it rested upon a classist frame of reference, the rise of a truly popular aesthetics liberated Peru's listening masses from the hegemony of the old Andean elite.

These developments speak to the continuing dynamism of Peru's Andean community, which continues to change at a dizzying pace. Peru's economy has boomed since 2001, and its working-class citizens have gained more than enough capital to influence the direction of public cultural activity. The brief flowering of Ayacuchano music might be taken as nothing more than an indication of popular culture's ephemeral nature, further evidence that structures of feeling continually give way before new objective circumstances.

Indeed, by 2012 contemporary Ayacuchano huayno no longer seemed a stable and distinct musical genre, much less one organized around an active performing scene. In record stores, music by the Gaitán Castros, Duo Ayacucho, and their followers was classified under the catch-all headings of folklore and/or fusión, the former encompassing all music based on traditions of the Peruvian Andes, while the latter applied to pan-Andean music as well as music using pan-Andean stylistics to spice up recordings that were otherwise based on traditional, electronic, popular, or New Age elements. Meanwhile, artists who had been associated with the Ayacuchano current a decade before were reinventing themselves, with such performers as Los Apus or Milder Oré borrowing rhythms and instrumentation from the dominant huayno norteño style. Perhaps most important, Julián Fernández's successor at Dolly Records, Arturo Chiclla, had turned back to the Ayacuchano style of the midcentury "Golden Age." Using his label's resources to produce and promote performers who acted as standard-bearers of traditional Ayacuchano huayno, including older artists such as Isabel Gamboa and Trio Ayacucho, he reduced the prevalence of or avoided entirely the sounds of pan-Andean music, balada, jazz, blues, and pop that had inflected his label's recordings in the 1990s and early 2000s because he felt they had resulted in too many recordings that were overloaded and *cursi* (corny).

Despite these changes, the patterns of distinction that Dolby/Dolly and its associated artists helped to stabilize in that era still structure Peru's Andean music scene. The associated sounds remain in circulation, albeit in greatly reduced form. A sense of intellectual exceptionalism continues to align the work of Ayacuchano artists with pan-Andean performers, and guitarists representing the former style, such as Manuelcha Prado and Julio Humala, continue to appear in the performance space of Yawar, Peru's stalwart pan-Andean performing ensemble. Some artists, such as Saywa and Damaris, continue to combine Ayacuchano with cosmopolitan sounds, ranging ever farther afield in search of novelty but sticking with those elements that connote sophistication and discernment in the world-music marketplace. In the case of Damaris, such work gained international recognition at the prestigious Viña del Mar International Song Festival, where her song "Tusuy Kusun" (*sic*), combining Andean, Afro-Peruvian, and global pop elements, was awarded the festival's top "folk song" prize in 2008. Even the musical efforts of the actress Magaly Solier, internationally recognized for her performances in films such as *Madeinusa* and *La teta asustada* and widely hailed as a global public symbol of Andean indigeneity, borrows heavily from the decidedly nonindigenous language of 1990s-era Ayacuchano huayno—indeed, the supporting players on her 2009 recording *Warmi* are drawn from Dolby's 1990s-era pool of performers.

Furthermore, the work of all of these artists appears alongside Ayacuchano and pan-Andean classics in the fusión bins of record stores such as Lima's Phantom chain, while that of huayno norteño artists does not, suggesting the perdurance of older classification schemes. This certainly does not mean that huayno norteño artists have remained resistant to musical change: their work, too, increasingly relies upon sounds borrowed from international pop and balada music. Some of them have even begun to borrow elements of Ayacucho's sound and marketing strategy in order to argue for their music's social cachet, referring to their style as "elegant," in contradistinction to that of lesser peers, and incorporating the distinctive Ayacuchano guitar sound into their sonic palette. Overall, stylistic boundaries have loosened up since the era when different currents of huayno music were strongly defined in regional terms. However, the underlying distinction associated with the previous era, whereby "elegant" variants of Andean music were counterpoised to the music of the popular classes, remains a basic principle by which the overall scene is configured.

Ayacuchano huayno and pan-Andean music remain prized symbols of discernment, precisely because the vocal commitment to artistry on the part of their apologists provides both those who make the music and those who consume it with a kind of cultural capital that is forsworn by the populists of the chicha and huayno norteño scene. In this sense, the subject positions associated with each stylistic field remain available for uptake by members of the public, and together these genres continue to map out the field of oppositions within which stances toward Andean heritage are formulated and inhabited by individual consumers. Indeed, the return of chicha and the rise of huayno norteño have each sharpened the distinction between class fractions that seek status through the acquisition and deployment of cultural capital, and those for whom such activities remain irrelevant before the accumulation of economic capital.[3]

These shifts in discourse also speak to the occupational hazards of working in and on the business of public culture. Media workers, artists, commentators, and other agents interact to build publics for their goods using the ideologies and technologies that are available to them at any given time. To the extent that they succeed, their efforts may profitably be analyzed as clues to the structure of the overall social field within which they work, as well as structuring devices that shape that very social field. However, such public constructions are fragile, undone by the fickleness of consumers and by changes in circumstance, any of which may redirect the meanings attached to a given cultural manifestation, its position within the public sphere, and the nature of the public that it gathers.

These circumstances testify to the themes of mediation that I have engaged in this book. They show how crucial mediators are in forging links between public cultural discourse and social structure, links that are no way inevitable or necessary, but are rather the product of determined agents taking advantage of broader changes to sell goods, define audiences, and perhaps mobilize people around their particular visions of cultural worth. The symbols and sites of identification that come to prominence in any given situation are forged by specifiable agents working in a particular situation, and the shape of their dissemination network will ultimately influence the nature of the community that they interpellate.

The Ayacuchano musicians and mediators that I have described should best be seen, then, as agents trying to manage the intersection of traditional values with new commercial opportunities, under conditions beyond their control, using strategies that ultimately failed to match the tenor of the social changes occurring under their noses. Indeed, the limited ability of the style's mediators to influence the overall direction of public discourse stands in poor contrast to the image of cultural leadership proffered by its proponents. But this matter is hardly relevant to the style's public. The mediators of contemporary Ayacuchano huayno provided the images by which a generation of upwardly mobile consumers came to enact their appreciation of Andean heritage. And it is difficult to argue that the strategies of musical appeal essayed within the more successful huayno norteño and chicha scenes are more realistic, or more socially representative, than the Ayacuchano currents that the newer styles have displaced. In analyzing the telenovelas centered on the lives of Chacalón and Dina Paucar, Vich (2006a) has warned against easy praise for what may seem to be realistic, sincere attempts at capturing the life world of the Andean populace. These narratives, and the work of the artists they portray, are widely admired for moving beyond the limiting frame of Andean folkloric representation and delineating the marginality, urban blight, and modern desires that actually characterize the milieu of most Andean citizens. But his analysis underscores the extent to which their stories, based on the glorification of material success through hard work and personal effort, deemphasize the closed social structures that limit class mobility in the first place.

More important, it might be argued that any claim that cumbia or huayno norteño artists represent a "more authentic" vision of Andean society is spurious, insofar as their musical scene, too, tends to homogenize what it claims to represent. Attention to the proletarian world depicted in their songs and their associated narratives is laudable, but the thorough focus on this milieu in contemporary Andean public culture has obscured the actual class diversity of the Andean community. Any regime of collective representation brings with it limitations and blind spots, holes into which disappear registers of experience particular to subgroups within the community portrayed. For this reason, it is worth attending to the critiques of huayno norteño and chicha imagery that have been essayed by Ayacuchano musicians. Attacks by such artists as Ernesto Camassi against attire and musical choices that they find ridiculous represent more than elitism and unsavory prejudice—though they are this too. They show the perdurance of a mode of cultural defense that took shape in an earlier time, among a generation for whom the tools of folkloric investigation represented a weapon against mainstream prejudices, and not an aesthetic straitjacket; for whom the right to artistic and personal dignity was predicated upon their ability to embody the essence of a cultural formation that was distinct from the criollo social milieu. The palpable sense of bitterness that appears in their dismissal of chicha and huayno norteño artists may reflect resentment as they lose control of Andean representation to an underclass in ascension.

But it is also the lament of people who are losing a myth of musical politics that they have lived deeply, as their voice becomes a tiny remnant trace of grandeur lost, echoing within a yawning chasm of global and local popular culture.

In their very resistance to adaptation, the strategies of contemporary Ayacuchano artists and mediators call attention to the radical impulse that once lay at the heart of folkloric musical discourse. By defending highland rights to cultural distinctiveness over the early to mid twentieth century, by rooting this defense in the replication of inherited traditions when faced by the apparent homogenizing thrust of global popular culture, Andean elites labored to resist the bigoted authority of Peru's dominant criollos. This drive foundered in the late twentieth century, when the essentializing limits of its preservationist discourse became clear to academic commentators and public intellectuals alike. But efforts to defend it in the present day should not be dismissed as mere attempts to shore up elite authority. Besides being uncharitable to those who have staked their careers on ideological certainties that have come to seem outdated, such a stance underestimates the extent to which any cultural politics depends upon the circumstances of its emergence, and the extent to which it will necessarily yield before a new cultural politics when those circumstances change.[4] Indeed, the currently fashionable thesis according to which chicha and huayno norteño artists speak in the legitimate voice of Peru's Andean masses may itself come to appear insufficiently critical, for these artists too are manufactured products of the culture industry, their media personas crafted to sell records and concert tickets, rather than social uplift.

It is more useful to recognize the way that the opposition between a musical politics of folkloric authenticity and one of populist representation together organize contemporary debates about Andean and Peruvian society. When viewed in this light, contemporary Ayacuchano huayno, pan-Andean music, and fusión are best distinguished from their cumbia and huayno norteño alters by the different paths these styles take to legitimizing contemporary Andean subject positions, rather than by any claims to superior social relevance. Though the two streams are readily differentiated at the sonic level, they share fundamental assumptions about the need to modernize Andean music. In Turino's terms (2000), both are grounded in the cosmopolitan cultural formation of globalizing capitalism and the transnational popular culture industry. Though their aesthetics of Andean cosmopolitanism are discrepant, both seek to create a vernacular modernity for popular uptake and in this sense might be regarded as functionally indistinguishable.

Nevertheless, precisely to the degree that huayno and cumbia–huayno norteño use different means to gather its public, these two stylistic formations organize new lines of division within the Andean community, which is why the work of production that lies behind such discrepant cosmopolitanisms requires further explication. When local media agents domesticate transnational materials, bringing new markers of distinction into a scene with established social divisions, they mediate the kind of ongoing social differentiation that thrives within societies riven by inequality. Nor are these the only lines of fracture within the Andean public sphere, which is divided into many different subsectors and organized around competing narratives of Andean present and future (see Tucker 2011). Many different narratives of Andean identity are being constructed and circulated within and beyond Peru, and it is in the dialogue between them that the future of Andeanness will emerge.

If this process is to be understood, then we require analyses that proceed along the lines suggested in this book. Andean life is increasingly lived in tandem with media consumption, and it will be critical to note the role of popular media agents in defining the narratives that circulate in the public sphere. The relationship between style, ideology, and consuming community is one that is cultivated by determined agents who shepherd musical sound and the listening public toward one another, creating logical identifications between the two by harnessing social change to market dynamics. It will be necessary to show how these media agents define their intended audiences and which sectors of the Andean public thereby accrue around competing definitions of Andean legitimacy—to show how these processes respond to changes in the socioeconomic organization of the Andean community, and also to changes in technological capability. In short, we urgently require studies that show how musical styles get mapped onto discrepant publics, in changing social circumstances, as local mediators compete to meet and satisfy the emergent desires of consuming communities.

NOTES

INTRODUCTION

1. This is not to overlook the existing tradition of scholarship on musical change in urban settings (i.e., Erlmann 1991, 1996b; Romero 2001; Turino 1990, 1993; Waterman 1990), but rather to note that studies of media networks per se remain rare. Even innovative scholarship on urban musics tends to focus on particular sites within large conurbations, rather than the process by which sounds scatter and recruit listeners (see Jottar 2009a, 2009b; Novak 2010; Sakakeeny 2010).
2. Andeanness has also been an important symbol in the indigenous revitalization movements of neighboring Ecuador and Bolivia (Becker 2008; Pallares 2002). By contrast, indigenous politics have gained little traction in Andean Peru (see Pajuelo 2007).
3. De la Cadena (2000) has persuasively argued that indigenismo ultimately reinscribed mestizo dominance, while Mendoza (2008) has argued instead that the movement included significant Indian input and therefore can be seen as a truly intersubjective site of self-fashioning for highland citizens. The question of indigenismo's sincerity and its effects on indigenous empowerment are important issues that lie beyond the purview of this book. For analyses of similar movements in Bolivia and Argentina, see Bigenho 2002; Ríos 2008.

CHAPTER ONE

1. On identity, see Brubaker and Cooper 2000; Hall and du Gay 1996; Ortner 1999. Exemplary ethnographies of media and identity include Abu-Lughod 2005; Dávila 2001; Hirschkind 2006; Mazzarella 2004.
2. Habermas ([1959] 1989) is mainly concerned with the bourgeois, literate café culture that arose in the wake of the French Revolution and its later evolution.
3. Critics particularly reject Habermas's demand that participants in public discourse bracket the "private" aspects of their life experience in favor of interests pertinent to all, thus shielding public discourse from the "merely parochial" claims of gender, ethnicity, or class (see Fraser 1990; Warner 2002). Indeed, by deciding, a priori, what is a truly collective concern and what is not, Habermas betrays an "inattention to agency, to the struggles by which both the public sphere and its participants are actively made and remade" (Calhoun 1992: 37) and ensures that his model responds to highly particular upper- or middle-class male concerns.

4. The classic accounts are those of Adorno (e.g., 2001), but for later studies see Chapple and Garofalo 1977; Frith 1978; Manuel 1991. Within Peru, Lloréns Amico (1983) has sketched out the early history of the local recording industry, and Romero (2001) has described José María Arguedas's role in the founding of that industry. However, only Lloréns Amico's 1991 article on migrant radio deals with the issues of mediation that concern me here.
5. On media use, see Ang 1985; Frith 1978, 1996; Hall 1973; Hebdige 1979; Middleton 1990; Radway 1984. On the music industry, see Hennion 1983, 1989; Negus 1992, 1999; Peterson 1978, 1997.
6. Other exemplary recording studies include Greene and Porcello 2005; Neuenfeldt 2001; Scales 2002.
7. Scholars of radio have typically come from sociology or media studies. See Ahlkvist 2001; Berland 1993a, 1993b, 1998; Hennion and Méadel 1986; Hilmes and Loviglio 2002b.
8. After a long period dominated by fears of cultural "greyout" (cf. Nettl 1983), Stokes (2004) has noted a tendency toward two visions of globalization in recent scholarship, a "pessimistic" one concerned with the uniformity that lies beneath an apparent, surface-level diversity (Erlmann 1996a; Feld 2000; Turino 2000) and a "celebratory" vision confident in celebrating globalization's provision of resources to subalterns seeking to work past local cultural limitations (for example, Galinsky 2002; Lipsitz 1994).
9. My use of the term "cosmopolitan" follows the colloquial understanding, rather than the relatively restricted sense developed by Turino (2000). Turino's "cosmopolitans" draw upon translocal resources of selfhood without surrendering to a homogenizing discourse of globalization, and his formulation mitigates the imprecisions fostered by most discussions of globalization, where the term designates incorporation into the Euro-American sphere of influence, and where those who are not "globalized" lie outside history. This analysis is sophisticated, but the term is so often used, in Peru and elsewhere, according to its popular definition as something "having worldwide rather than limited or provincial scope or bearing" (*Merriam-Webster's Collegiate Dictionary*, 11th ed.), and this notion is so central to recent developments in Peruvian music, that I do not believe that it is helpful to confuse matters by attempting to use the term in two distinct senses. Further, most Peruvians I know do take the baseline of cosmopolitanism to be participation in a transnational popular culture associated with the United States and other Latin American countries.
10. Policy waxed and waned in tenor, granting varying degrees of power and legitimacy to indigenous leaders. Moreover, it can be argued that indigenous peoples were not fully reduced to subaltern status until after independence, when the new state removed colonial protections and privileges for Indians (Thurner 1997). For excellent studies of Andean society in this period, see Baker 2008; Stavig 1999; Stern 1982; Walker 1999.
11. My understanding of racialization follows the work of Wade (1993, 1997), who views racial differentiation as a process through which social attributes, physical attributes, descent, and class status are read onto subaltern populations in evolving patterns that nevertheless preserve older colonial hierarchies. See also Omi and Winant (1986) 1994.
12. Weismantel (2001) has criticized scholars who, drawing upon American race categories, describe Andean mestizos as racially interstitial, instead of taking their own claims to whiteness at face value. However, her analysis draws heavily on fieldwork

in Ecuador and Bolivia and very thinly upon Peru's distinct situation. It elides the kinds of experiences that I describe here, which do not place mestizos into the stable interstitial position that she rightly dismisses, but rather make their identities as "whites" something that is difficult to claim before national elites.

13. Orlove (1998) describes the micropolitics of such identity work by hypothesizing a conversation between unknown individuals who meet on a deserted road and are faced with the task of determining their relative status so that each will know how to behave. In his realistic account, leather shoes and the casual demonstration of formal schooling become central to evaluating social and ethnic positions. Andean identities, in other words, are established by comparison rather than by absolute criteria: an individual's position within the mestizo-Indian hierarchy is continually reformulated in the course of social interactions (see also Mishkin 1963; Mayer 1970). Nevertheless, each interaction ends up by reproducing the binary opposition between Indian and non-Indian.

14. Or, as Lomnitz has noted, "a *mestizo* is not exactly a thing that really exists, but a representation" (2009), a means of expressing one's felt relation to local histories of cultural mixture, racial hierarchy, and power.

15. The great intellectual José María Arguedas observed ([1958] 1977) that Andean society has generated many different kinds of mestizo cultures, each unique in its stance toward cultural mixture, and it might be noted here that scholars have rarely attempted to characterize the differences that exist within both Indian and mestizo communities throughout the Andes.

16. Very few scholars have taken care to explore this distinction, which sets Peruvian discourses of mestizaje apart from the more well-known discourses of mestizaje that guide public discourse in countries like Brazil, Mexico, and Cuba. José Guillermo Nugent's account is the most incisive, placing explicitly racialized notions of mestizaje, like the highly influential one articulated by Mexican scholar José Vasconcelos, in contradistinction to Peruvian usage, where "talk of a mestizo race has been carefully avoided, in favor of a mestizo 'culture' that joins two races which do not mix: whites and Indians" (Nugent 1992: 47–48).

17. I would like to thank Benjamin Teitelbaum for helping me to find the language in which to express this concept.

18. See Bellenger 2007; Bigenho 2002; Ritter 2002; Schechter 1992; Stobart 2006; Turino 1993. My own research has elsewhere engaged extensively with issues of music and indigenous identity (Tucker 2011), and for that reason I choose to reserve my discussion here to the more fraught links between music and Andean elite identity, the complexities of which are formidable and deserve a book-length treatment on their own. In general, my Peruvian friends who espouse a self-consciously subaltern identity, whether as "cholos" or "Indians" or "Quechuas," are somewhat ambivalent about the contemporary Ayacuchano style's success in displacing other kinds of voices from the Peruvian public sphere, but not about the style on its own merits, which they might dismiss as "commercial" or "boring" but never as a falsification of Andean identity. Indeed, in my experience indigenous Peruvians typically feel much less obliged to deny the existence of a distinct Andean mestizo culture than do either criollo citizens or certain scholars who have written upon the subject. The effects of the public cultural displacement wrought by contemporary Ayacuchano huayno were brought home to me most clearly one day when I dropped by the Quechua-language broadcaster Radio Quispillacta in Ayacucho. My friend Graciano Machaca, director of the station, was hosting a journalist from Lima who I believe had come

to prepare a report on the station's efforts at revitalizing the Quechua language and indigenous musical genres such as chimaycha in the local countryside. I observed as Machaca gave her a long disquisition on the importance of the language and the distinct nature of indigenous culture, only to have her finish by asking if the station could provide her with examples of "traditional Andean music," such as that of the Gaitán Castro brothers—foremost interpreters of mestizo-cosmopolitan, contemporary Ayacuchano music and a dominant presence in Lima's Andean public sphere. The silence that followed was stony as Machaca and his colleague Edilberto appeared to swallow their frustration before politely answering that the music she had asked for did not really represent the kind of indigenous revitalization work they were involved in. The incident was a testament to the uphill battle faced by indigenous citizens in Peru seeking to make their distinct identities heard above the homogenizing sounds of such genres as contemporary Ayacuchano huayno and huayno norteño.

19. See Doughty 1970; Mangin 1964; Matos Mar 1968; Núñez Rebaza 1990.
20. Regional clubs remain important among Andean migrants in Lima, though they are nowhere near as central as they apparently once were, since they tend to attract the patronage of first-generation migrants, rather than the second-, third-, and fourth-generation migrants who form Lima's majority. They remain centers for traditional performance as well, though they are not averse to hiring representatives of more modern traditions. Many Ayacuchano clubs host annual *carnaval* celebrations, festivals for community patron saint days, and other kinds of events centered on folkloric performance. They have been particularly active in hosting *danzaq* (scissors dancers) competitions in recent years; indeed, this flashy performance genre has become something of an all-purpose symbol of Andean authenticity, and after a Peruvian network produced a serialized drama inspired by the career of the renowned scissors dancer Qori Sisicha, it attained a cachet that would have been almost unimaginable decades earlier.
21. See Adams and Valdivia 1991; Degregori, Blondet and Lynch 1986; Vich 2001; for music, see Hurtado Suarez 1995; Romero 2001; Turino 1990, 1991, 1993.
22. This desertion was largely due to the devastation wrought by Peru's defeat in the War of the Pacific (1879–83).
23. The brief synthesis presented here is largely based on Degregori 1997; Gorriti Ellenbogen 1999; Palmer 1994; Poole and Rénique 1992. A much fuller account is presented in the final report of Peru's Truth and Reconciliation Commission (CVR 2003).
24. The group's understanding of Peruvian society, which combined Maoist thought with the 1930s-era writings of the Peruvian communist José Carlos Mariátegui, was long out of date. At the time, Peru was ruled by a leftist dictatorship that had attempted to redress indigenous and peasant grievances, and though ultimately ineffectual, it certainly represented a turn away from a "feudal" situation.
25. One of the most gruesome aspects of the Shining Path's method was that they counted on such an eventuality, hoping that the indiscriminate response of the armed forces would drive peasants away from state protection.
26. The lingering effects of the violence are plainly implicated in certain contemporary social problems that afflict the region. Most young Ayacuchanos, though, do not treat it as the overdetermining factor in their biographies, but rather as one more in a long line of injustices heaped upon Andean Peru, a view that underlines the central finding of the Truth and Reconciliation Commission: that the root causes of the conflict lay in the region's enduring economic and social exclusion.

27. Toledo was born in the Andes, but he grew up on the north coast, far from the centers of indigenous Andean life. Within Peru, he is not considered to be indigenous, and his use of Andean imagery was often mystifying to his constituents, as he used mestizo music in a confused bid to shore up his credentials as an Andean Indian and participated in kitschy commemorations of indigeneity that revealed his stereotyped, Hollywoodesque understanding of Andean life.
28. The political situation during Toledo's tenure in particular recalls Hale's (2002) and Hale and Millamán's (2006) critiques of ethnic politics, which decry the self-serving treatment of minority peoples by neoliberal politicians, who pass themselves off as social activists by patronizing subaltern culture while supporting policies that disadvantage those very communities.

CHAPTER TWO

1. Unless otherwise noted, references to casual conversations such as the one cited here and to formal interviews pertain to research activities conducted in Ayacucho and Lima between 2000 and 2003. Interview subjects are thanked in the acknowledgments.
2. The vals is a sung genre based on the European waltz, typically performed to the accompaniment of one or more guitars, which enliven the basic (ternary) waltz rhythm with syncopated cross-rhythms and flashy solo passages, and perhaps a *cajón*, which does the same. The most widely celebrated valses tend to be love songs, often songs of heartbreak, and are interpreted in an appropriately nostalgic fashion. The marinera, Peru's official national dance, is typically performed using the same resources, but with a far more extensive use of hemiola in guitar and cajón parts. Lyrics are based on Spanish poetic forms such as the seguidilla, and in ages past performances might have involved some competitive interaction between different performers. Both genres are held to have arisen in the mixed-race (black and white) precincts of working-class Lima, but together they came, by the mid-twentieth century, to stand for the distinctive criollo culture of the Peruvian coast. See Feldman 2001; León 1997, 2003.
3. Other highland genres are mostly limited to particular social or regional contexts, and Romero (1999) suggests that this is the reason for the trans-Andean importance of huayno. Such generality contrasts starkly with the specificity of the *yaraví* or the *qachwa* or *ccachua* (a song and round dance particular to Quechua-speaking communities), tied to the urban-mestizo and rural-indigenous communities, respectively, or the *herranza* and the *carnaval*, heard during animal branding and carnival season. The most thorough analyses of huayno's structural principles have been published in Spanish by Peruvian scholars: see Romero 2002; Vásquez Rodríguez and Vergara Figueroa 1990. However, see also Romero 1999, 2001; Turino 1984, 2007.
4. Songs that are not set in an AABB pattern almost always use a variant that preserves the binarism of this arrangement: an ABAB arrangement is not uncommon, and in Ayacucho, musicians sometimes repeat the last line for emphasis, resulting in an AABBB structure overall.
5. Often this effect, sometimes called the "Andean cadence," is drawn out further in a contrast between the third and fourth phrases of the strophe. In this case, a small variation is introduced such that the third phrase ends within the area of the song's major tonic, and the fourth phrase comes to rest in the area of the relative minor tonic.
6. Falconí distinguished his contemporary compositions from traditional songs by noting that earlier huayno was "a romantic, personal thing. In the early part of the century,

they were songs to distract oneself, to let each another know what was going on emotionally, inside." Similarly, Turino has related that his teacher told him simply, "When I am sad, I compose a huayno" (2001: 237).
7. Fugas often consist of preexisting pieces, sometimes another huayno.
8. Huayno's absence from texts before late colonial times probably means that it was a marginal genre prior to that period, if it existed at all (Romero 2002). Many writers nevertheless claim a pre-Columbian origin, building speculative genealogies based on observations recorded in early Spanish chronicles and word lists in colonial-era dictionaries (Camassi Pizarro 2007; Gradante n.d.). Such claims do not bear scrutiny, given the paucity and vagueness of descriptions drawn from chronicles (see Stevenson 1968), or sources such as González Holguín's 1608 Quechua dictionary (González Holguín and Porra Barrenechea 1952), where it is defined only as a couples dance. Further, although Andean pentatonicism was once assumed to be an Inca legacy, this has been definitively shown to be false, and archaeological evidence overwhelmingly shows that pre-Columbian instruments were not tuned to a pentatonic scale (Olsen 2002; Haeberli 1979). Many contemporary indigenous genres too are tetratonic or tritonic, and even rural indigenous huayno tunes draw upon pandiatonic, pentatonic, and tetratonic scales (Romero 2002).
9. Most musicians in twentieth-century Ayacucho bore nicknames. "Chipi" means "monkey," in Quechua; Prado's given name was Arturo. In his own youth, Prado was a friend and sometime musical partner of Falconí's father, a well-regarded vocalist.
10. In particular, Carranza noted the extensive use of nature metaphors, giving as an example the common trope of referring to a female beloved as a "dove" (*cuculí* or *urpi* in Quechua).
11. In a 1990 edition of Robles's writings, a melody appears on p. 80 that was later recorded by the Duo Hermanos García Zárate as the huayno "Guitarra ama waqaychu" (Don't Cry, Guitar). On p. 96 appears a tune fragment from the huayno "Ripuy ripuy," recorded by Trio Ayacucho in 2002. Elsewhere, Robles notates tunes that are related to the Ayacuchano yaraví "El imposible," and the Cuzqueño huaynos "Cuculí" and "Saqsaywaman." Camassi Pizarro (2007) has stated that Ayacuchano tunes attributed to a Manuel Soto in the d'Harcourt collection are recognizable in contemporary performers as well.
12. In their study of rural indigenous music, the Montoyas affirm that musical continuity from the nineteenth century to the present is well attested (Montoya, Montoya, and Montoya 1997). Elsewhere Roel Pineda's main consultant, an organist at San Jerónimo church in Cusco, dated his huayno repertoire back to 1905 (Roel Pineda 1959), and the Escobars' 1981 collection (Escobar and Escobar 1981) alludes to a collection of huaynos dated 1903.
13. Vivanco singles him out in his list of outstanding performers from the early twentieth century (1988), calling him an expert in the guitar tuning once called *decente*, which the performer Ernesto Camassi and others told me was once archetypal among Ayacucho's gentlemanly class.
14. I heard different accounts of this matter. Carlos Falconí told me that his father would rail at him for speaking Quechua, and his bandmate Ernesto Camassi noted some stigma attached to the language as well. However, their former classmate María Luisa Bustamante told me that it was spoken freely in her home; no stigma was attached to it whatsoever. I would suggest that this points to the distinct cultural orientations within class groups that often go missing in accounts of Andean society.

15. Early scholars instead thought that jocose, picaresque huaynos were most typical of Ayacucho's tradition, for instance. See del Pino 1949; Pozo 1954.
16. The title derives from a sacred class of Inca temple servants. These tunes are all sometimes performed as fox-trots, the international popularity of which coincided with the heyday of indigenista composition.
17. Despite this experience, it should be noted that as of January 2012, this group is in fact alive and well, and perhaps even larger than it was a decade beforehand. And it is still holding rehearsals in its space near Ayacucho's main plaza.
18. Vivanco asserted that this ensemble was faithful to the style heard during his youth in Ayacucho, in the 1920s and 1930s (see Vilcapoma 1999). A similar ensemble can be heard on Yma Sumac's recordings of the 1940s, which were directed by her husband, the Ayacuchano musician and estudiantina veteran Moisés Vivanco.
19. A cover of the pan-Andean tinku "Celia" by the metal band Alkoholika was a minor hit in Bolivia at the time.
20. See Stobart 2006; Turino 1993.
21. Many Ayacuchanos interpret the success of Picaflor de los Andes, widely regarded as the greatest huayno performer of all time, as the result of the way that he combined Ayacucho's vocal style with the vigorous instrumentation of the Central Andes.
22. In point of fact, the genre that Central Andean groups play is typically called *huaylas*. It is identical to huayno in verse structure, as well as melodic and harmonic principles, but it tends to be distinguished by faster tempos and very active instrumental accompaniment, with saxes and clarinets often playing ornamented, energetic, jagged lines full of stuttering, repeated notes that echo the stomping footwork of the accompanying dance. See Romero 2001.
23. Musicians from Áncash, such as Jilguero del Huascarán and Pastorita Huaracina, were especially popular in the 1950s, and the music of the central highlands ruled from the 1960s through the 1980s. The northern harp-based style that currently dominates Peru is discussed below.
24. This widely admired ensemble disappeared in the mid-1960s.
25. Medina is often erroneously credited with the song's composition. Parra Carreño, Cabrera, and Pozo (1939) described the song as a very old tune, long familiar to his audience. Ernesto Camassi thought that both Medina and Las Lindas Satankas (the Melendez sisters) were *muy rústicas* (very hickish), perhaps indicating that indigenous performers were not entirely absent from the competition. Medina's performance can be heard on the compilation *The Secret Museum of Mankind, vol. 4*.
26. See Romero (2001) for a full recounting of this pivotal event.
27. As Romero (2001) has noted, the era's musicians did not exactly chafe at these restrictions: indigenista hegemony had certainly marginalized other traditions, and performers of more quotidian styles of music were grateful for Arguedas's arbitration. And performers did not necessarily need to represent their home region, instead being judged by their fidelity to the style of the region they claimed to represent onstage. Many artists who became known as Central Andean performers were from Ayacucho, including Orlando Sauñe, of Estudiantina Perú, and Picaflor de los Andes.
28. Romero argues that the Central Andean style that emerged on disc at this time was continuous with earlier music of the region, and the same seems to be true for Ayacucho. He also points out that there are no pre-1950s field recordings that might document a conjectural, "purer" aesthetic that has since been corrupted (2001: 118).
29. Such handles are commonly used by Peruvian record companies to brand their artists.

30. This distinction does not hold up fully in practice, but nearly all of the venues where I have found performances of traditional Ayacuchano huayno fall into this category. They include the concert hall of the Instituto Cultural Peruano-Norteamericano, the Teatro Ricardo Palma, the Teatro Pardo y Aliaga, the auditorium of the National Museum, and the auditorium of the María Angola hotel, in Lima; and the Municipal Auditorium, the patio of the Colegio San Antonio, the auditorium of the local branch of the National Institute of Culture, the auditorium of the Cooperativa Santa Magdalena, and the Condorcunca Music Conservatory, and several lecture halls at the UNSCH, in Ayacucho.

31. The relation between the decline of the harp in Ayacucho and the rise of the harp-based huayno norteño style to be discussed below is unclear: my friend Otoniel Ccayanchira, an Ayacuchano harpist, maintained that the northern style had attracted local talent away from Ayacucho's distinctive harp tradition, but local memories tended to bespeak a dearth of local harpists that long antedated the rise of huayno norteño.

32. The Lira Paucina, a trio from rural southern Ayacucho, had already recorded in the 1950s, but their style is different from that of the city and does not enter into the series of imageries and oppositions that concern me here. The Smithsonian Folkways title *Mountain Music of Peru*, a field recording from the same era, bears a number of recordings from Ayacucho that are very different in tone from the commercial records of the late 1960s and 1970s.

33. These characteristics have led many to debate whether such songs are huaynos at all, though the composers and their public certainly understand them as such. For more thorough discussions of these songs and these times, see Ritter 2002, 2006; Vásquez Rodriguez and Vergara Figueroa 1988.

34. Recounting his motivations, Falconí touched upon ideas of testimony and collective catharsis, asking, "Who was going to assume the defense of the people who were being brutalized? The artists. Who else was going to do it?" "Chipillay Prado" itself was one of Falconí's testimonial songs, a fact unknown to me until we discussed it, since its later verses had never been recorded. Following the opening two verses, with their themes of tradition and emotional release, the song turns instead to the goals of the new huayno movement, suturing old and new concerns:

    Payhinam ñuqa takini, manañam llakiymanñachu
    Payhinam ñuqa tocani, manañam waqaymanñachu
    Masmi kallpanchakuni, llaqtallay pichaykunaypaq,
    Masmi kallpanchakuni, suwata qarqullanaypaq

    Atuqta manchakuq kani, uywayta aysarikuptin (*bis*)
    Lorom atuqta maslIan, llapantam payqa qatirun
    Lorom atuqta maslIan, ñuqapaq yarqayta saqin

    [I sing like him, I will pine no more
    I sing like him, I will weep no more
    Instead I will save my strength, to clean out my town
    Instead I save my strength, to evict the thieves

    Once I feared the fox, stealer of lambs
    But now the parrot has turned thief, stealing all
    But now the parrot has turned thief, leaving me with nothing]

    The fox is a stock figure of Andean myth and legend, appearing as both a dangerous predator and an admirable trickster. The Quechua term *uywa*, which I have translated

here as "lamb," is actually a class term for the young and defenseless, including animals and humans alike. *Loro* (parrot) is a slang term for military officials, recalling their green uniforms.
35. Few found such suggestions as *huayno moderno* or *huayno juvenil* (teen huayno) to be very persuasive, and neither do I.
36. Ayacucho's kena players tended to favor a vibratoless, whistling timbre and extensive use of trills instead of the portamentos and scalar fireworks of pan-Andean performers, while charango players plucked huaynos in parallel thirds, enlivened by tremolo on sustained tones, and finishing performances with a faster strummed fuga section. Such performers, and such performances, still exist, though they are increasingly rare.
37. A number of scholars have explored the relationship between chicha and its descendant, *tecnocumbia*, which flourished in the late 1990s (Bailón 2004; Quispe Lázaro 2000, 2002; Romero 2002; Salcedo 2000).
38. The origin of the term is usually tied to a 1960s hit by the group Los Demonios del Corocochay. Despite loose usage, many commentators reserve it for those variants that project self-consciously Andean roots.
39. See Bullen 1993; Degregori 1984; Franco 1991; Matos Mar 1984; Quijano 1980; Turino 1990.
40. Comparable examples abound in greater Latin America: a partial list might include *merengue* vs. *bachata* (Austerlitz 1997; Pacini Hernandez 1995); *tejano* vs. *orquesta* vs. *banda* music (Peña 1985, 1999; Simonett 2001); and *salsa dura* vs. *salsa romántica* (Aparicio 1998; Manuel 2006; Washburne 2008).
41. See Bendix 1997 for an account of the radicalism inherent in the folkloric scholarship that underpinned these ideas. Roel Mendizábal 2000 provides a complementary history, emphasizing folklore's progressivism in a racially and culturally stratified society like Peru.
42. As far as I know, performers elsewhere do not call it by this name, but refer to it as *huayno con arpa* (huayno with harp), *tecno-huayno*, or simply huayno.
43. This harp is hardly the only instrument associated with the northern region, which like Ayacucho department houses many different musical traditions. Indeed, in recent years the harp of huayno norteño has been increasingly displaced by the *requinto*, itself an adaptation of another northern instrumental aesthetic.
44. Traditionally, tritonic santiago music is sung during the ritual marking of animals throughout the Andes. It has also been adapted into a popular genre throughout the Andes, where it typically relies upon the same instrumentation as local huayno music while preserving the original genre's constant, driving beat and upbeat, playful mood.
45. This evaluation, which I often received from listeners of Lucy's generation, was not exactly a recognition of my talents, but rather the result of hearing me perform in a style that has not been current since the 1970s heyday of García Zárate himself.
46. See Nettl 1983 for an early statement; Erlmann 1996a and Turino 2000 for more sophisticated readings.

CHAPTER THREE
1. See Coronado 2009; de la Cadena 2000; Mendoza 2000, 2008; Tamayo Herrera 1982; Tarica 2008.
2. The term "huamanguino" calls to mind the colonial name of the city and is still used to distinguish ancestral city-dwellers from recent arrivals. Here, I use the terms

"huamanguino" and "huamanguinismo" to describe the people and their urban elite cultural formation, reserving "Ayacuchano" to describe the geographic space of the city and the department.

3. Indeed, the very notion that "mestizos" might think of themselves as indigenous—not aboriginal—to the Andes contests the dichotomous view of Peruvian history that many writers implicitly espouse, in which Andean mestizos are considered non-Andean precisely to the extent that they consider themselves nonaboriginal.

4. The university was first closed in 1876 because of state fiscal problems. It was briefly reopened at the war's end in 1883 before being permanently shut down in 1886.

5. Though he did not specify the source of his data, Carlos Falconí told me that by the end of the nineteenth century "hundreds" of pianos had been imported to Ayacucho. His childhood memories and the musical accounts in *Revista Huamanga* show that pianos were played in many houses, schools, and social organizations of Ayacucho's elite. As of 2012, one such piano was still in service at the Ayacuchano restaurant Wallpa Sua, where local performers enlivened weekend nights with renditions of local music in the style that might have been heard in Anchorena's own salon.

6. This excepts those educated intellectuals who do seize upon it as a self-conscious marker of identity. The related Quechua word *misti* derives from the Spanish term and is typically used by Quechua-speakers to denote Peru's directing class. When I first arrived in Ayacucho, I told Carlos Falconí that I was interested in such race categories; he was incredulous at the idea that I would ask people if they were mestizos. Visibly agitated at such a faux pas, despite his own proud use of the label, he told me that "*nobody* in Ayacucho will call himself a *mestizo*. Go ahead, *haz la prueba* [try it]."

7. A typical list of such markers, derived from a single work on an Ayacuchano musician (Vilcapoma 1999), includes the following, for persons of the non-indigenous elite: *clase media* (middle class), *clase señorial* (gentlemanly class), *con apellido* (with a good last name), *de prestigio* (prestigious), *un niño de ciudad* (a city child), *de abolengo* (of noble heritage), *los urbanos de clase media* (the urban middle class), *(hablando) no de limeño, ni de serrano, sino un intermedio, como mestizo ayacuchano* ([speaking] not as a person from Lima, nor as a highlander, but in between, as an Ayacuchano mestizo), *no un provinciano* (not provincial), *con corbata* (wearing a tie), *bien puesto* (well put together), *digno representante de la familia Vivanco, de esos españoles de la prosapia de Ayacucho* (worthy representative of the Vivanco family, of those Spanish inheritors of Ayacucho), *blancos* (whites), *mistis* (roughly translated, a non-Indian person with power), *el sector ilustrado* (the educated sector), *la clase feudal terrateniente* (the feudal landowning class), *poseedora de casonas y haciendas* (owners of big houses and estates), *renegaba de su pasado y desdeñaba al indio* (who despised their past and looked down upon the Indian), *muy conocida* (very well-known), *grupo de poder* (group in power), *vecinos* (neighbors, translated literally; a colonial term used to distinguish Spanish settlers from local Indians within a given jurisdiction), *el grupo dominante local y sus intelectuales* (the dominant local group and its intellectuals), *aristocracia huamanguina* (the huamanguino aristocracy), and *buena sociedad* (good society). Terms used for Indians or people who occupy the lower rungs of society include *provinciano* (provincial), *los sectores bajos* (the lower classes), *los cholos del barrio* (the half-breeds of the slums), *(bautizado) con bombos y platillos* ([baptized] with drums and cymbals, that is, not quietly and decently), *el pueblo* (the commoners), *ignorante* (ignorant; used in relation to the indigenous inhabitants of the high puna regions), *sin colegio* (without schooling), and *estratos mestizos y indios* (mestizo and Indian classes; used in opposition to the term "gentlemanly" [*señorial*]).

8. Feldman (2001) describes how this category, as used in Lima, came to be framed in opposition to the increasing presence of Andean migrants in Lima's city-space around the mid-twentieth century.
9. This usage survives in daily conversation. Indicating its reputation for liveliness and respectability, one friend described the neighborhood where I lived in Ayacucho as "San Blas criollo," and another used the term to distinguish the huayno of the city—*huayno criollo*—from the indigenous version of the countryside. Scholars who follow the dominant usage, further binding the term's self-conscious elitism to the capital and its culture, may end up by flattering the very pretension to Limeño dominance upon which this usage rests.
10. Franck, for instance, complained about the "unbroken, dismal, tuneless, indigenous wail" of Anchorena's celebrating porters.
11. Many artists complain about this tendency, asserting that a sense of ownership has led certain people to hoard songs that have gone unheard for ages and are no longer known to the general populace.
12. In the years since, his talented son has taken up the harp and become a preserver of the style as well.
13. Sullca can be heard on the Nonesuch recording *Kingdom of the Sun: Peru's Inca Heritage* (1969).
14. This dearth probably derived partly from the nature of their social circles: certainly, I attended such parties at other peoples' houses and occasionally heard news of more.
15. Despite their service in elite contexts, harpists were mainly drawn from rural indigenous communities or the urban underclass. They were also often disabled, and many well-known harpists have been afflicted with blindness or kyphosis (curvature of the spine).
16. Turino's charango teacher, Julio Benavente Díaz, similarly recalled the Cuzqueño landlords who, as children, adopted elements of indigenous music from the Indian servants on their parents' haciendas.
17. Chuchón gathered her huayno repertoire into a book, *Sentimiento Ayacuchano* (Chuchón Huamaní 2007). Her memories are probably inflected by her social position: it is unlikely that women of lesser pedigree were strongly discouraged from going into the street. Market stalls, for instance, have been run by indigenous and mestiza women for centuries. Franck saw enough of them that he was moved to ridicule their headwear.
18. Between 1919 and 1944 as many as four newspapers at a time served this city of under fifteen thousand, attesting to a disproportionately active writing public (Cavero Carrasco and Cavero Carrasco 2007: 39).
19. "Mariscal," in this quote, is the high school Mariscal Cáceres, which is the same Colegio Nacional San Ramón, discussed below, that Vivanco had attended a decade or more prior: it changed its name in 1938.
20. Rivera taught him only in serenatas to his future wife, which perhaps led Vivanco to study with one Teodoro Martínez as well.
21. Bustamante (1935) noted that Anchorena published these tunes, but it is unclear whether the first two pieces are Anchorena's compositions or simply publications financed by him.
22. Such as Alicia Fernández, Celmira Cárdenas, Carmen Fajardo, and Lola Martínez, or the national girls' choir, all of whom appear in later events. Again, see Parra Carreño, Cabrera, and Pozo 1938: 28.

23. Besides those named, prominent members of the founding board included the teachers Lucio Alvizuri and Manuel Bustamante. Later members included the jurist Juan José del Pino, as well as many teachers at the Colegio San Ramón (after 1938, the Colegio Nacional Mariscal Cáceres), including the writer Néstor Cabrera, Luis Cavero, Moisés Cavero, Osmán del Barco, Leoncio Jerí Untiveros, Carlos Mendívil, Luis Milóm Bendezú, Rómulo Parodi, and Carlos Vivanco.
24. More concrete recommendations touched upon the ongoing appeal for the reopening of the UNSCH, indigenous education, and the diversion of water to the city from the Cachi River, among other perennial issues.
25. In point of fact, Ayacucho does not possess significant natural resources, though Pozo and others claimed it did.
26. These nationalist aspects of indigenismo are well outlined by de la Cadena (2000) and Mendoza (2000, 2008).
27. Some Ayacuchanos had already created indigenista-style artworks, such as Moisés Cavero's 1914 Quechua-language play *Qisampi sapan urpikuna*.
28. For a discussion of the full resonance of the term *gamonal*, see Mayer 2009: 88. Many great works of indigenista literature revolve around the subjugation of Indians by these overbearing landlords. A 1935 article in *Revista Huamanga* entitled "Fiesta en Tambo," in fact, describes one of the festival's benefits as providing a defense against *gamonalismo*.
29. Alternately, they may raise the question of whether indigenismo itself is an adequate title for the many movements toward Andean valorization that existed at this time.
30. The debate, which continues today, usually pits the contemporary towns of Huamanguilla and Quinua as the probable sites of this initial settlement.
31. Urrutia (1994) provides the best review of the evidence for the Pokras' nonexistence.
32. Similarly, Alvizuri (1935) dwelled on the definition of indigeneity in order to argue that, strictly speaking, the term applied to anyone who was born into a given area and who therefore belonged there.
33. Mendoza's (2008) account of early indigenismo in Cusco similarly indicates the distance that lies between later interpretations and the intentions of its progenitors. She also describes earlier attempts to create art objects based on indigenous patterns, including nineteenth-century "Inca operas," and if the indigenista period saw the emergence of orchestrated pseudo-indigenous music for popular consumption, it is not unlikely that this was but the most recent trend in a long-standing pattern of cultural interaction.
34. Anchorena was a composer of indigenista tunes. Bustamante played with the indigenista Compañia Pachamama and with the Estudiantina Típica Ayacucho. And on a visit to Ayacucho, the writer Aurelio Miró Quesada noted recreational music making in the home of Juan José del Pino, though he did not specify the nature of the music he heard (Miró Quesada [1938] 2004).
35. Elsewhere, references appear decrying the influence of jazz, tango, and the one-step.
36. Bustamante declares that this was later published in *El Peru Ilustrado* in September 1887.
37. The list of performers appears in an accompanying piece, entitled "Audición Musical," where González is listed as performing "vernacular music" along with "los señores La Rosa Oré y Crisóstomo Pillpi."
38. The sort of list pioneered here by Bustamante appears in many later writings, including Vivanco 1971; Vivanco 1988; García Miranda and Wong Gutiérrez 1999.
39. In Anchorena's examples, happy songs might celebrate survival after thunderous

nights in the wilds of the primitive cavern; sad ones might lament the sight of an aging wife, a reminder of impending mortality.

40. Arguedas's ideas can be found in "Notas elementales sobre al arte popular religioso y la cultura mestiza de Huamanga" ([1958] 1977). Camassi and Falconí, among others, cited them to me nearly verbatim.
41. If this recalls Bustamante's (1935) redundantly melancholy examples of vernacular music, elsewhere Parra Carreño (1939) indulges in the same self-contradictions as the earlier author, claiming instead for huayno an immense variety.
42. This is likely to be true, in a sense. Given the regular circulation of people between these cities (Huancayo was on the road from Lima to Ayacucho), it is to be expected that tunes circulated freely between them, and it is exceptionally difficult to state with any clarity the origin of a particular verse or song.
43. Turino (1984) referred to this conundrum as a contest between the "identity factor" and the "hegemony factor."
44. Recent commentators have differed on the matter of the musical style favored by the CCA, without engaging deeply with the material that was actually played. Millones has noted that indigenista-style composition provided an effective *dar salida* (way out) for highland mestizos such as the members of the CCA, desirous to identify with Andean heritage while maintaining a discreet distance from Indian identification with its heavy stylization (2005: 218). Gamarra, by contrast, acknowledges that performances often featured the huamanguino elite's own practices (*expresiones propias*; Gamarra Carrillo 2007: 138), while noting that often these were shared with indigenous peoples.
45. Fajardo (1940: 51) goes on to state that Jáuregui's talent and fame are such "that we might say that the artistic personality of certain Ayacuchanos who have attained celebrity is that of Jáuregui." Without further specification it is impossible to know whom he is referring to, but it is reasonable to assume that he means Moisés and possibly Alejandro Vivanco, other indigenista-style performers who attained far greater fame.
46. On its fourth anniversary, José Antonio Escarcena noted "the interest that the Center is raising in the study and interpretation of huamanguino folklore," but he also noted critics who accused them of becoming an academic institution, only suitable for intellectuals (1938: 15). His membership report revealed that the society included just sixty-eight associates, of whom only twenty-two regularly came to meetings. Even Ernesto Camassi, who sought to revive the society in the 1990s, noted that their events had mainly been confined to places like the Club 9 de diciembre, Ayacucho's most exclusive salon.
47. As early as 1935 an anonymous squib in *Revista Huamanga* acknowledged the salutations of periodicals in Cusco, and its circulation eventually reached other national and international centers as well.
48. Similarly, Pereyra describes how the CCA and its allies "defined for Ayacucho a cultural mestizaje that had begun with colonization and [which] enunciated the supposed cultural and biological inferiority of Ayacuchano peasants" (Pereyra Chávez 2007: 143).

CHAPTER FOUR

1. Typically, the term "record label" refers to the trademark under which the products of a particular company are marketed, as well as the human and technical infrastructure that lies behind that trademark.

2. For studio ethnographies that explore these and other points in detail, see Greene 2002; Greene and Porcello 2005; Meintjes 2003; Scales 2002.
3. See Frith 1996; Negus 1999; Peterson 1997.
4. IEMPSA was founded in 1945 as a local distributor for the international conglomerate Odeón, operating initially under the name of the parent company. It began to finance recordings of Peruvian music in 1946, sending the singer Jesús Vásquez to Odeón's Buenos Aires studios, where she recorded several pieces of música criolla, accompanied by the Puneño composer and arranger Jorge Huirse, and at least one huayno. In 1949 the company bought its own microphones and a portable four-track machine, and began recording in Lima's Cine Coloso and, later, Cine Metro movie theaters, after evening shows let out. After 1962, the company built a record studio and acquired an eight-track machine to produce hi-fi recordings. In the meantime, the emergence of the Virrey label, founded in 1953 by air force officers (Land Vásquez 1992), Discos Smith, and eventually Sono Radio opened up the market considerably. See also Lloréns Amico 1983, Romero 2001, and Turino 1993 for sketchy accounts of early Peruvian recording.
5. The break between one era and the next was not entirely clean. Indigenista ensembles still performed for audiences within and beyond the capital. And alongside folkloric huayno records, IEMPSA released albums by respected indigenista ensembles such as Sol del Perú in the early 1950s, as well as in later years.
6. This period has been dealt with more extensively in Turino 1988.
7. Many performers told me that record company personnel might demand that they record particular songs because they were already associated with the artists or their home region, because they were beloved by the employee making the request, or because they would generate a hit record. But record company executives were mainly interested in waxing an accomplished performance, and in this early period that rarely meant significant demands for change in a given artist's style or musical resources.
8. Like Romero's consultants who were involved with Central Andean music (2001), my friends and acquaintances in Ayacucho maintained that the era's recordings were little different from musical practice in their homes and places of leisure.
9. Figures on record production are notoriously hard to come by in Peru. However, Land Vásquez (1992) estimated that IEMPSA devoted 50 percent of its production capacity to huayno music and related genres in the years before 1975. By comparison, he estimated that the label Virrey devoted 55 percent of its capacity to the same music between 1964 and 1975.
10. Such a profile was not unheard of among huayno musicians, but it was hardly common. By comparison Pastorita Huaracina, the first outstanding star of the recorded huayno era, had been a domestic worker, and Picaflor de los Andes, regarded by common consensus as the greatest performer of the Golden Age, worked as a truck driver.
11. For a cogent discussion of academic folklore's intellectual politics in this era, see Roel Mendizábal 2000. Given Ayacucho's intellectual focus on the Hispanic inheritance rather than the indigenous past, local folkloric investigations differed in important ways from the Cuscocentric efforts described by Roel, with their search for "totalizing" frames of interpretation based on readings of indigenous lifeways. Nevertheless, the notion of shared, collective patterns of consciousness, housed in folkloric objects which must therefore be faithfully recreated for public consumption, was substantially similar.

12. García Zárate had been performing for some fifteen years by the time this recording was released, but he had recently become the director of Sono Radio's Andean music division. Such directors were usually recognized performers: IEMPSA's Gilberto Cuevas was a member of the huayno group Los Errantes, and the company also employed the highland guitarist Antonio Gutiérrez. These artistic directors acted as talent scouts, oversaw the recording process, and determined what music should make it to the marketplace. It is, therefore, very likely that García Zárate's recent employment weighed heavily in the label's decision to release his album.
13. These were not the first recordings made by Ayacuchano musicians. To the 1928 RCA sides by Las Lindas Satankas and Tani Medina, the 78s from the 1940s by the Estudiantina Municipal, and Yma Sumac's 1940s-era recordings with Moisés Vivanco's conjunto might be added those of the kena player Alejandro Vivanco, who made some indigenista recordings in the 1950s, and Gaspar Fajardo Andía, a guitarist from the Ayacuchano town of Huanta who recorded some solo guitar music in the same decade. Finally, the Trio Lira Paucina recorded in the 1950s as well, and though the band members hailed from the far south of Ayacucho department, they shared performance techniques and repertoire with Ayacucho itself. Despite these precedents, Ayacuchano performers date the true advent of Ayacuchano recording to the 1960s.
14. Peru's record companies aimed tended to seek out and record representative performers from many different subregions. Some artists and styles, however, achieved success well beyond their geographic point of origin. Lima's coliseos were ruled by performers from northern Áncash department, such as Pastorita Huaracina, Jilguero del Huascarán, and the Conjunto Atusparia in the 1950s, only to cede preeminence during the 1960s to such performers as Picaflor de los Andes, Flor Pucarina, and Estudiantina Peru, whose Central Andean music dominated the huayno scene until the 1980s. Vivanco (1971) argues that these changes corresponded to the arrival in Lima of migrant waves from the regions in question.
15. See Degregori 2000a (especially pp. 37–47) for a description of this period. Ayacucho at this time attracted established and upcoming leaders of Andean scholarship, including R. Tom Zuidema, Billie Jean and William Isbell, Irene Silverblatt, Steve Stern, David Scott Palmer, John Earls, and Jan Szeminski.
16. The Tuna is exceptional among local groups in that it maintains the estudiantina sound of the early twentieth century. Upon hearing them in 1988, Alejandro Vivanco stated that "[he] was gratified to see how, hearing the same melodies 50 years later, some groups of my hometown are interpreting them in exactly the same way" (Vilcapoma 1999: 83). This list of important former members is too long to enumerate, but prominent names include those of Ángel Bedrillana, Óscar Figueroa, the Gaitán Castro brothers, and Mario Laurente. García Zárate himself appeared as a special guest on their first album.
17. Gamarra was not, in fact, an original member. He was brought in because of his superior guitar skills to replace Carlos Flores, who left the trio shortly after the group's first series of recordings for the IEMPSA label.
18. In pursuit of poetic perfection, the group was not above tinkering with songs they considered worthy but poetically deficient. Both Camassi and Falconí told me that they made metrical or lexical adjustments in places where they deemed it necessary.
19. Unusually for a song from this landlocked region, "Vapor brillante" describes a steamship carrying the speaker's love interest away. According to Falconí and Camassi, this dates it to Peru's nineteenth-century guano boom, during which many local men traveled to the coast seeking jobs in the offshore industry.

20. Repeatedly, Falconí and Camassi assured me that this quality had assured the group's success, though it disappointed listeners such as Falconí's father, who dismissed it as so much distasteful shouting.
21. Guitarists who admired Gamarra, as well as Gamarra himself, told me that these passages often appeared to derive from jazz, tropical music, Argentinean zamba, or other foreign musical styles somewhat distant from the local huayno scene. He insisted, however, that his musical inspirations came unbidden, and that he never set out to copy any particular style.
22. Indeed, Nery published at least one scholarly article in a local journal on folkloric method and cultural analysis (Zoila García, personal communication).
23. It has become part and parcel of his legend that the young Raúl García Zárate taught himself. According to his peers, though, he learned many guitar techniques from older and often unacknowledged peers, including Alberto "Raktaku" Juscamayta and Arturo "Chipi" Prado.
24. Sometimes these small enterprises were run by recording artists, such as Antonio Gutierrez's Volcán label or Erasmo Medina's Ollanta label.
25. Despite that fact that she came from the coastal city of Nazca, Martina Portocarrero had become identified as a Shining Path supporter and had already recorded songs associated with the guerrillas, including "Flor de retama" and "Yerba Silvestre"—the latter authored by the Shining Path lieutenant Edith Lagos. Even the García Zárates had produced a somewhat unsuccessful recording of "El hombre," a song later associated with the era's political conflicts, in the early 1970s. And the Trio Los Labradores de Huanta had recorded "Flor de retama" shortly after it was composed, in the early 1970s.
26. In point of fact, the money to found the business came from Fernández's wife, Rosa Chiclla.
27. Dolby also recorded many groups from the Ayacuchano countryside and seasonal music such as songs for *carnaval*.
28. The artist was usually given a preestablished number of cassettes gratis, which he or she could then sell off independently. The label retained all other rights over royalties and profits.
29. This was no idle concern: the composer Walter Humala spent several years incarcerated for this crime.
30. It is unlikely that they heard pan-Andean music for the first time in Lima. Like other Andean cities, Ayacucho had long been home to pan-Andean performers and performance venues, and recordings by representative artists circulated there.
31. The fact that the main hit of the hypersexualized "lambada craze" of the 1980s was based upon Los Kjarkas's saya "Llorando se fue" speaks to the international currency of these images (Templeman 1996, 2005; Wara Céspedes 1993).
32. Sanjuanito music features relatively rapid, very simple and repetitive, apparently always pentatonic melodies with extensive use of the "Andean cadence" over a binary rhythmic pattern that accents the upbeats, making it eminently suitable for dance clubs. Tinkus also tend toward pentatonicism, but the genre is most distinguished by its rhythm, which features a square, insistent, four-beat thrum played at a very fast tempo.
33. For an exploration of balada, see Party 2006.
34. In a later live recording, this parallel was made even more explicit when the duo added a rock drum kit, saxophone, and synthesizer.
35. Camassi maintained that "Mi propuesta" was not a huayno at all, but a takirari, a Bolivian genre and a pan-Andean staple.

36. This roster included the guitarists Óscar Figueroa, Fíler Ordóñez, and Manuelcha Prado; the bassist Julio Lingan; and the wind player Fredy Gómez, among others.
37. This is Fernández's own description of the passage.
38. So much so that when the label Mundo Music released a box set in 2003 containing remastered recordings by the Tuna of the UNSCH, they dubbed the instrument into the mix.
39. Similarly, despite a general antipathy to electronic sounds, synthesized string orchestras were generally ruled acceptable since they carried the sophisticated connotations of symphonic music. The sounds of a standard rock 'n' roll drum kit eventually came to be permissible as long as they remained unobtrusive.

CHAPTER FIVE

1. The station broadcast from Cerro El Pino, a small hill in a rough neighborhood—a location calculated to dissuade police interference. It covered only part of the enormous migrant district of Lurigancho but all of the city's central districts, from Rímac to Barranco, as well as substantial portions of the northern, southern, and eastern cones, the historical centers of migrant life.
2. The station was eventually shut down, apparently at the instigation of the consortium that owned Zeta, whose member stations ran congratulatory commercials after the raid saluting the newfound zeal of the authorities.
3. This was a growing trend. In Lima I twice watched Prado's peer Max Castro escorted on and off stage by a phalanx of handlers, who warded off young admirers. At other shows, including performances by Castro and Ángel Bedrillana, I saw members of their fan clubs arrive with placards bearing messages of love and appreciation.
4. Although many Peruvians experience huayno through live performance, recordings, or television shows, none of these approaches the importance of radio. Until recently, televised huayno shows were confined to early hours, while even pirated CDs remained a luxury not often purchased by those with severely constrained budgets. Most Peruvian radio studies have focused exclusively on Lima: see Arnold 1998 for an exception. Most have treated matters of Andean musical content in terms of airtime percentage, decrying its marginalization and arguing for greater coverage of Peruvian musics in the name of communicative democracy or strengthening national identity (Alfaro, Tellen, Pinilla, and Gogin 1990; Bolaños 1995; Zúñiga 1999). An exception is the work of Lloréns Amico, discussed below.
5. In surveys of several dozen randomly selected households that I conducted while living in Ayacucho, every one of them reported listening to radio for more than two hours a day, but most numbers were far higher. Some gave figures in the double digits.
6. In a typical testimonial, the DJ Ricardo Daryx, an employee of a competing station, responded to my query about the reasons for the style's success by saying, "Simple: it was Frecuencia A. How else would it have happened?"
7. Lima's FM dial hosted dozens of stations dedicated to rock, pop, tropical music, and news, but few huayno stations, and those that existed mostly played northern huayno music during this period. The exception was the government-operated Radio Nacional, perennially low in the ratings, which had several early-morning shows, typically hosted by intellectuals, and eventually a show hosted by the Gaitán Castro brothers—which most attributed to their friendship with President Alejandro Toledo. Most of the people who broadcast contemporary Ayacuchano huayno could not afford to purchase airtime on mainstream stations, and they operated as pirates.

AM radio, by contrast, hosted a number of huayno stations, but they were largely avoided by contemporary huayno broadcasters owing to the rural-folkloric connotations of the AM band. In Ayacucho, the FM dial was less full, and there were many legal stations that played huayno music.

8. The few, invaluable studies that exist tend not to focus on day-to-day operations or the act of broadcasting itself, but rather to provide histories of influential broadcasters and their relationship to particular styles (Laird 2005; McCann 2004; Simonett 2001). Conversely, studies of talk radio, such as those collected in Scannell 1991, do not address music, and the large literature on early American radio mainly features radio dramas and more diffuse issues such as the emergence and structure of the network system (Douglas 2004; Hilmes 1997; Smulyan 1994).

9. In part, too, this is a matter of historical timing: when popular culture and media finally became legitimate objects of scholarly attention, radio had also been eclipsed in economic power and social cachet, though not in usage, by later media. See Hilmes and Loviglio 2002a.

10. The style of the more successful shows was inevitably parroted, diluting the idiosyncrasy of the originals and narrowing the diversification of the airwaves. But this process might be treated as an important sociological fact as well as a capitalist strategy, a way to explore how individual actors take advantage of technological change to produce lasting effects on the social categories available to wider publics.

11. There are a large number of excellent popular, semiacademic, and/or autobiographical works on such influential music DJs as Alan Freed (Jackson 1991) or Wolfman Jack (Douglas 1999; Jack 1995).

12. Much of this section is synthesized from Alegría 1988 and Bustamante 2005.

13. It was granted to the Peruvian Broadcasting Company, an affiliate of England's Marconi Wireless Company.

14. In his attempts to forge a national community through radio's collective address, Leguía's activities echo those of contemporary and later leaders in Brazil (McCann 2004), Mexico (Hayes 2000), the United States (Hilmes 2002), and Afghanistan (Baily 1994).

15. In fact, the government had appropriated OAX in the 1920s, relaunching it as Radio Nacional in 1937, when regulations were passed that privatized the airwaves, reserved one frequency for the state, and specified the medium's duty to safeguard the national interest. See Stein 1986 for an account of Lima's working-class mobilizations in this period.

16. Some early programs were run as promotional spaces by the agencies that sold receivers, as well as some that distributed records locally.

17. The survey was conducted by the newspaper *La Crónica* and the broadcaster Radio Central: in point of fact, música criolla shared first place with radio dramas. Bustamante lists the música criolla musicians Flora Cevallos, Carlota Calderón, Esther Cornejo, Las Costeñitas, Rosita Delgado, Pedro Espinel, Las Estrellitas, La Limeñita, Maruja López, Eduardo Márquez Talledo, Yolanda Matos, Filomeno Ormeño, Delia Vallejos, and Jesús Vásquez as performers who appeared on the radio during this period (2005: 213–14).

18. Examples include Radio Abancay, Radio Juliaca, and Radio Ayacucho. Peru's state television station was also founded at this time in partnership with UNESCO.

19. Coronado had won a prize at the 1931 Pampa de Amancaes competition commemorating the Día del Indio and was thereafter contracted by the impresario Juan Lepiane to perform in indigenista shows throughout the capital. He entered the ensemble at

Radio Nacional in 1932 and later performed on other radio stations with the Quinteto Cuzco.

20. Alejandro Vivanco stated that Moisés Vivanco was the first Andean guitarist to perform on Peruvian radio, in 1934, though he does not specify further (Vilcapoma 1999: 80).
21. Almost everyone in Ayacucho old enough to remember this era told me about listening to the station.
22. It is unclear whether Pizarro charged for the service, but such payments eventually became a widespread practice and an important means for hosts to generate revenue.
23. This regime would change with the founding in Lima in 1962 of Radio Agricultura's all-day huayno broadcasts.
24. The Radio Victoria chain, along with subsidiaries like Radio Ayacucho, was nationalized under the leftist regime of Velasco Alvarado, which did encourage the broadcast of Andean music, and though its rules were widely flaunted, Radio Nacional did continue to broadcast some huayno music into the twenty-first century (Lloréns Amico 1983, 1991; Turino 1990). Among others, Ernesto Camassi of Trio Ayacucho also had a radio show on this station for some time.
25. Indeed, Picaflor de los Andes recorded his first album in 1963, the year that La Voz was founded.
26. Cruz claimed that the station had actually been fined for this offense. I was not able to ascertain the truth of this rather incredible story, but several friends confirmed it, meaning that it has the force of folkloric truth if not fact.
27. There they continue to dominate in the twenty-first century, though they have been increasingly joined by huayno norteño, which appealed more to the succeeding generation of rural peasants and migrants. Indeed, one radio director, in response to my question about his station's programming choices, stated bluntly that they tried to reach "all social sectors" by broadcasting a little of everything: "Ayacuchano music for the educated, [Central Andean] music for older peasants, and huayno norteño for younger migrants." It is well worth noting that that Radio La Voz also broadcasts many other kinds of music, including rural-indigenous music rarely heard anywhere else—most prominently on the show *Takiyninchik*, hosted by the anthropologist Uriel Salcedo.
28. No radio director was able to tell me why this price decrease happened at this time. However, Fernando Cruz told me that "an FM station could be set up, equipped, and begin running with $3,000 or $4,000, while founding an AM station meant an investment of around $20,000 to $30,000." Further, an AM antenna required a hectare of open high ground, whereas smaller FM antennas could be set up on rooftops in the city center.
29. Radio listenership is difficult to assess in Peru, and most mediators rely on word of mouth or personal observation, especially in such a small market as Ayacucho. Many radio directors were distrustful of the methods employed by ratings agencies, believing that their informal, man-on-the-street surveys were poor gauges of listenership. Most believed, furthermore, that the employees of such organizations took bribes from radio managers looking to boost ratings and, hence, advertising contracts. And all recognized that, inasmuch as these agencies refused to report publicly the ratings of Peru's many pirate stations, their results were irremediably flawed.
30. I believe that these were meant to signal "summer" to listeners, despite the fact that Ayacucho is over a hundred miles from the ocean.

31. The joke may be that the woman addressed by name is compared to one of the bovines at the upcoming bullfight.
32. "Conejo" is a relatively common nickname for someone with overjet, also known as buck teeth.
33. One typical, randomly selected two-hour broadcast from January 29, 2003, included commercials for an afternoon of bullfighting in the town of Huascahura, the *chicharronería* (pork butcher shop) Los Cerezos, the computing institution Cibernet, an eye clinic, the bus company Expreso Molina ("Don't travel in any old bus!"), the outdoor bar Los Algarrobos, the beverage company Fruti Kola, the local Dolby JR record store, the seafood restaurant Cevichería Miguelito, a local credit institution, Ayacucho's water service, a glass company, Restaurant Las Américas, a gas delivery company, a school offering driving lessons, a cosmetology program, several clothing stores specializing in jeans and youth fashions, and a live concert of local sanjuanito bands in the nearby valley of Muyurina.
34. Sales figures may have been available from record companies, but owing to the overwhelming disproportion between legal and pirate sales, they were properly regarded as completely useless.
35. For foundational accounts dealing with such problems of tradition and authenticity, see Handler and Linnekin 1984; Hobsbawm and Ranger 1983. The basic paradoxes presented there—that the desire to maintain "pure" traditions is itself a modern impulse, and that conceptions of tradition and authenticity themselves change over time in response to new conditions—have nowhere been stated more effectively.
36. There were notable exceptions, such as the program *Suri Sikuris*, run by the three Arone brothers, all of whom had an intellectual bent and a very serious interest in traditional music.
37. I saw such influence in action only once, when, in Argumedo's absence, his brother entered the broadcast booth at Frecuencia A to object to a huayno-rock fusion track that a DJ had just placed on the air, shouting "This is a huayno station! Huayno!"
38. Very successful performers, in 2003, charged up to $2,500–$3,000 for a single show in Ayacucho.
39. Indeed, I saw representatives of the artists Max Castro and Ángel Bedrillana each come by local radio stations to protest that they were not promoting upcoming concerts with the requisite zeal.

EPILOGUE

1. See the discussion in chapter 2.
2. Most of my Peruvian acquaintances dated this uptick in interest to the death in a car accident of the entire cumbia group Néctar.
3. In this sense, these two styles parallel Bourdieu's distinction between the restricted field of artistic production, and the popular field, recalling his point that the overall structure of any given social field will be reproduced within its various subsectors as well.
4. I mean here to echo the concerns raised by Mendoza 2008 with regard to recognizing the radical and positive values of folkloric discourse, as against scholars who have only criticized folkloric representation for its conservative tendencies.

BIBLIOGRAPHY

Abu-Lughod, Lila. 2005. *Dramas of Nationhood: The Politics of Television in Egypt.* Chicago: University of Chicago Press.
Adams, Norma, and Néstor Valdivia. 1991. *Los otros empresarios: Ética de migrantes y formación de empresas en Lima.* Lima: Instituto de Estudios Peruanos.
Adorno, Theodor W. 2001. *The Culture Industry: Selected Essays on Mass Culture.* London: Routledge.
Ahlkvist, Jarl A. 2001. "Programming Philosophies and the Rationalization of Music Radio." *Media, Culture & Society* 23 (3): 339–58.
Alegría, Alonso. 1988. *O-A-X: Crónica de la radio en el Perú (1925–1980).* Lima: Radioprogramas Editores.
Alfaro, Rosa María, Rubén Tellen, Helena Pinilla, and Gina Gogin. 1990. *Cultura de masas y cultura popular en la radio peruana: Diagnóstico para construir una alternativa radial.* Lima: Calandria/Tarea.
Alfaro Rotondo, Santiago. 2006. "El lugar de las industrias culturales en las políticas públicas." In Cortés and Vich, *Políticas culturales,* 137–76.
Alomía Robles, Daniel, and Armando Robles Godoy. 1990. *Himno al sol: La obra folclórica y musical de Daniel Alomía Robles.* Lima: Consejo Nacional de Ciencia y Tecnología.
Altamirano, Teófilo. 1984. *Presencia andina en Lima metropolitana: Un estudio sobre migrantes y clubes de provincianos.* Lima: Pontificia Universidad Católica del Perú, Fondo Editorial.
Alvizuri, Lúcio. 1935. "El neoindianismo en Ayacucho." *Revista Huamanga* 4: 85–88.
Anchorena, Carlos. 1939. "Disertación que, sobre 'Música Peruana,' diera el Doctor Carlos Anchorena en el 'Club Social Iquitos.'" *Revista Huamanga* 27: 11–15.
Ang, Ien. 1985. *Watching "Dallas": Soap Opera and the Melodramatic Imagination.* London: Methuen.
———. 1991. *Desperately Seeking the Audience.* London: Routledge.
Aparicio, Frances R. 1998. *Listening to Salsa: Gender, Latin Popular Music, and Puerto Rican Cultures.* Hanover, NH: University Press of New England.
Appadurai, Arjun. 1986. *The Social Life of Things: Commodities in Cultural Perspective.* Cambridge: Cambridge University Press.
———. 1996. *Modernity at Large: Cultural Dimensions of Globalization.* Minneapolis: University of Minnesota Press.
Appadurai, Arjun, and Carol Breckenridge. 1995. "Public Modernity in India." In *Consuming*

Modernity: Public Culture in a South Asian World, edited by Carol A. Breckenridge, 1–15. Minneapolis: University of Minnesota Press.

Arguedas, José María. 1966. "Raúl García, un intérprete de la música completa de Ayacucho." *El Comercio*, Sunday supplement, June 16: 20.

———. (1958) 1977. "Notas elementales sobre el arte popular religioso y la cultura mestiza de Huamanga." In *Formación de una cultura nacional indoamericana*, 148–72. México: Siglo Veintiuno Editores. Citations refer to the 1977 edition.

———. (1940) 1989. "La canción popular mestizo e india en el Perú: su valor documental y poetico." In *Indios, mestizos y señores*, 45–47. Citations refer to the 1989 edition.

"Audición musical." 1939. *Revista Huamanga* 27: 22–35.

Austerlitz, Paul. 1997. *Merengue: Dominican Music and Dominican Identity*. Philadelphia: Temple University Press.

Bailón, Jaime. 2004. "La chicha no muere ni se destruye, sólo se transforma: Vida, historia y milagros de la cumbia peruana." *Íconos (Ecuador)* 18: 53–62.

Baily, John. 1994. "The Role of Music in the Creation of an Afghan National Identity." In *Ethnicity, Identity, and Music: The Musical Construction of Place*, edited by Martin Stokes, 45–60. Oxford: Berg.

Baker, Geoffrey. 2008. *Imposing Harmony: Music and Society in Colonial Cuzco*. Durham: Duke University Press.

Balbi, Carmen Rosa. 1997. "Una ciudadanía descoyuntada o redifinida por la crisis? De 'Lima la horrible' a la identidad chola." In *Lima: Aspiraciones, reconocimiento y ciudadanía en los noventa*, edited by Carmen Rosa Balbi, 11–28. Lima: Pontificia Universidad Católica del Perú, Fondo Editorial.

Barnes, Ken. 1988. "Top 40 Radio: A Fragment of the Imagination." In *Facing the Music*, edited by Simon Frith, 8–50. New York: Pantheon Books.

Becker, Marc. 2008. *Indians and Leftists in the Making of Ecuador's Modern Indigenous Movements*. Durham: Duke University Press.

Bellenger, Xavier. 2007. *El espacio musical andino: Modo ritualizado de producción musical en la isla de Taquile y la región del lago Titicaca*. Lima: IFEA and Pontificia Universidad Católica del Perú.

Bendix, Regina. 1997. *In Search of Authenticity: The Formation of Folklore Studies*. Madison: University of Wisconsin Press.

Berland, Jody. 1993a. "Contradicting Media: Toward a Political Phenomenology of Listening." In *Radiotext(E)*, edited by Neil Strauss, David Mandl, and Bart Plantenga, 209–17. New York: Columbia University Press.

———. 1993b. "Radio Space and Industrial Time: The Case of Music Formats." In *Rock and Popular Music: Politics, Policies, Institutions*, edited by Tony Bennett, 105–18. London: Routledge.

———. 1998. "Locating Listening: Technological Space, Popular Music, Canadian Mediations." *Cultural Studies* 2 (3): 343–58.

Bigenho, Michelle. 2002. *Sounding Indigenous: Authenticity in Bolivian Music Performance*. New York: Palgrave.

Bolaños, César. 1995. *La música nacional en los medios de comunicación electrónicos de Lima metropolitana*. Lima: Facultad de Ciencias de la Comunicación, Centro de Investigación Social, Universidad de Lima.

Bourdieu, Pierre. 1977. *Outline of a Theory of Practice*. Cambridge: Cambridge University Press.

———. 1984. *Distinction: A Social Critique of the Judgement of Taste*. Translated by Richard Nice. Cambridge, MA: Harvard University Press.

———. 1993. *The Field of Cultural Production: Essays on Art and Literature*. New York: Columbia University Press.
Brubaker, Rogers, and Frederick Cooper. 2000. "Beyond 'Identity.'" *Theory and Society* 29 (1): 1–47.
Bull, Michael, and Les Back. 2003. *The Auditory Culture Reader*. Oxford: Berg.
Bullen, Margaret. 1993. "Chicha in the Shanty Towns of Arequipa, Peru." *Popular Music* 12 (3): 229–44.
Burga, Manuel. 2010. "Estudiantes de Huamanga." *La República*, May 13. http://www.larepublica.pe/columnistas/aproximaciones/estudiantes-de-huamanga-13-05-2010.
Bustamante, Emilio. 2005. "Los primeros veinte años de la radio en el Perú." *Contratexto* 13: 206–20.
Bustamante, Manuel E. 1935. "Breves referencias sobre la música vernacular." *Revista Huamanga* 4: 25–33.
Caballero Martín, Víctor. 1995. *Ayacucho: Las migraciones y el problema laboral*. Lima: Chirapaq and Centro de Culturas Indias.
Cabrera, Néstor. 1938. "Los tunantes: Tradición ayacuchana." *Revista Huamanga* 14: 11–14.
Calhoun, Craig. 1992. "Introduction: Habermas and the Public Sphere." In *Habermas and the Public Sphere*, edited by Craig Calhoun, 1–48. Cambridge, MA: MIT Press.
Camassi, Ernesto, and Trio Ayacucho. [c. 1967–75]. *Aquí estamos mejor* [album cover text]. Discos Sono Radio LP SE 9449. Lima: Discos Sono Radio.
Camassi Pizarro, Ernesto W. 2007. *Historia del wayno huamanguino*. Lima: Ediciones Altazor.
Cavero Carrasco, Ranulfo, and Rómulo Cavero Carrasco. 2007. *Retablo de memorias: Indígenas e indigenismo en Ayacucho*. Huamanga: Universidad Nacional de San Cristóbal de Huamanga.
"Centro Cultural Ayacucho." 1934. *Revista Huamanga* 1: frontispiece.
Chapple, Steve, and Reebee Garofalo. 1977. *Rock 'n' Roll Is Here to Pay: The History and Politics of the Music Industry*. Chicago: Nelson-Hall.
Chuchón Huamaní, Serafina. 2007. *Sentimiento ayacuchano*. Lima: Ediciones Altazor.
Colloredo-Mansfeld, Rudolf Josef. 1999. *The Native Leisure Class: Consumption and Cultural Creativity in the Andes*. Chicago: University of Chicago Press.
Corbin, Alain. 1998. *Village Bells: Sound and Meaning in the Nineteenth-Century French Countryside*. Translated by Martin Thom. New York: Columbia University Press.
Coronado, Jorge. 2009. *The Andes Imagined: Indigenismo, Society, and Modernity*. Pittsburgh: University of Pittsburgh Press.
Cortés, Guillermo, and Victor Vich, eds. 2006. *Políticas culturales: Ensayos críticos*. Lima: IEP Ediciones, Instituto Nacional de Cultura, and Organización de Estados Iberoamericanos.
Cotler, Julio. 1978. *Clases, estado y nación en el Perú*. Lima: Instituto de Estudios Peruanos.
d'Harcourt, Raoul, and Marguerite d'Harcourt. 1925. *La musique des Incas et ses survivances*. Paris: P. Geuthner.
Dávila, Arlene M. 2001. *Latinos, Inc.: The Marketing and Making of a People*. Berkeley and Los Angeles: University of California Press.
de la Cadena, Marisol. 2000. *Indigenous Mestizos: The Politics of Race and Culture in Cuzco, Peru, 1919–1991*. Durham: Duke University Press.
de Mata Peralta Ramírez, Juan. 1995. *Tradiciones de Huamanga*. 2 vols. Lima: Gráfica N & R Editores.
Degregori, Carlos Iván. 1984. "Huayno, Chicha: El nuevo rostro de la música peruana." *Cultura Popular (CELADEC)* 13–14: 187–93.
———. 1997. "The Maturation of a Cosmocrat and the Building of a Discourse Community:

The Case of Shining Path." In *The Legitimization of Violence*, edited by David E. Apter, 33–82. New York: New York University Press.

———. 2000a. "Panorama de la antropología en el Perú: del studio del Otro a la construcción de un Nosotros diverso." In Degregori, *No hay país más diverso*, 20–73.

Degregori, Carlos Iván, ed. 2000b. *No hay país más diverso: Compendio de antropología peruana*. Lima: Desarrollo de las Ciencias Sociales en el Perú.

Degregori, Carlos Iván, Cecilia Blondet, and Nicolás Lynch. 1986. *Conquistadores de un nuevo mundo: De invasores a ciudadanos en San Martín de Porres*. Lima: Instituto de Estudios Peruanos.

del Pino, Juan José. 1946. "Cual es el sentido psicológico de la música ayacuchana? Introducción." *Revista Huamanga* 58: 23–28.

———. 1949. "Cual es el sentido psicológico de la música ayacuchana? Factores étnicos y sociales determinantes de la transformación de la música aborigen en la propiamente huamanguina." *Revista Huamanga* 62: 21–25.

DESCO. 2005. "40 aniversario." *Revista Quehacer* 155: 54–59.

Diez Hurtado, Alejandro. 2003. *Elites y poderes locales: Sociedades regionales ante la descentralización; Los casos de Puno y Ayacucho*. Lima: SER/DFID.

Donham, Donald L. 1990. *History, Power, Ideology: Central Issues in Marxism and Anthropology*. Cambridge: Cambridge University Press.

Dornfeld, Barry. 1998. *Producing Public Television, Producing Public Culture*. Princeton: Princeton University Press.

Doughty, Paul. 1970. "Behind the Back of the City: Provincial Life in Lima, Perú." In *Peasants in Cities: Readings in the Anthropology of Urbanization*, edited by William Mangin, 30–46. Boston: Houghton Mifflin.

Douglas, Susan J. 1999. *Listening In: Radio and the American Imagination, from Amos 'n' Andy and Edward R. Murrow to Wolfman Jack and Howard Stern*. New York: Times Books.

Douglas, Susan J. 2004. *Listening In: Radio and the American Imagination*. Minneapolis: University of Minnesota Press.

Erlmann, Veit. 1991. *African Stars: Studies in Black South African Performance*. Chicago: University of Chicago Press.

———. 1996a. "The Aesthetics of the Global Imagination: Reflections on World Music in the 1990s." *Public Culture* 8 (3): 467–87.

———. 1996b. *Nightsong: Performance, Power, and Practice in South Africa*. Chicago: University of Chicago Press.

———. 2004. *Hearing Cultures: Essays on Sound, Listening, and Modernity*. Oxford: Berg.

Escarcena, José Antonio. 1938. "Memoria leída en la sesión solemne del 12 de octubre de 1938, por el doctor J. Antonio Escarcena, presidente del 'Centro Cultural Ayacuchano.'" *Revista Huamanga* 16: 13–17.

Escobar, Gloria, and Gabriel Escobar. 1981. *Huaynos del Cusco*. Cusco: Editorial "Garsilaso."

Fajardo, J. Víctor. 1940. "La obra artística del folklorista José María de Jáuregui." *Revista Huamanga* 30: 51–52.

———. 2000. "A Sweet Lullaby for World Music." *Public Culture* 12 (1): 145–71.

Feldman, Heidi Carolyn. 2001. "Black Rhythms of Peru: Staging Cultural Memory through Music and Dance, 1956–2000." Ph.D. diss., University of California, Los Angeles.

Ferrier, Claude. 2010. *El huayno con arpa: Estilos globales en la nueva música popular andina*. Lima: Instituto de Etnomusicología and Instituto Francés de Estudios Andinos.

Franck, Harry Alverson. 1917. *Vagabonding Down the Andes*. New York: Century.

Franco, Carlos. 1991. *Imágenes de la sociedad peruana: La "otra" modernidad*. Lima: Centro de Estudios para el Desarrollo y la Participación.

Fraser, Nancy. 1990. "Rethinking the Public Sphere: A Contribution to the Critique of Actually Existing Democracy." *Social Text* 2: 56–80.
Frith, Simon. 1978. *The Sociology of Rock*. London: Constable.
———. 1996. *Performing Rites: On the Value of Popular Music*. Oxford: Oxford University Press.
Fuenzalida, Fernando. 1970. "Poder, raza, y étnia en el Perú contemporáneo " In *El indio y el poder en el Perú*, edited by José Matos Mar, 15–86. Lima: Instituto de Estudios Peruanos.
Fuller, Norma. 2002. "El papel de las clases medias en la producción de la identidad nacional." In *Interculturalidad y política: Desafíos y posibilidades*, edited by Norma Fuller, 419–40. Lima: Pontificia Universidad Católica del Perú; Universidad del Pacífico, Centro de Investigación; and Instituto de Estudios Peruanos.
Gal, Susan, and Kathryn A. Woolard. 2001. "Constructing Languages and Publics: Authority and Representation." In *Languages and Publics: The Making of Authority*, edited by Kathryn A. Woolard, 1–12. Manchester: St. Jerome.
Galinsky, Philip. 2002. "Music and Place in the Brazilian Popular Imagination: the Interplay of Local and Global in the *mangue bit* Movement of Recife, Pernambuco, Brazil." In Walter Aaron Clark, *From Tejano to Tango: Latin American Popular Music*, 195–216. New York: Routledge.
Galindo Vera, Vidal. 2000. *Bibliografía de la revista "Huamanga."* Lima: Representaciones e Impresiones San Miguel.
Gálvez Carrillo, M. Jesús. 1945. "Araskaska: Apunte ayacuchano." *Revista Huamanga* 62: 34–36.
Gamarra Carrillo, Jefrey. 1996. "El espacio regional como pretexto: Historia y producción cultural en Ayacucho 1900–1950." In *La tradición andina en tiempos modernos*, edited by Hiroyasu Tomoeda and Luis Millones, 133–58. Osaka: National Museum of Ethnology.
———. 2007. "Las veladas literario-musicales como espacios de construcción de identidades en Ayacucho del siglo XX: Elementos de la historia cultural regional." In *El desarrollo de las ciencias sociales en Ayacucho: la Universidad Nacional de San Cristóbal de Huamanga*, edited by Luis Millones, Jefrey Gamarra, and José Ochatoma Paravicino, 169–78. Lima: Fondo Editorial de la Facultad de Ciencias Sociales, UNMSM.
———. 2010. *Generación, memoria y exclusión: La construcción de representaciones sobre los estudiantes de la Universidad de Huamanga (Ayacucho, 1959–2006)*. Huamanga: UNSCH.
García Canclini, Néstor. 2001. *Consumers and Citizens: Globalization and Multicultural Conflicts*. Minneapolis: University of Minnesota Press.
García, José Uriel. 1973. *El nuevo indio*. Lima: Editorial Universo.
García Miranda, Juan José. 1991. *Huamanga en los cantos de arrieros y viajantes*. Lima: Lluvia Editores.
García Miranda, Juan José, and Jorge Wong Gutiérrez. 1999. *Ayacucho canta y baila*. Lima: Instituto Nacional de Cultura, Club Departamental Ayacucho, Comisión XLVII Jornadas Ayacuchanas.
García Zárate, Raúl. 1973. *Raúl García y su guitarra andina* [album cover text]. Sono Radio LP SE 9326. Lima: Sono Radio.
———. 1979. *Recital folklórico* [album cover text]. Sono Radio LP SE 9558. Lima: Sono Radio.
García Zárate, Raúl, and Javier Echecopar. 1988. *Música para guitarra del Perú*. Lima: Saywa Centro Peruano de Música.
Ginsburg, Faye D., Lila Abu-Lughod, and Brian Larkin. 2002. "Introduction." In *Media Worlds: Anthropology on New Terrain*, edited by Faye D. Ginsburg, Lila Abu-Lughod, and Brian Larkin, 1–56. Berkeley and Los Angeles: University of California Press.

Glave, Luis Miguel, and Jaime Urrutia. 2000. "Radicalismo político en élites regionales: Ayacucho 1930–1956." *Debate Agrario* 31: 1–37.
González Holguín, Diego, and Raúl Porras Barrenechea. 1952. *Vocabulario de la lengua general de todo el Perú llamada lengua qquichua o del Inca*. Lima: Impr. Santa María.
Gootenberg, P. 1991. "Population and Ethnicity in Early Republican Peru: Some Revisions." *Latin American Research Review* 26 (3): 109–57.
Gorriti Ellenbogen, Gustavo. 1999. *The Shining Path: A History of the Millenarian War in Peru*. Chapel Hill: University of North Carolina Press.
Gradante, William. 2007–12. "Huayno." *Grove Music Online*. http://www.oxfordmusiconline.com/subscriber/article/grove/music/13458.
Grandin, Ingemar. 2005. "The Soundscape of the Radio: Engineering *Modern Songs* and Superculture in Nepal." In Green and Porcello, *Wired for Sound*, 222–44.
Greene, Paul D. 2002. "Nepal's *Lok Pop* Music: Representations of the Folk, Tropes of Memory, and Studio Technologies." *Asian Music* 34 (1): 43–65.
———. 2005. "Mixed Messages: Unsettled Cosmopolitanisms in Nepali Pop." In Green and Porcello, *Wired for Sound*, 198–221.
Greene, Paul D., and Thomas Porcello. 2005. *Wired for Sound: Engineering and Technologies in Sonic Cultures*. Middletown, Conn.: Wesleyan University Press.
Green, Shane. 2006. "Negotiating Multicultural Citizenship and Ethnic Politics in 21st Century Latin America." In *Latin America after Neoliberalism: Turning the Tide in the 21st century?*, edited by Eric Hershberg and Fred Rosen, 276–97. New York: New Press.
Habermas, Jürgen. (1959) 1989. *The Structural Transformation of the Public Sphere: An Inquiry into a Category of Bourgeois Society*. Cambridge: MIT Press.
Haeberli, Joerg. 1979. "Twelve Nasca Panpipes: A Study." *Ethnomusicology* 23 (1): 57–74.
Hale, Charles R. 2002. "Does Multiculturalism Menace? Governance, Cultural Rights and the Politics of Identity in Guatemala." *Journal of Latin American Studies* 34:485–524.
———. 2006. *Más que un Indio = More than an Indian: Racial Ambivalence and Neoliberal Multiculturalism in Guatemala*. Santa Fe: School of American Research Press.
Hale, Charles R., and Rosamel Millamán. 2006. "Cultural Agency and Political Struggle in the Era of the Indio Permitido." In *Cultural Agency in the Americas*, edited by Doris Sommer, 281–304. Durham: Duke University Press.
Hall, Stuart. 1973. *Encoding and Decoding in the Television Discourse*. Birmingham: University of Birmingham.
Hall, Stuart, and Paul du Gay. 1996. *Questions of Cultural Identity*. London: Sage.
Handler, Richard, and Joyce Linnekin. 1984. "Tradition, Genuine or Spurious." *Journal of American Folklore* 97: 273–90.
Hayes, Joy Elizabeth. 2000. *Radio Nation: Communication, Popular Culture, and Nationalism in Mexico*. Tucson: University of Arizona Press.
Hebdige, Dick. 1979. *Subculture: The Meaning of Style*. London: Methuen.
Hendy, David. 2000. "Pop Music Radio in the Public Service: BBC Radio 1 and New Music in the 1990s." *Media, Culture & Society* 22 (6): 743–61.
Hennion, Antoine. 1983. "The Production of Success: An Anti-Musicology of the Pop Song." *Popular Music* 3:158–93.
———. 1989. "An Intermediary between Production and Consumption: The Producer of Popular Music." *Science, Technology and Human Values* 14 (4): 400–424.
Hennion, Antoine, and Cecile Méadel. 1986. "Programming Music: Radio as Mediator." *Media, Culture & Society* 8 (3): 281–303.
Hilmes, Michele. 1997. *Radio Voices: American Broadcasting, 1922–1952*. Minneapolis: University of Minnesota Press.

———. 2002. "Rethinking Radio." In Hilmes and Loviglio, *Radio Reader*, 1–20.
Hilmes, Michele, and Jason Loviglio. 2002a. "Introduction." In Hilmes and Loviglio, *Radio Reader*, xi–xv.
———, eds. 2002b. *Radio Reader: Essays in the Cultural History of Radio*. New York: Routledge.
Himpele, Jeff D. 2008. *Circuits of Culture: Media, Politics, and Indigenous Identity in the Andes*. Minneapolis: University of Minnesota Press.
Hirschkind, Charles. 2006. *The Ethical Soundscape: Cassette Sermons and Islamic Counterpublics*. New York: Columbia University Press.
Hobsbawm, Eric, and Terence Ranger. 1983. *The Invention of Tradition*. Cambridge: Cambridge University Press.
Howard, Philip N., and Steve Jones. 2004. *Society Online: The Internet in Context*. Thousand Oaks, Calif.: Sage.
Hurtado Suarez, Wilfredo. 1995. *Chicha peruana: música de los nuevos migrantes*. Lima: ECO, Grupo de Investigaciones Económicas.
Itier, César. 2007. *El hijo del oso: La literatura oral quechua de la región del Cuzco*. Lima: IFEA, Instituto de Estudios Peruanos, Fondo Editorial de la Pontificia Universidad Católica del Perú, and Fondo Editorial de la Universidad Nacional Mayor de San Marcos.
Itier, César, and Nemesio Zúñiga Cazorla. 1995. *El teatro Quechua en el Cuzco*. Lima: Institut Français d'études andines/Centro de Estudios Regionales Andinos "Bartolomé de las Casas."
Jackson, John A. 1991. *Big Beat Heat: Alan Freed and the Early Years of Rock and Roll*. New York: Schirmer Books.
Jack, Wolfman. 1995. *Have Mercy! Confessions of the Original Rock 'n' Roll Animal*. New York: Warner Books.
Johnson, Randal. 1993. "Editor's Introduction: Pierre Bourdieu on Art, Literature, and Culture." In *The Field of Cultural Production: Essays on Art and Literature*, edited by Pierre Bourdieu and Randal Johnson, 1–25. New York: Columbia University Press.
Jottar, Berta. 2009a. "The Acoustic Body: Rumba Guarapachanguera and Abakuá Sociality in Central Park." *Latin American Music Review* 30 (1): 1–24.
———. 2009b. "Zero Tolerance and Central Park Rumba Cabildo Politics." *Liminalities: A Journal of Performance Studies* 5: 1–24.
Kingdom of the Sun: Peru's Inca Heritage. 1969. Nonesuch LP H-72029. New York: Nonesuch.
Knauft, Bruce M. 2002. *Critically Modern: Alternatives, Alterities, Anthropologies*. Bloomington: Indiana University Press.
Koc Menard, Nathalie. 2001. "Recomposición de la ciudad de Huamanga." In *Baldomero Alejos: Ayacucho, 1924–1976*, ed. Mayu Mohanna, 129–32. Lima: ICPNA.
Kunreuther, Laura. 2006. "Technologies of the Voice: FM Radio, Telephone, and the Nepali Diaspora in Kathmandu." *Cultural Anthropology* 21 (3): 323–53.
Lacey, Kate. 2002. "Radio in the Great Depression: Promotional Culture, Public Service, and Propaganda." In Hilmes and Loviglio, *Radio Reader*, 21–40.
Laird, Tracey E. W. 2005. *Louisiana Hayride: Radio and Roots Music along the Red River*. Oxford: Oxford University Press.
Land Vásquez, Ladislao H. 1992. "Los caminos de la música: Los géneros populares andinos en un medio urbano." Bachelor's thesis, Universidad Nacional Mayor de San Marcos.
Larkin, Brian. 2008. *Signal and Noise: Media, Infrastructure, and Urban Culture in Nigeria*. Durham: Duke University Press.

León, Javier. 1997. "El que no tiene de inga, tiene de mandinga: Negotiating Traditon and Ethnicity in Peruvian Criollo Popular Music." Master's thesis, University of Texas at Austin.

———. 2003. "The Aestheticization of Tradition: Professional Afroperuvian Musicians, Cultura Reclamation, and Artistic Interpretation." Ph.D. diss., University of Texas at Austin.

Liechty, Mark. 2003. *Suitably Modern: Making Middle-Class Culture in a New Consumer Society*. Princeton, NJ: Princeton University Press.

Límaco, César Augusto. 1959. "Homenaje al 'Centro Cultural Ayacucho.'" *Revista Huamanga* 25: 33–34.

Limansky, Nicholas. 2008. *Yma Sumac: The Art behind the Legend.* New York: YBK.

Lipsitz, George. 1994. *Dangerous Crossroads: Popular Music, Postmodernism, and the Poetics of Place.* London: Verso.

Lloréns Amico, José Antonio. 1983. *Música popular en Lima: Criollos y andinos.* Lima: Instituto de Estudios Peruanos.

———. 1990. "Voces provincianas en Lima: Migrantes andinos y comunicación radial." *Revista Peruana de Ciencias Sociales* 2 (1): 119–54.

———. 1991. "Andean Voices on Lima Airwaves: Highland Migrants and Radio Broadcasting in Peru." *Studies in Latin American Popular Culture* 10: 177–89.

Lomnitz, Claudio. 2009. "Tiempo mexicano: Transnacionalidad y frontera en la formación de ladependencia como forma cultural." Paper given at the Thirteenth Congreso de Antropología en Colombia: Antropología y nuevas experiencias sociales, September 30–October 3, Bogotá.

Mangin, William. 1964. "Clubes de provincianos en Lima." In *Estudios sobre la cultura del Perú*, 298–305. Lima: Universidad Nacional Mayor de San Marcos.

Mannheim, Bruce. 1986. "Popular Song and Popular Grammar, Poetry and Metalanguage." *Word* 37 (1–2): 45–75.

Manuel, Peter. 1991. "Latin Music in the United States: Salsa and the Mass Media." *Journal of Communication* 41 (1): 104–16.

———. 1993. *Cassette Culture: Popular Music and Technology in North India.* Chicago: University of Chicago Press.

———. 2006. *Caribbean Currents: Caribbean Music from Rumba to Reggae.* Philadelphia: Temple University Press.

Matos Mar, José. 1968. "Dominación, desarrollos desiguales y pluralismo en la sociedad y cultura peruana." In *Perú problema: Cinco ensayos*, edited by José Matos Mar, 13–52. Lima: Instituto de Estudios Peruanos.

———. 1984. *Desborde popular y crisis del estado: El nuevo rostro del Perú en la década de 1980.* Lima: Instituto de Estudios Peruanos.

Mayer, Enrique. 1970. "Mestizo e indio: El contexto social de las relaciones interétnicas." In *El Indio y el poder en el Perú rural*, edited by José Matos Mar, 87–152. Lima: Instituto de Estudios Peruanos.

———. 2009. *Ugly Stories of the Peruvian Agrarian Reform.* Durham: Duke University Press.

Mazzarella, William. 2003. *Shoveling Smoke: Advertising and Globalization in Contemporary India.* Durham: Duke University Press.

———. 2004. "Culture, Globalization, Mediation." *Annual Review of Anthropology* 33 (1): 345–67.

McCann, Bryan. 2004. *Hello, Hello Brazil: Popular Music in the Making of Modern Brazil.* Durham: Duke University Press.

Meintjes, Louise. 2003. *Sound of Africa! Making Music Zulu in a South African Studio.* Durham: Duke University Press.

Méndez Gastelmundi, Cecilia. 1993. *Incas sí, indios no: Apuntes para el estudio del nacionalismo criollo en el Perú.* Lima: Instituto de Estudios Peruanos.

Mendoza, Zoila S. 2000. *Shaping Society through Dance: Mestizo Ritual Performance in the Peruvian Andes.* Chicago: University of Chicago Press.

———. 2008. *Creating Our Own: Folklore, Performance, and Identity in Cuzco, Peru.* Durham: Duke University Press.

Meneses Rivas, Max. 1998. *La utopia urbana: El movimiento de pobladores en el Perú.* Lima: Brandon Enterprises Editores.

Middleton, Richard. 1990. *Studying Popular Music.* Milton Keynes: Open University Press.

Miller, Daniel. 1994. *Modernity, an Ethnographic Approach: Dualism and Mass Consumption in Trinidad.* Oxford: Berg.

———. 1995. "Consumption and Commodities." *Annual Review of Anthropology* 24: 141–61.

Miller, Kiri. 2008. "Grove Street Grimm: *Grand Theft Auto* and Digital Folklore." *Journal of American Folklore* 121 (481): 255–85.

———. 2012. *Playing Along: Digital Games, YouTube, and Virtual Performance.* New York: Oxford University Press.

Millones, Luis. 2005. "La nostalgia del pasado glorioso: Ayacucho 1919–1959." In *Pasiones y desencuentros en la cultura andina*, edited by Luis Millones and Hiroyasu Tomoeda, 195–232. Lima: Fondo Editorial del Congreso de la República.

Miró Quesada, Aurelio. (1938) 2004. "Ayacucho." In *Antología de Huamanga*, 202–21. Lima: Fundación Manuel J. Bustamante. Citations refer to the 2004 edition.

Mishkin, Bernard. 1963. "The Contemporary Quechua." In *Handbook of South American Indians*, edited by Julian H. Steward, 2:411–500. New York: Cooper Square.

Montoya, Rodrigo, Luis Montoya, and Edwin Montoya. 1997. *La sangre de los cerros: Antología de la poesía quechua que se canta en el Perú (Urqukunapa yawarnin).* Lima: Universidad Nacional Federico Villareal.

The Secret Museum of Mankind, vol. 4. 1997. Yazoo CD 7010. United States: Yazoo Records.

Murray, Matthew. 2002. "'The Tendency to Deprave and Corrupt Morals': Regulation and Irregular Sexuality in Golden Age Radio Comedy." In Hilmes and Loviglio, *Radio Reader*, 135–56.

Nabeshima, Hirotsugu. 1992. "Radio Tawantinsuyo, Peru." *LA DXing* 5: 66–67.

Negus, Keith. 1992. *Producing Pop: Culture and Conflict in the Popular Music Industry.* London: E. Arnold.

———. 1999. *Music Genres and Corporate Cultures.* London: Routledge.

Neira, Hugo. 2004. "Del desborde de Matos Mar a los desbordes: Llave y polladas—retorno a la cuestión de la anomia." In *Desborde popular y crisis del estado: Veinte años después*, edited by José Matos Mar, 163–82. Lima: Fondo Editorial del Congreso del Perú.

Nettl, Bruno. 1983. *The Study of Ethnomusicology: Twenty-nine Issues and Concepts.* Urbana: University of Illinois Press.

Neuenfeldt, Karl. 2001. "Cultural Politics and a Music Recording Project: Producing Strike Em! Contemporary Voices from the Torres Strait." *Journal of Intercultural Studies* 22 (2): 133–45.

———. 2005. "Nigel Pegrum, 'Didjeridu-Friendly Sections,' and What Constitutes an 'Indigenous' CD: An Australian Case Study of Producing 'World Music' Recordings." In Greene and Porcello, *Wired for Sound*, 84–102.

Neyazi, Taberez Ahmed. 2010. "Cultural Imperialism or Vernacular Modernity? Hindi Newspapers in a Globalizing India." *Media, Culture & Society* 32 (6): 907–24.

Novak, David. 2010. "Playing Off Site: The Untranslation of *onkyō*." *Asian Music: Journal of the Society for Asian Music* 41 (1): 36–59.

Nugent, Guillermo. 1992. *El laberinto de la choledad*. Lima: Fundación Friedrich Ebert.

Núñez Rebaza, Lucy. 1990. *La vigencia de la danza de tijeras en Lima metropolitana*. Lima: Pontificia Universidad Católica del Perú.

Olsen, Dale A. 1986. "Towards a Musical Atlas of Peru." *Ethnomusicology* 30 (3): 394–412.

———. 2002. *Music of El Dorado: The Ethnomusicology of Ancient South American Cultures*. Gainesville: University Press of Florida.

Omi, Michael, and Howard Winant. (1986) 1994. *Racial Formation in the United States: From the 1960s to the 1980s*. 2nd ed. New York: Routledge & Kegan Paul. Citations refer to the 1994 edition.

Orlove, Benjamin S. 1998. "Down to Earth: Race and Substance in the Andes." *Bulletin of Latin American Research* 17 (2): 207–22.

Orozco, Crescencio, and Trio Ayacucho. 1982. *Juntos como siempre* [album cover text]. Discos Sono Radio LP SE 9767. Lima: Sono Radio.

Ortner, Sherry B. 1999. *The Fate of "Culture": Geertz and Beyond*. Berkeley and Los Angeles: University of California Press.

Pacini Hernandez, Deborah. 1995. *Bachata: A Social History of Dominican Popular Music*. Philadelphia: Temple University Press.

Pajuelo, Ramón. 2007. *Reinventando comunidades imaginadas: Movimientos indígenas, nación y procesos sociopolíticos en los países centroandinos*. Lima: Instituto Francés de Estudios Andinos, UMIFRE 17, and Instituto de Estudios Peruanos.

Pallares, Amalia. 2002. *From Peasant Struggles to Indian Resistance: The Ecuadorian Andes in the Late Twentieth Century*. Norman: University of Oklahoma Press.

Palma, Ricardo. (1893) 2009. *Tradiciones peruanas II*. Barcelona: Linkgua Ediciones S.L. Citations refer to the 2009 edition.

Palmer, David Scott. 1994. *The Shining Path of Peru*. 2nd ed. New York: St. Martin's Press.

Parker, David Stuart. 1998. *The Idea of the Middle Class: White-Collar Workers and Peruvian Society, 1900–1950*. University Park: Pennsylvania State University Press.

Parra Carreño, Alfredo. 1938. "Los pokras son kechuas o aymaras?" *Revista Huamanga* 15: 4–19.

———. 1940. "Cantos de Huamanga." *Revista Huamanga* 36–37: 22–27.

———. 1945. "Centro Cultural Ayacuchano." *Revista Huamanga* 62: 37–40.

Parra Carreño, Alfredo, Néstor Cabrera, and Manuel J. Pozo. 1939. "Audición musical." *Revista Huamanga* 27–30: 22–35.

Party, Daniel. 2006. *Bolero and Balada as the Guilty Pleasures of Latin American Pop*. Ph.D diss., University of Pennsylvania.

Peña, Manuel H. 1985. *The Texas-Mexican Conjunto: History of a Working-Class Music*. Austin: University of Texas Press.

———. 1999. *The Mexican American Orquesta: Music, Culture, and the Dialectic of Conflict*. Austin: University of Texas Press.

Pereyra Chávez, Nelson E. 2007. "Sociedad, identidad e imágenes: La fotografía de Ayacucho (1863–1940)." In *El desarrollo de las ciencias sociales en Ayacucho: La Universidad Nacional de San Cristóbal de Huamanga*, edited by Luis Millones, Jefrey Gamarra, and José Ochatoma Paravicino, 127–58. Lima: Fondo Editorial de la Facultad de Ciencias Sociales, UNMSM.

Perlacios Campos, Juan Moisés. N.d. *Personalidades de Huamanga*. Lima: Nova Graf.
Peterson, Richard A. 1978. "The Production of Cultural Change: The Case of Contemporary Country Music." *Social Research* 45 (2): 293–314.
———. 1997. *Creating Country Music: Fabricating Authenticity*. Chicago: University of Chicago Press.
Pinney, Christopher. 2001. "Introduction: Public, Popular, and Other Cultures." In *Pleasure and the Nation: The History, Politics, and Consumption of Public Culture in India*, edited by Rachel Dwyer and Christopher Pinney, 1–34. New Delhi: Oxford University Press.
Pisani, Michael. 2005. *Imagining Native America in Music*. New Haven: Yale University Press.
Poole, Deborah. 1997. *Vision, Race, and Modernity: A Visual Economy of the Andean Image World*. Princeton: Princeton University Press.
Poole, Deborah, and Gerardo Rénique. 1992. *Peru: Time of Fear*. London: Latin American Bureau.
"Por los fueros de la tradición". 1955. *Revista Huamanga* 85: 1–2.
Pozo, Manuel J. 1934. "Discurso en la fundación." *Revista Huamanga* 1: 1–4.
———. 1954. "Poesía y música vernacular: El triste de nuestros altiplanos y el huayno de la ciudad." *Revista Huamanga* 83: 11–18.
Quijano, Aníbal. 1980. *Dominación y cultura*. Lima: Mosca Azul Editores.
Quispe Lázaro, Arturo. 2000. "Rossy War y la chicha amazónica." *Revista Quehacer* 125: 106–11.
———. 2002. "La tecnocumbia: Integración o discriminación solapada?" *Revista Quehacer* 135: 107–13.
Radway, Janice A. 1984. *Reading the Romance: Women, Patriarchy, and Popular Literature*. Chapel Hill: University of North Carolina Press.
Ríos, Fernando. 2008. "La Flûte Indienne: The Early History of Andean Folkloric-Popular Music in France and Its Impact on *Nueva Canción*." *Latin American Music Review* 29 (2): 145–81.
Ritter, Jonathan. 2002. "Siren Songs: Ritual and Revolution in the Peruvian Andes." *British Journal of Ethnomusicology* 11 (1): 9–42.
———. 2006. "A River of Blood: Music, Memory, and Violence in Ayacucho, Peru." Ph.D. diss., University of California, Los Angeles.
Riva-Agüero, José de la. (1955) 1995. *Paisajes peruanos*. Lima: Pontificia Universidad Catolica del Peru, Instituto Riva-Agüero.
———. (1955) 2004. "Iglesias y casas, y aspecto general de la ciudad." In *Antología de Huamanga*, 181–191. Lima: Fundación Manuel J. Bustamante. Citations refer to the 2004 edition.
Roel Mendizábal, Pedro. 2000. "De folklore a cultura híbridas: Rescatando raíces, redefiniendo fronteras entre nos/otros." In Degregori, *No hay país más diverso*, 74–122. Desarrollo de las Ciencias Sociales en el Perú.
Roel Pineda, Josafat. 1959. "El wayno del Cuzco." *Folklore Americano* 6 (7): 129–245.
Rofel, Lisa B. 1994. "Yearnings: Televisual Love and Melodramatic Politics in Contemporary China." *American Ethnologist* 21 (4): 700–722.
Romero, Raúl R. 1999. "Andean Peru." In *Music in Latin American Culture: Regional Traditions*, edited by John M. Schechter, 383–423. New York: Schirmer Books.
———. 2001. *Debating the Past: Music, Memory, and Identity in the Andes*. New York: Oxford University Press.

———. 2002. "Panorama de los estudios sobre música andina en el Perú." In *Sonidos Andinos: Una antología de la música campesina del Perú*, edited by Raúl R. Romero and Rosa Alarco, 11–70. Lima: Pontificia Universidad Católica del Perú, Instituto Riva-Agüero, Centro de Etnomusicología Andina.

Rothenbuhler, Eric W., and Tom McCourt. 2002. "Radio Redefines Itself, 1947–1962." In Hilmes and Loviglio, *Radio Reader*, 367–87.

Sakakeeny, Matt. 2010. "'Under the Bridge': An Orientation to Soundscapes in New Orleans." *Ethnomusicology* 54 (1): 2–27.

Salazar Bondy, Sebastián. 1964. *Lima la horrible*. Lima: Populibros.

Salcedo, José María. 2000. "La misma chicha con distinto tecno." *Revista Quehacer* 125: 92–97.

Samuels, David William. 2004. *Putting a Song on Top of It: Expression and Identity on the San Carlos Apache Reservation*. Tucson: University of Arizona Press.

Sandoval, Pablo. 2000. "Los rostros cambiantes de la ciudad: Cultura urbana y antropología en el Perú." In Degregori, *No hay país más diverso*, 278–329.

Scales, Christopher A. 2002. "The Politics and Aesthetics of Recording." *World of Music* 44 (1): 41–60.

Scannell, Paddy. 1991. *Broadcast Talk*. London: Sage.

Schechter, John Mendell. 1992. *The Indispensable Harp: Historical Development, Modern Roles, Configurations, and Performance Practices in Ecuador and Latin America*. Kent, OH: Kent State University Press.

Simonett, Helena. 2001. *Banda: Mexican Musical Life across Borders*. Middletown, Conn.: Wesleyan University Press.

Sitjar Terre, Ana María. 1939. Letter. *Revista Huamanga* 21: 7–8.

Smulyan, Susan. 1994. *Selling Radio: The Commercialization of American Broadcasting, 1920–1934*. Washington, DC: Smithsonian Institution Press.

Spitulnik, Debra Anne. 1994. "Radio Culture in Zambia: Audiences, Public Words, and the Nation-State." Ph.D. diss., University of Chicago.

Squier, Susan Merrill. 2003. *Communities of the Air: Radio Century, Radio Culture*. Durham: Duke University Press.

Starn, Orin. 1991. "Missing the Revolution: Anthropologists and the War in Peru." *Cultural Anthropology* 6 (1): 63–91.

Stavig, Ward. 1999. *The World of Túpac Amaru: Conflict, Community, and Identity in Colonial Peru*. Lincoln: University of Nebraska Press.

Stein, Steve. 1986. *Lima Obrera, 1900–1930*. Lima: Ediciones El Virrey.

Stern, Steve J. 1982. *Peru's Indian Peoples and the Challenge of Spanish Conquest: Huamanga to 1640*. Madison: University of Wisconsin Press.

Sterne, Jonathan. 2003. *The Audible Past: Cultural Origins of Sound Reproduction*. Durham: Duke University Press.

Stevenson, Robert. 1968. *Music in Aztec and Inca Territory*. Berkeley and Los Angeles: University of California Press.

Stobart, Henry. 2006. *Music and the Poetics of Production in the Bolivian Andes*. Aldershot, England: Ashgate.

Stokes, Martin. 2004. "Music and the Global Order." *Annual Review of Anthropology* 33 (1): 47–72.

Straw, Will. 1991. "Systems of Articulation, Logics of Change: Communities and Scenes in Popular Music." *Cultural Studies* 5 (3): 368–88.

Sturm, Circe. 2002. *Blood Politics: Race, Culture, and Identity in the Cherokee Nation of Oklahoma*. Berkeley and Los Angeles: University of California Press.

Takenaka, Ayumi, Karsten Paerregaard, and Ulla Berg. 2010. "Peruvian Migration in a Global Context." *Latin American Perspectives* 37 (5): 3–11.

Tamayo Herrera, José. 1982. *Historia social e indigenismo en el altiplano.* San Isidro: Ediciones Treintaitrés.

Tarica, Estelle. 2008. *Inner Life of Mestizo Nationalism.* Minneapolis: University of Minnesota Press.

Templeman, Robert W. 1996. "Renacimiento de la saya: El rol que juega la música en el movimiento negro en Bolivia." *Anales de la Reunión Anual de Etnología, 1995,* 2: 89–94.

Thornton, Sarah. 1996. *Club Cultures: Music, Media, and Subcultural Capital.* Hanover, NH: University Press of New England.

Thurner, Mark. 1997. *From Two Republics to One Divided: Contradictions of Postcolonial Nationmaking in Andean Peru.* Durham: Duke University Press.

Trio Ayacucho. [c. 1966–70]. *Remembranza huamanguina* [album cover text]. Discos Sono Radio LP SE 9483. Lima: Discos Sono Radio.

Tsing, Anna Lowenhaupt. 2005. *Friction: An Ethnography of Global Connection.* Princeton: Princeton University Press.

Tucker, Joshua. 2011. "Producing the Andean Voice: Popular Music, Folkloric Performance, and the Possessive Investment in Indigeneity." Unpublished manuscript.

———. 2013. "From *The World of the Poor* to the Beaches of 'Eisha': Chicha, Cumbia, and the Search for a Popular Subject in Peru." In *All Cumbias, the Cumbia: The Transnationalization of a Latin American Musical Genre,* edited by Héctor Fernández L'Hoeste and Pablo Vila. Durham: Duke University Press.

Turino, Thomas. 1984. "The Urban-Mestizo Charango Tradition in Southern Peru: A Statement of Shifting Identity." *Ethnomusicology* 28 (2): 253–70.

———. 1988. "Music of Andean Migrants in Lima, Peru: Demographics, Social Power, and Style." *Latin American Music Review* 9 (2): 127–50.

———. 1990. "'Somos el Perú' (We Are Peru): Cumbia Andina and the Children of the Andean Migrants in Lima." *Studies in Latin American Popular Culture* 9: 18–25.

———. 1993. *Moving Away from Silence: Music of the Peruvian Altiplano and the Experience of Urban Migration.* Chicago: University of Chicago Press.

———. 1999. "Signs of Imagination, Identity, and Experience: A Peircian Semiotic Theory for Music." *Ethnomusicology* 43 (2): 221–55.

———. 2000. *Nationalists, Cosmopolitans, and Popular Music in Zimbabwe.* Chicago: University of Chicago Press.

———. 2001. "Music in Latin America." In *Excursions in World Music,* edited by Bruno Nettl, Charles Capwell, Philip V. Bohlman, Isabel K. F. Wong, and Thomas Turino, 227–54. Upper Saddle River, NJ: Prentice Hall.

———. 2003. "Nationalism and Latin American Music: Selected Case Studies and Theoretical Considerations." *Latin American Music Review* 24 (2): 169–209.

———. 2007. *Music in the Andes.* New York: Oxford University Press.

———. 2008. *Music as Social Life: The Politics of Participation.* Chicago: University of Chicago Press.

Turkle, Sherry. 2005. *The Second Self: Computers and the Human Spirit.* Cambridge, MA: MIT Press.

Turow, Joseph. 1990. "The Critical Importance of Mass Communication as a Concept." *Information and Behavior* 3: 9–20.

Urrutia, Jaime. 1994. "Los pocras o el mito de los huamanguinos." In *La diversidad Huamanguina: Tres momentos en sus orígenes,* 26–29. Lima: IEP.

———. 1985. *Huamanga: Región e historia, 1536–1770*. Ayacucho: Universidad Nacional de San Cristóbal de Huamanga.
———. 2001. "Sociedad en Huamanga: Una mirada desde su élite." In *Baldomero Alejos: Ayacucho, 1924–1976*, 120–23. Lima: ICPNA.
van den Berghe, Pierre L., and George P. Primov. 1977. *Inequality in the Peruvian Andes: Class and Ethnicity in Cuzco*. Columbia: University of Missouri Press.
Varallanos, José. 1988. *El condor pasa: Vida y obra de Daniel Alomía Robles, músico, compositor y folklorista*. Lima: Taller Gráfico P. L. Villaneuva.
Vásquez Rodríguez, Chalena, and Abilio Vergara Figueroa. 1988. *Chayraq! Carnaval ayacuchano*. Lima: Centro de Desarrollo Agropecuario/Asociación de Publicaciones Educativas.
———. 1990. *Ranulfo, el hombre*. Lima: Centro de Desarrollo Agropecuario.
Velarde, Hernán, and Raúl García Zárate. 1970. *Recital de guitarra* [album cover text], Sono Radio LP catalog no. SE 9276. Lima: Sono Radio.
Vich, Víctor. 2001. *El discurso de la calle: Los cómicos ambulantes y las tensiones de la modernidad en el Perú*. Lima: Pontificia Universidad Católica del Perú, Universidad del Pacífico, and Instituto de Estudios Peruanos.
———. 2006a. "Dina y Chacalón: El secuestro de la experiencia." *Hueso Húmero* 48 (May): 80–95.
———. 2006b. "Gestionar riesgos: Agencia y maniobra en la política cultural." In Cortés and Vich, *Políticas culturales*, 45–70.
Vilcapoma, José Carlos. 1999. *La quena de todos los tiempos: Alejandro Vivanco, vida y obra*. Lima: Nuevo Mundo Ediciones.
Vivanco, Alejandro. 1971. "El migrante de provincias como intérprete de folklore andino en Lima." Bachelor's thesis, Universidad Nacional Mayor de San Marcos.
———. 1988. *Cien temas del folklore peruano*. Lima: Bendezú.
Wade, Peter. 1993. *Blackness and Race Mixture: The Dynamics of Racial Identity in Colombia*. Baltimore: Johns Hopkins University Press.
———. 1997. *Race and Ethnicity in Latin America*. London: Pluto Press.
Walker, Charles. 1999. *Smoldering Ashes: Cuzco and the Creation of Republican Peru, 1780–1840*. Durham: Duke University Press.
Wallach, Jeremy. 2005. "Engineering Techno-Hybrid Grooves in Two Indonesian Sound Studios." In Greene and Porcello, *Wired for Sound*, 138–55.
Wang, Jennifer Hyland. 2002. "'The Case of the Radio-active Housewife': Relocating Radio in the Age of television." In Hilmes and Loviglio, *Radio Reader*, 343–66.
Wara Céspedes, Gilka. 1984. "New Currents in 'música folklórica' in La Paz, Bolivia." *Latin American Music Review* 5 (2): 217–42.
———. 1993. "'Huayño,' 'Saya' and 'Chuntunqui': Bolivian Identity in the Music of 'Los Kjarkas.'" *Latin American Music Review* 14 (1): 52–101.
Warner, Michael. 2002. "Publics and Counterpublics." *Public Culture* 14 (1): 49–90.
Washburne, Christopher. 2008. *Sounding Salsa: Performing Latin Music in New York City*. Philadelphia: Temple University Press.
Waterman, Christopher Alan. 1990. *Jùjú: A Social History and Ethnography of an African Popular Music*. Chicago: University of Chicago Press.
Webb, Richard. 2009. "El izquierdista Riva-Agüero." *El Comercio*, December 28. http://elcomercio.pe/impresa/notas/izquierdista-riva-aguero/20091228/386744.
Weismantel, Mary. 2001. *Cholas and Pishtacos: Stories of Race and Sex in the Andes*. Chicago: University of Chicago Press.
Weismantel, Mary, and Stephen F. Eisenman. 1998. "Race in the Andes: Global Movements and Popular Ontologies." *Bulletin of Latin American Research* 17 (2): 121–42.

Wightman, Ann M. 1990. *Indigenous Migration and Social Change: The Forasteros of Cuzco, 1570–1720*. Durham: Duke University Press.

Yelvington, Kevin A. 1991. "Ethnicity as Practice? A Comment on Bentley." *Comparative Studies in Society and History* 33 (1): 158–69.

Zúñiga, Pilar. 1999. *La música y los medios de comunicación*. Lima: Universidad de San Martin de Porres, Facultad de Ciencias de la Comunicación.

INDEX

Page numbers in italics *indicate musical examples.*

Abu-Lughod, Lila, 15
"Adíos pueblo de Ayacucho" (huayno), 56, 77, 88, *139*
Afro-Bolivian music, 66, 128, 200n31
Afro-Peruvian music, 52
Ahlkvist, Jarl A., 171–72
Alatrista, Juan (apocryphal figure), 100, 103
Alkoholika, 191n19
"Almendras, ciruelas" (huayno), 87
Almonacid, Saturnino, 106, 122
Alomía Robles, Daniel, 40; "El condor pasa," 45
Alvarado, Taca, 90, 100
Alvizuri, Lúcio, 196n23; "El neoindianismo en Ayacucho," 97–98, 99, 196n32
"Amor, Amor" (huayno), 129–30, *130*
Amor, amor (Hermanos Gaitán Castro album), 129–31
"Amor herido" (huayno), 173
Amor Serrano (telenovela), 177, 178
Áncash, huayno from, 55, 72, 191n23
Anchorena, Carlos Alberto: as composer, 103, 107–8, 196n34, 196–97n39; "Disertación sobre música peruana," 105; musical interests, 81–82, 83, 84, 94, 106, 195n21; *tradiciones* written by, 102
Andean cadence, 189n5, 200n32
Andean identity: categories used, 22–24, 187n18, 194nn6–7; class and, 79–80, 82–84, 94–96, 182–84; competing narratives, 184; competing visions, 5, 19, 23–24, 51–52; cumbia as element in, 178–79; dress and, 115–16, 182–83;
in Ecuador and Bolivia, 185n2 (intro.); huayno as marker, 12, 70–71, 89, 93–94, 178–79; *indigenismo* movement and, 6, 30–33, 49–50, 79–80, 96–99, 106–7; local music genres, 189n3; micropolitics of, 187n13; modernity and, 15–17, 114; pan-Andean music and, 50–51, 131–32; racialization of, 20–21, 79–80, 82–84, 106–7, 110, 183, 187n16, 194n3; second-generation migrants' taste shifts, 157; taste distinctions and, 12; *telurismo* and, 104–5
Andean pentatonicism, theory of, 190n8
andinismo movement, 99
andino, lo, 5
Angulo, Víctor, 116
animadores, 73, 74–75
Apus, Los, 179
araskaska dance, 104
Arequipa, recording studios in, 126
Argentinean *zamba*, 61
Arguedas, José María: on Andean mestizo cultures, 187n15; "Basic Notes on the Popular Religious Art and the Mestizo Culture of Huamanga," 85–86, 197n40; commentary on García Zárate's guitar playing, 123–24; on huayno as identity marker, 40, 54; role in Peruvian record industry, 56, 186n4, 191n27; writings on huayno, 105
Argumedo, Isaac, 157, 161, 162, 204n37
Arone, Martín, 53
Arone brothers, 204n36
Arriola, Pedro, 66, 131, 133, 134, 142

Arriola, Rodolfo, 2
Así cantan los pueblos andinos del Perú (radio program), 157
Ayacuchano huayno: aesthetics of, 54–55, 58–60, 71, 77, 103–6, 111, 140–44; arrangements of, 124; bilingual texts in, 54; class and, 24, 29–36, 94–96, 116–17, 124–25, 135, 144; composers of, 107–8; contemporary, 64–66, 112, 115, 128–44, 153, 168–70, 179–80; dancing and, 89, 128; disidentification of, 168–70; Dolby JR recordings of, 126–44; early twentieth-century performers, 87, 103; elements of, 6; elite nature of, 54, 60–61, 70, 79, 94–96, 107–8, 116–17, 124–25, 135, 181, 183, 197n44; foreign sound recordings of, 55–56; golden age of, 115–26; guitar technique, 41, 54, 58–59, 88–89, 90, 120–24; historical factors in, 4–5, 119; *huayno criollo* as term for, 195n9; huayno norteño aesthetics compared with, 23, 73–76, 142–43; indigenous huayno compared with, 54, 189–90n6; institutions dedicated to maintenance of, 59; justification of new elements in, 141–42; Lima performances of, 4, 12, 57–58, 61, 89, 111; mainstream positioning of, 133–35; musicians' nicknames, 190n9; non-Ayacucho performers of, 143–44; pan-Andean music influences in, 65–66, 114, 128–30, 141, 169–70, 173, 179; political subjects, 61–64, 111, 127–44; public performance of, 95–96, 107–8, 118–19, 169; radio broadcasts of, 3, 12, 13, 14–15, 145, 153, 160–68; recording studios' standard accompaniment of, 116, 133; recordings of, 2, 13–15, 115–44, 199n13; revival of, 7, 29–30; rural variants, 60; salons and, 91, 93–96, 102, 120, 197n46; style evolution, 2–3, 51–52; testimonial songs, 64, 111, 192–93n34; vocal interpretation in, 54; waves of popularity, 57, 64; writings on, 102–8. See also specific composers and performers
"Ayacucho" (pan-Andean song by IAO), 174
Ayacucho (García Zárate album), 117, 123–24
Ayacucho, Battle of, 26, 80, 84
Ayacucho, Peru: cantinas and *tiendas* as performance venues, 89–90; churches in, 26–27; conservatory, 59; early twentieth-century decline, 79, 80–81; economic problems and employment, 27; education's importance in, 27–28, 70, 91–92, 95, 96–99; emigration of aristocracy from, 83; geography of, 27; historical factors, 4–5, 26–30; *huamanguino* identity, 21–22, 79–110; huayno norteño live performances, 169–70; leftist activity in, 85; Lima's influence on, 4; musical life in twentieth-century, 6, 51–52; musical practice in early twentieth-century, 86–93; newspapers in, 195n18; pan-Andean music in, 200n30; performance venues for huayno, 192n30; pianos valued in, 81–82, 194n5; Pokras and, 101–2; population increase, 28; Quechua language spoken in, 44; race, class, and status in, 80–84, 94–96, 106–7; radio broadcasts in, 157–60; sacred music in, 104; salons in, 91, 93–96, 102, 107, 197n46; serenades in, 90–91; Shining Path guerrillas and, 26, 28–29, 61–64, 127, 188nn24–26
Ayacucho en el corazón de todos (radio show), 149, 160–63
"Ayla," 173
Ayvar, Luis, 173

balada, 36; aesthetics of, 114; Ayacuchano huayno and, 65; contemporary Ayacuchano huayno influenced by, 130–31, 136–38
bandurria(s): in Ayacuchano huayno, 89; in *indigenista* music, 46
Bareto, 178
Bedrillana, Ángel, 126, 132–33, 199n16, 201n3, 204n39
Bedrillana, Castro, 201n3
Bedrillana, Keti, 171–72, 175
Benavente Díaz, Julio, 195n16
Benavides, Óscar R., 154
Bendezú, Luis Milóm, 196n23
Bendix, Regina, 193n41
Bolívar, Simón, 84
Bolivia: Andeanness in, 185n2 (intro.), 186–87n12; pan-Andean music in, 66; *takirari* genre, 61; *tundiki* genre, 128
bombos: in contemporary Ayacuchano huayno, 65; in pan-Andean music, 50–51
Bourdieu, Pierre, 11–12, 204n3

Bravo de Rueda, Jorge: "Vírgenes de sol," 45
Brazil, *mestizaje* [*mestiçagem*] in, 187n16
Burga, Manuel, 118
Bustamante, Emilio, 202n17
Bustamante, Manuel: "Breves referencias sobre la música vernacular," 94, 103–4, 195n21, 197n41; on CCA founding board, 196n23; as performer, 196n34; *tradiciones* written by, 102
Bustamante, María Luísa, 117–18, 190n14

Cabrera, Néstor, 108, 191n25, 196n23; "Los tunantes," 100
cajón, 189n2
Calderón, Carlota, 202n17
Camasca family, 60
Camassi, Ernesto: Arguedas's influence on, 197n40; on *decente* guitar tuning, 190n13, 191n25, 197n46, 200n35; García Zárate's style viewed by, 125; huayno norteño and chicha criticized by, 75, 182; live performance by, 87–88; radio show, 203n24; in Trio Ayacucho, 119–20, 131, 190n11, 200n20
Campo de Marte bandshell (Lima), 133–34, 144
"Canción indígena" (*indigenia* salon piece), 94
Cárdenas, Celmira, 195n22
Caribeña, La (Ayacucho radio station), 147–48, 170
carnaval, 189n3, 200n27
Carranza, Luis, 40, 105
Castro, Max, 126, 170, 201n3, 204n39
Cavero, Luis, 196n23
Cavero, Moisés, 98, 196n23; *Qisampi sapan urpikuna*, 196nn27
Cavero Carrasco, Ranulfo, 98–99, 109
Cavero Carrasco, Rómulo, 98–99, 109
ccachua saratipiy, 94
ccachua, 189n3
Ccayanchira, Otoniel, 87, 192n31
"Celia" (*tinku*), 191n19
Centro Cultural Ayacuchano, 6, 92–104; *conjunto filarmónico* project, 106; founding of, 82, 93–95, 196n23; huayno style favored by, 197n44; importance of, 80, 92–93; influence of, 109–10, 197n48; intellectual agenda, 85, 96–99, 118, 121–22, 197n45; purpose of, 95–96; salons, 94–96, 107–8; work of, 84
Centro Qosqo de Arte Nativo, 49

Cevallos, Flora, 202n17
Chacalón, 67, 68, 69, 70–71, 178–79, 182
Chacalón: El ángel de los pobres (miniseries), 70–71, 178–79, 182
charango(s): in Ayacuchano huayno, 54, 88–89; in contemporary Ayacuchano huayno, 65, 129–30, 133, 137; in *indigenista* music, 45, 46; in pan-Andean music, 50–51, 129; in regional huayno, 60
chicha, 6, 66–72; aesthetics, 66, 71, 143; Ayacucho radio broadcasts, 170; changes in, 70–72; class and, 24, 35, 69–70, 182–83; cosmopolitanism of, 67–68, 128, 178; elements in, 66–67; genres influencing, 67; taste and, 181; *technocumbia* and, 193n37; telenovela character as performer of, 178–79, 182
Chiclla, Arturo, 179–80
Chiclla, Rosa, 200n26
"Chiki tuku" (huayno), 42, 42–44, 59–60
Chile, pan-Andean music in, 66
chimaycha, 188n18
"Chipillay Prado" (Falconí huayno), 38, 39–42, 44, 59–60, 192–93n34
cholos, 23, 187n18
Chuchón, Oriol, 90–91, 100
Chuchón Huamaní, Serafina, 90–91, 195n17
"Chullalla sarachamanta" (huayno), 46, 46–49, 52
circulatory loops, 5
class: changes in Ayacucho, 80–84; consumption and, 25–26, 31–32, 36, 153, 158–59; diversity of, 182–83; *indigenismo* and, 30–31, 94–96; taste and, 12, 35–36, 69–70, 71, 73–76, 124–25, 135, 144, 159, 170, 177–79; terms used for, 83. *See also decente*, concept of
Club 9 de diciembre (Ayacucho), 197n46
Coco C (DJ), 162–63
Colegio San Antonio (Ayacucho), 192n30
Colegio San Ramón, 92, 95, 195n19, 196n23
comercial (term), 136, 140–41
Compañía Pachamama, 196n34
Compañía Peruana de Radiofusión S.A., 154
Condorcunca Music Conservatory (Ayacucho), 192n30
"condor pasa, El" (Alomía Robles), 45
"Con el mayor cariño" (huayno), 119, *120*

Conjunto Ancashino Atusparia, 155, 199n14
Conjunto Típico Huaracino, 155
Cooperativa Santa Magdalena (Ayacucho), 192n30
Corantes, Raffo, 173
"Corazón mío" (huayno norteño), 130
Cornejo, Esther, 202n17
Coronado, Florencio, 155, 202-3n19
cosmopolitanism, 15-17, 29-30; of chicha, 67-68, 128, 178; in contemporary Ayacuchano huayno, 112, 128-29, 130-32, 134, 142-43, 168-70; modernization and, 183; as term, 186n9
Costeñitas, Las, 202n17
criollos: Afro-Peruvian musical genres of, 36-37; emigration from highlands, 27, 83-84; intermarriage of, 20; status of, 19, 183, 195n9
Criollos, Los, 154
criollo y tunante (term), 84
Crónica, La, 202n17
Cruz, Fernando, 23, 76, 157-58, 169-70, 203n28
Cruz, Totito, 72
cuarteta, 89
Cuarteto de Cámara Incaico, 155
Cuba, *mestizaje* in, 187n16
"Cuculí" (huayno from Cusco), 190n11
Cuevas, Gilberto, 116, 199n12
cultural production, Bourdieu's studies of, 11-12
cumbia, 178, 184; performances in Lima, 2; rhythm, 67, 67
Cusco, Peru: huaynos of, 106; *indigenismo* movement in, 94, 97, 196n33; pan-Andean music in, 65-66, 128; Radio Cusco in, 154; Radio Tawantinsuyo, 155; recording studios in, 126

Damaris, 180
Dan, Leo, 157
Daryx, Ricardo, 201n6
decente, concept of: applied to Ayacuchano huayno, 135; concert attendance and, 61; guitar tuning and, 190n13; mestizos and, 20-21, 23-24, 25, 27, 28, 83; second-generation migrants, 69
De la Cadena, Marisol, 185n3 (intro.), 196n26
del Barco, Osmán, 196n23

Delgado, Rosita, 202n17
del Pino, Juan José: on CCA founding board, 196n23; "Cual es el sentido psicológico de la música ayacuchana?," 105; "Momumentos coloniales de Huamanga," 99; salons at home of, 196n34; *tradiciones* written by, 102, 106
Demonios del Corocochay, Los, 193n38
despedidas, 86-88
Díaz, Eladio, 139-41, 142-43
DINSA label, 125
disc jockeys in Peru: importance of, 7; influence of, 13, 148-49, 160-63, 171-76, 175; as mediators, 149-53, 160-68, 171-76, 175, 202n11; style of, 152-53, 163-64; techniques of, 4, 167-68
Discos Smith, 115, 198n4
Dolby (later Dolly) JR label, 14-15, 126-44; audience base, 127, 138-39; business model of, 126-27; competitors to, 135; decentralized recording process, 115; founding of, 126; genre identity construction at, 113-15, 138; influence of, 7; in 1990s, 132-35; promotion of Ayacuchano huayno, 112, 126-45; recording genre mix, 127; renaming of, 138; return to traditionalism, 179-80; tradition vs. innovation at, 136, 139-44
Dolorier, Hugo, 165, 166
Dolorier, Ricardo, 62
Dolorier, Ronald, 165
Dornfeld, Barry, 138
drum machine, in huayno norteño, 73, 74-75
Duo Ayacucho, 136-38, 164; "Paloma, torcaza" as performed by, 137, 137-38
Duo Hermanos García Zárate: Fernández's admiration for, 135; recordings, 60, 117, 120-26, 190n11, 200n25; "Umpa rosas" as performed by, *123*; unique performance qualities, 125. See also García Zárate, Nery; García Zárate, Raúl

Earls, John, 199n15
Echecopar, Javier, 124-25
Ecuador: Andeanness in, 185n2 (intro.), 186-87n12; pan-Andean music in, 66
electric bass: in contemporary Ayacuchano huayno, 133, 142; in huayno norteño, 72-73, 74-75

Escarcena, José Antonio, 197n45
Espinel, Pedro, 202n17
Estación, La (Lima club), 111
Estrellitas, Las, 202n17
estudiantina ensembles, 46, 49–50; Ayacuchano huayno instruction, 59, 92, 118; dated character of, 49; performance of huayno, 60, 89, 199n16; recordings by, 115, 117
Estudiantina Municipal de Ayacucho, 51–52, 92, 108, 121, 191n17, 199n13
Estudiantina Perú, 158, 191n27, 199n14
Estudiantina Típica Ayacuchana, 56, 196n34
"Éxitorama" (radio show), 157
"Expreso Puquio" (huayno), 173, 174

Fajardo, Carmen, 195n22
Fajardo Andía, Gaspar, 199n13
Fajardo de Castro, Magdalena, 93
Falconí, Carlos: Arguedas's influence on, 197n40; childhood of, 89, 91–92, 190n14; contemporary compositions distinguished from traditional music, 189–90n6; on dearth of Ayacuchano huayno radio programming, 159; García Zárate's style viewed by, 125; on his musical motivations, 192–93n34; huaynos composed by, 39–42; huayno style, 43–44, 58; on Peruvian identity categories, 194n6; political huaynos, 61; on popularity of pianos in Ayacucho, 194n5; sound recordings, 64; in Trio Ayacucho, 119–20, 200n20
Falconí, Robert, 89
Feldman, Heidi Carolyn, 195n8
Felices, Telésforo, 92, 122
Fernández, Alicia, 195n22
Fernández, Hamylton, 140
Fernández, Julián: directorial role as record producer, 114, 133, 135–38, 141; founding of Dolby JR, 126; promotional activities, 133–35; radio program produced by, 160
festejo, 52
fiesta de la música, La (radio program), 173
Figueroa, Óscar, 62, 131, 138, 199n16, 201n36
"Flor de retama" (huayno), 57–58, 62, 62–64, 200n25
floreos (ornamentation), 58–59, 125

Flores, Arturo, 129
Flores, Carlos, 199n17
Flor Pucarina, 115–16, 158, 199n14
folklorismo movement, 99
fox-trots, 154, 191n16
Franck, Harry, *Vagabonding Down the Andes*, 81–83, 195n10, 195n17
Frankfurt School, 13
Frecuencia A Record (radio station), 204n37; aesthetic control, 201n6; as bellwether, 149; Huamán's show on, 161–68, 173; influence of, 14–15; pressures felt by, 174; role in Ayacucho's musical life, 171, 176
Frecuencia A Record (television station), 70–71
Freed, Alan, 202n11
friction, Tsing's concept of, 15, 17
Frith, Simon, 11
fuga (of huayno), 39, 190n7, 193n36
Fujimori, Alberto, 127–28
Fuller, Norma, 25
fusión, 65, 179, 180, 183

Gaitán Castro, Diosdado, 132
Gamarra, Amílcar, 61, 119–20, 199n17, 200n21
Gamarra Carrillo, Jefrey, 91, 95, 96, 98, 118–19, 197n44
Gamarra-Salerno duo, 154
Gamboa, Isabel, 179
gamonales, 98, 196n28
García, José Uriel: "El nuevo indio," 97–98
García Zárate, Nery, 58, 120–26; background and early career, 120–22; commemoration of, 59; recordings, 51–52, 117, 122–26. *See also* Duo Hermanos García Zárate
García Zárate, Raúl, 120–26; audience for, 58–59, 193n45; background and early career, 120–22, 200n23; class of, 159; on melancholy in huayno, 44; as paragon, 77; radio performances, 155; recordings, 52, 117, 122–26, 139, 199n16; solo guitar album, 60, 123–24, 199n12. *See also* Duo Hermanos García Zárate
genre: Frith's concept of, 11; importance for sound recordings and marketing, 113–14; limits of, 17
Glave, Luis Miguel, 92–93

global pop, Ayacuchano huayno and, 64–66, 76. *See also specific genres and performers*
globalization, 15–17, 144, 179–84; conflicting visions of, 186n8
Gómez, Fredy, 137, 201n36
Gómez Negrón, Pancho, 155
González, Francisco, 94, 103, 107–8
González, Mina, 72
González Holguín, Diego, 190n8, 196n37
Great Depression, 154
Greene, Paul D., 114–15
guapeo, 55
Guardia, Jaime, 60
guiro, in huayno norteño, 73
guitar(s): Ayacucho technique, 41, 54, 58–59, 88–89, 90, 120–24, 129–30; *bordón*, 142; in contemporary Ayacuchano huayno, 65, 133; in estudiantina ensembles, 46; García Zárate's performance on, 121; in *indigenista* music, 45; in pan-Andean music, 50–51; use in huayno genre, 39, 41
"Guitarra ama waqaychu" (huayno), 190n11
Gutiérrez, Antonio, 116, 199n12, 200n24
Guzmán, Abimael, 28–29, 127

Habermas, Jürgen, 9–11, 185nn2–3 (ch. 1)
habitus, 12
Hale, Charles R., 189n28
harp(s): in Ayacuchano huayno, 87, 88–89, 192n31; in huayno norteño, 72–73, 192n31, 193n43; in *indigenista* music, 45, 46; performers on, 195n15; in regional huayno, 54, 60, 72
"Helme" (huayno), 94, 108
"Hermanochay," 132
Hermanos Gaitán Castro, 164; "Amor, Amor" as performed by, *130*; early career, 199n16; huayno style of, 111–12; radio show hosted by, 201n7; recordings, 127, 129–31, 129–32, 136, 137, 179; stage attire of, 131; style of, 131–32, 134, 188n18; telenovela character associated with, 177
Hernández, Rosario, 140
herranza, 189n3
Hilmes, Michele, 176
Hispanist heritage, 6, 198n11
"hombre, El" (huayno), 200n25

hora del charango, La (radio program), 155
house parties in Ayacucho, 86–89, 94
Huamán, Carlos, 61–62
Huamán, Miguel Ángel, 149, 158–61, 164–68, 172–76
huamanguinismo: foundations of, 79, 84–86; legacy of, 109–10; meaning of, 21–22, 26, 80, 84–85, 193–94n2; music's role in, 85–110, 197n45
Huancavelica, Peru, 80
Huancayo, Peru: huaynos of, 106, 197n42; recording studios in, 126
Huanta, Peru, 62
Huaracina, Pastorita, 72
huaylas, 191n22
huayno: as Andean identity marker, 12, 39–45, 60, 70–71, 79–80, 106–7, 170–75, 184; chicha and, 69, 128; circulation of, 89; consolidation of, 40–41; cumbia and, 178; melancholy of, 40; modal ambivalence, 38, 44–45; modernity and, 15, 168–70, 172–73; origins of, 190n8; overview of, 6, 37–45; performances in Lima, 2; picaresque, 191n15; regional styles of, 36, 45, 53–61, 129–30; rhythm, 39, *39*; stage attire for, 115–16; standardization of regional styles, 56, 70, 133, 191n27; subject matter in, 44; texts, 38, 39–40, 41–42, 62–64, 111, 127–28; timbre in indigenous performance, 54; *wanka* style, 55. *See also* Ayacuchano huayno; huayno norteño
huayno con arpa, 193n42
huayno norteño, 72–76; aesthetics of, 66, 73–76, 111–12, 170–71; Ayacuchano huayno aesthetics compared with, 23, 75–76, 111, 142–43; Ayacucho radio broadcasts, 170; class and, 24, 35, 170, 182–83; cumbia and, 178, 184; Hermanos Gaitán Castro's performances of, 130–31; instrumentation in, 72–73, 193nn42–43; live performances in Ayacucho, 169–70; popularity of, 178–79; radio programming of, 203n27; stage attire, 73, 75; standard rhythm, 72–73, *73*; stylistic changes in, 180, *181*
Huirse, Jorge, 198n4
Humala, Julio, 180
Humala, Walter, 61, 200n29

IAO (pan-Andean duo), 173–74
identity construction: audiences and, 11–12; huayno norteño and, 73; mediators and, 9, 13–15; micropolitics of, 187n13; modernity and, 15, 114–15, 168–70, 172–73; music's role in, 23–24, 32–33, 70–71, 85–86, 117–19, 182–84; selection of materials, 26, 114, 125; taboo nature of terminology, 22. *See also* Andean identity
IEMPSA record company, 51–52, 56, 115, 117, 119–20, 198n9, 198nn4–5, 199n12
Illanes, Julia, 139
"imposible, El" (*yaraví*), 190n11
Inca, cultural reverence for, 19, 31
incasimo movement, 99
Indians, Andean indigenous: abjection of, 19, 20, 21; *indigenismo* movement's arrangement of music, 45–46; music of, 187–88n18, 203n27; subaltern representation of, 5, 22–23, 51, 187n18; taboo nature of terminology, 22
indigenismo movement, 45–53; Andean identity and, 6; in Ayacucho, 79–80, 84–86, 196nn26–29, 197n44; in Cusco, 196n33; Hispanism and, 98–99, 198n11; ideals of, 30–31; latter-day, 30–33; music in, 45, 49–50, 55–56, 85–86, 92–95, 196n33; musical *huamanguinismo* and, 102–8; nationalist aspects of, 196n26; pan-Andean music and, 50–51; Pokras and, 101–2; recordings of, 115, 198n5; sincerity of, 185n3 (intro.); *tradiciones* in, 99–100
indigenista folklore, 6
Instituto Cultural Peruano-Norteamericano, 3, 192n30
instrumentation: for Ayacucho house parties, 88–89; in chicha, 67; in contemporary Ayacuchano huayno, 65, 133, 141–43, 201n39; of estudiantina ensembles, 46; of *indigenista* parlor music, 45; in pan-Andean music, 50–51, 65; of regional huayno styles, 54, 60
intermedios, 89
Inti-Illimani, 66, 132
Isbell, Billie Jean, 199n15
Isbell, William, 199n15

JAFE studio, 126
Jaivas, Los, 136
"Jarana" (huayno), *121–22*
Jauja, huayno from, 55
Jáuregui, José, 94, 103, 104, 107–8, 197n45
Jilguero del Huascarán, 115–16, 191n23, 199n14
Juntos como siempre (Trio Ayacucho album), 119
Juscamayta, Alberto "Raktaku," 87–88, 200n23

kenas: in contemporary Ayacuchano huayno, 65, 89, 129–30, 133, 137, 141, 193n36; in *indigenista* music, 45, 46; in pan-Andean music, 50–51; performance techniques, 193n36; in regional huayno, 60
Kjarkas, Los, 66, 128, 200n31

Lagos, Edith, 200n25
"Lágrimas de Ñusta" (huayno), 92
laúdes: in Ayacuchano huayno, 89; García Zárate's performance on, 121; in *indigenista* music, 46
Laurente, Mario, 118–19, 199n16; García Zárate's style viewed by, 125
Lecuona Cuban Boys, 154
Leguía, Augusto B., 49, 55–56, 153, 202n14
Lepiane, Juan, 202–3n19
Lima, Peru: Andean radio programming in, 155–56, 201nn6–7; Andean region as viewed by, 19; Ayacuchano huayno performances in, 4, 12, 57–58, 61, 89, 111, 116, 127–44, 133–35, 192n30; Ayacucho aristocracy's emigration to, 83; Barranco district, 3; chicha performance in, 67, 68–69; criollo community in, 36–37; Cruz de Motupe district, 3; demographic geography, 2, 24–25; as focal point for public culture industry, 24–26; harp and vocalist ensembles, 55; huayno from, 72; *indigenismo* movement in, 94, 97; informal marketplace in, 25–26; La Victoria district, 127; Lince district, 57–58; Lurigancho district, 3; Miraflores district, 3; *peñas* as performance venues, 118–19; record stores in, 180; small urban centers influenced

Lima, Peru (*cont.*)
    by, 4; sound recording companies in, 115, 127–44; soundscapes of, 1–2, 3–4
Limeñita, La, 202n17
Lindas Satankas, Las, 55–56, 191n25, 199n13
Lingan, Julio, 201n36
linguistic parallelism in huayno texts, 41–42
Lira Paucina, 60, 192n32
"Llorando se fue" (Los Kjarkas *saya*), 200n31
Lloréns Amico, José Antonio, 54, 156, 186n4
Loayza, Alfredo, 147, 148–49
Lomnitz, Claudio, 187n14
López, Maruja, 202n17

Machaca, Graciano, 187–88n18
"Madre" (huayno norteño), 74
magia del canto andino, La (radio program), 171–72
mandolin(s): in Ayacuchano huayno, 54, 89; in estudiantina ensembles, 46
manolacha, 87–88
María Angola Hotel (Lima), 3, 192n30
Mariátegui, José Carlos, 188n24
marinera, 89, 189n2
Márquez Talledo, Eduardo, 202n17
Martínez, Lola, 195n22
Martínez, Teodoro, 195n20
Más música de Ayacucho (García Zárate album), 117
Matos, Yolanda, 202n17
Matos Mar, José, 25
Matta de Turner, Clorinda, 103
"Maywa maywachallay verde" (Jáuregui), 94
mediators: identity construction and, 9, 13, 30–33, 70–71, 77, 181–82; public sphere and, 9–11; radio DJs as, 149–53, 160–68, 171–76, 175, 202n11; radio stations as, 147–76; recording studios and labels as, 112–15, 138–39, 144–45; recruitment of consumers, 5, 7–8, 10–11, 12, 113–14, 150, 153, 158–59; studies of, 185n1 (intro.). *See also* radio, Peruvian; sound recording industry in Peru
Medina, Erasmo, 200n24
Medina, Pío Max, 93
Medina, Tani, 56, 88, 92, 103, 191n25, 199n13

Medina family, 60
Melendez sisters, 191n25
Mendieta, Walter, 139
Mendívil, Carlos, 196n23
Mendoza, Zoila S., 128, 185n3 (intro.), 196n26, 196n33
mestizaje process: *indigenismo* movement characterization of, 97, 197n48; Peruvian differences from other countries, 187n16; racialization and, 21, 79–80, 82–84, 106–7, 110, 183, 187n16
mestizo peoples, highland: *decente* concept and, 20–21, 23–24, 25, 27, 28, 83; identity issues, 5, 8, 19–20, 30–33, 183, 194n3, 194nn6–7, 197n44; race and, 21, 82–84, 106–7, 110, 186–87n12; taboo nature of terminology, 22
Mexico, *mestizaje* in, 187n16
Meza, José, 129
Millamán, Rosamel, 189n28
Millones, Luis, 197n44
Miró Quesada, Aurelio, 196n34
Miró Quesada family, 109
misti, 194n6
modernity: Ayacuchano huayno and, 6; cosmopolitanism and, 16–17, 29–30, 114, 128–29, 168–70; identity and, 15, 70–71, 172–73; latter-day *indigenismo* and, 30–33; tradition and, 204n35
Montoya, Edwin, 60, 117, 118–19, 135, 139, 190n12
Montoya, Luis, 190n12
Montoya, Rodrigo, 190n12
Mountain Music of Peru, The (Folkways album), 192n32
Mundo Music, 201n38
Munguía, Nelly, 64, 126
Municipal Auditorium (Ayacucho), 192n30
Muñoz, Walter, 168–69
música criolla, 36–37, 54, 154, 178, 198n4, 202n17
musique des Incas et ses survivances, La, 40

National Institute of Culture (Ayacucho), 192n30
National Museum (Lima), 192n30
National School of Folklore (Lima), 49–50, 59, 139
Navarro del Águila, Ernesto, 91–92
Néctar, 204n2
Negus, Keith, 138

Nepali *lok pop* musicians, 114–15
Normal School (Lima), 95
Nueva Crema, La, 68
Nugent, José Guillermo, 187n16

OAX (radio station), 153–54, 202n15
Odeón company, 56, 198n4
Ollanta label, 125, 200n24
Opinión, La, 91
Ordóñez, Fíler, 201n36
Oré, Milder, 179
Orlove, Benjamin S., 187n13
Ormeño, Filomeno, 202n17
Orquesta Américas, 165
"Otra vez me equivoqué" (huayno norteño), 130

Pacheco, Lucio, 72
Pacheco, Tomás, 72
Palma, Ricardo, 99–100
Palmer, David Scott, 199n15
"Paloma, torcaza" (huayno), *137*, 137–38
Palomino, Trudy, 127
pan-Andean music, 6; aesthetics, 143; antagonism toward, 131–32; in Ayacucho, 200n30; contemporary Ayacuchano huayno influenced by, 65–66, 114, 128–30, 133, 169–70, 173, 179, 180; Dolby JR's recordings of, 136; indigenista performance and, 50–51, 52–53; modernity and, 15, 114; radio broadcasts, 173–74; taste and, 53, 181; world popularity of, 50–51, 66, 114, 128
pan flutes: in contemporary Ayacuchano huayno, 65, 133, 141; in pan-Andean music, 50–51
"Para todos hay mañana" (huayno), 103–4
"Para un viejo corazón" (huayno), 57, 132–33
parlor music, *indigenista* compositions as, 45
Parodi, Rómulo, 196n23
Parra Carreño, Alfredo: "Cantos de Huamanga," 105–6; CCA and, 95, 98, 99; comments on Andean musical traditions, 107, 108; *tradiciones* written by, 102, 191n25, 197n41
"Pasajero en el camino" (huayno), 130
pascalle, 89
Pastorita Huaracina, 115–16, 191n23, 198n10, 199n14
Paucar, Dina, 23, 74–75, 178, 182

payola, 174–75, 176
Peralta Ramírez, Mata: *tradiciones de Huamanga*, 100
Pereyra Chávez, Nelson E., 197n48
Peru: cosmopolitan dance genres in, 189n2; cosmopolitan pop genres in, 36, 128–29; education in traditional music and dance, 49–50; ethnic politics and, 189n28; map of, *18*; race, power, and geography in, 17–24, 79–80, 186–87n12; radio as nation-state project, 153–57; social imaginary of, 2–3; Truth and Reconciliation Commission, 188n23, 188n26
Peru Ilustrado, El, 196n36
Peruvian Broadcasting Company, 202n13
piano, in *indigenista* music, 45, 194n5
Picaflor de los Andes, 130, 158, 191n21, 191n27, 198n10, 199n14, 203n25
Pinares, Yolanda, 173
"Pirwalla pirwa" (huayno), 57
Pizarro Cerrón, Luis, 155–56
"Plegaria al sol" (*indigenia* salon piece), 94
Pokras, 101–2, 196n31
"Por maldad" (Chacalón), 69
Portocarrero, Martina, 64, 126, 200n25
Pozo, Manuel Jesús, 93–94, 95, 96–99, 102, 106, 191n25
Prado, Carlos, 137–38, 147–48, 170
Prado, Chipi, 40, 190n9, 200n23
Prado, Manuelcha: Falconí and, 41; live performances, 170, 180, 201n36; recordings, 42–44, 64, 173, 175, 177
public sphere, Habermas's study of, 9–11
Puno, pan flute ensembles from, 55
Puquio, Peru, 41

qachwa, 189n3
Qori Maki, 87
Quechua language: Andean identity and, 187–88n18; linguistic parallelism in genres, 42; nature metaphors in, 42; stigma attached to, 190n14; use by elites, 44; use in huaynos, 39, 43–44, 102
"Qué lindos son tus ojitos" (huayno norteño), 74
Quilapayún, 66

racialization, concept of, 20–21, 186n11. See also Andean identity; *mestizaje* process radio: consumer use of, 151–52; DJs as mediators, 149–53, 160–68, 171–76, 202n11; DJs' style, 152–53, 163–64; early broadcasting, 153–57; as educative media, 153–54; foreign genres on, 154; gender and, 152; geographic focus of, 150–51; horizontal context in, 151–52, 156–57; scheduling as framing device, 152; selection and contextualization process on, 14; studies on, 149–51, 175–76

radio, Peruvian: advertisements on, 168; Ayacuchano huayno broadcasts, 3, 12, 13, 14–15, 145, 147–76, 201–2n7; broadcasts in Ayacucho, 157–60; central importance of, 14, 148–49; consumer recruitment methods, 5, 7, 150, 153, 156, 158–59; DJs' influence, 148–49, 160–63, 171–76, 175; DJs' style, 152–53, 163–68; DJs' technical skills, 167–68; listenership assessment, 203n29; music programming, 1930s–1950s, 155–56; pan-Andean shows, 53; payola and, 174–75, 176; pirate stations, 13, 148–49, 201n7, 201nn1–2; promotion of Ayacuchano artists on, 147–48, 160–68, 171–72, 173, 174–75; promotion of recordings on, 133, 144, 145, 162, 173–74; time slots on, 148–49

Radio Abancay, 202n18
Radio Agricultura, 203n23
Radio Atlantis, 171–72
Radio Ayacucho, 157, 202n18, 203n24
Radio Central, 202n17
Radio Cinética, 160–61
Radio del Pacífico, 133–34
Radio Dusa, 154, 155
Radio El Sol, 155–56
Radio Gigante, 147
Radio Goicochea, 154, 155
Radio IncaSat, 170
Radio Internacional, 155
Radio Juliaca, 202n18
Radio La Caribeña, 163
Radio La Voz de Huamanga, 157–58, 203n27
Radio Lima, 155
Radio Mélody, 161, 173, 174
Radio Nacional, 155, 201n7, 202n15
Radio Quispillacta, 187n18

Radio San Cristóbal, 157
Radio Tawantinsuyo, 155
Radio Victoria (chain of radio stations), 154, 157, 203n24
Radio Wari, 159–60, 168–69
Radio Zeta, 147, 201n2
Raúl García y su guitarra (radio program), 155
RCA Victor, 55–56
reception, mediators' marketing and, 5, 31–32
Recital de guitarra (García Zárate album), 124
Recital folklórico (García Zárate album), 124
recopilaciones, 92
redondilla, 89
Revatta, Kiko, 57, 127, 132–33, 134
Revista Huamanga, 82, 97–107, 194n5, 196n28, 197n47
Rinconcito Ayacuchano, El (Lima club), 57–58
"Ripuy ripuy" (huayno), 190n11
Riva-Agüero, José de la: *Paisajes peruanos*, 79, 80, 81, 90
Rivera, Francisco "El Inkario," 92, 195n20
rock 'n' roll, 36, 67, 130; on Peruvian radio, 157
Rodrigo, Joaquín, 177
Roel Mendizábal, Pedro, 193n41
Roel Pineda, Josafat, 41, 190n12, 198n10
Román, Opa, 87, 90, 103
romance (poetic form), 39
Romero, César, 129, 131
Romero, Raúl R., 186n4, 189n3, 198n8
rural migrants to cities: as audience base for Dolby JR, 127, 133–35; chicha and, 67, 68–69; *cholos* term used for, 23, 187n18; cultural transformation and, 24–25; identity issues, 5, 57–58, 116; location of, 19; marginalization in Ayacucho, 28; movement of, 2; second-generation, 68–69, 157; solidarity clubs of, 25, 188n20; as taste community, 159

Sáez, Benjamín, 103
Salcedo, Uriel, 203n27
San Antonio Abad University (Cusco), 95
Sandoval, Pablo, 69
sanjuanito, 128, 200n32
San Marcos University (Lima), 95
San Miguel, Peru, 89

santiago, 74
Santos Montero, José, 104
"Saqsaywaman" (huayno from Cusco), 190n11
Sauñe, Orlando, 191n27
saya, 66, 128, 200n31
Saywa, 180
scene, Straw's concept of, 11–12
seguidilla, 189n2
señorial class, 22, 83
sentiment, quality of, 22, 55
serenata, 90–91, 94, 103, 195n20
serranismo movement, 99
Shapis, Los, 67, 73
Shining Path: Ayacucho and, 26, 28–29, 61–64, 127, 188nn24–26; Portocarrero and, 200n25
Silverblatt, Irene, 199n15
Sisicha, Qori, 188n20
ska, 178
sol de los Andes, El (radio program), 155–56
Sol del Perú, 198n5
solidarity clubs, cultural activities of, 25, 188n20
Solier, Magaly, 180
Son del Sol (Hermanos Gaitán Castro album), 111, 136
Sono Radio record company, 56, 115, 198n5, 199n12
Soto, Manuel, 190n11
sound recording industry, taste mediation of, 112–13. *See also* sound recording industry in Peru
sound recording industry in Peru: cassette technology, 125, 200n28; discourse of recording, 139–44; foreign record companies, 55–56; genres recorded, 198n9; independent labels, 13, 125–26, 126–44; marketing strategies, 13–14, 31–32, 199n14; piracy and, 125; promotion of Ayacuchano huayno, 60–61, 115–44, 199nn13–14; promotion of regional huayno styles, 45, 51–52, 53–61; record label as term, 197n1; standardization of Ayacuchano huayno, 133, 139–40. *See also* Dolby (later Dolly) JR label; *other labels and companies*
"Soy provinciano" (chicha), 68, 71
Spanish: arrival in Peru, 18–19; intermarriage of, 20; poetic forms, 39; privileging of heritage, 84–86, 99–102

Spitulnik, Debra Anne, 14, 151–52, 162
Stern, Steve, 199n15
Sterne, Jonathan, 176
Stokes, Martin, 186n8
Straw, Will, 11–12
Sucre, Naranjita de, 170–71
Sullca, Antonio "Sunqu Suwa," 87, 195n13
Sullca family, 60
Sumac, Yma, 92, 155, 191n18, 199n13
Sureños, Los, 139
Suri Sikuris (radio program), 204n36
Szeminski, Jan, 199n15

takirari, 61, 200n35
Takiyninchik (radio program), 203n27
taste: class and, 12, 69–70, 71, 73–76, 124–25, 135, 144, 159, 170, 177–79; communities, 158–59
Teatro Pardo y Aliago (Lima), 192n30
Teatro Ricardo Palma (Lima), 192n30
technocumbia, 193n37
techno-huayno, 193n42
Teitelbaum, Benjamin, 187n17
television: consumer recruitment methods, 5; telenovelas on, 70–71, 177–79, 182
telurismo, 104–5
Testimonio ayacuchano (album), 64
timbales, in huayno norteño, 73
tinku, 53, 66, 128, 191n19, 200n32
tobas, 66
"Todos juntos" (pan-Andean song), 136
Toledo, Alejandro, 30, 189nn27–28, 201n7
Torres, Felipe, 104
tradiciones, 99–100, 102–3
Tres de Huamanga, Los, 139
Trio Ayacucho: accompanimental singing style, 89, 120, 200n20, 203n24; Camassi and, 87–88, 131; dearth of performing opportunities, 159; distinct style of, 125; Falconí and, 58–59; Fernández's admiration for, 135; formation of, 119–20; Gamarra and, 61; "Jarana" as performed by, *121–22*; recordings, 60, 139, 141, 179, 190n11
Trio Lira Paucina, 199n13
Trio Los Estudiantes, 155
Trio Los Labradores de Huanta, 200n25
Trio Voces de Huamanga, 60, 117, 139
Tsing, Anna, 15
Tucno Rocha, Marco, 87–88

Tuna Universitaria de la UNSCH, 117, 118, 199n16, 201n38
tundiki, 128
Tupac Amaru label, 125
Turino, Thomas, 16, 183, 186n9, 190n6, 195n16, 197n43
"Tusuy Kusun" (Damaris), 180

Umaru, Peru, 90
"Umpa rosas" (huayno), 58, *123*
Universidad Nacional San Cristóbal de Huamanga: bankrupting of, 81; closure of, 109, 194n4; lecture halls, 192n30; reopening of, 27–28, 79, 93, 117–19; Tuna ensemble, 60, 117, 118, 199n16, 201n38
Untiveros, Leoncio Jerí, 196n23
Urrutia, Jaime, 92–93, 196n31
"Utku pankillay" (huayno), 87, 92
uywa, 192–93n34

Vallejos, Delia, 202n17
vals music, 37, 154, 189n2
"Vapor brillante" (huayno), 119, 199n19
Vasconcelos, José, 187n16
Vásquez, Jesús, 198n4, 202n17
Vásquez Rodríguez, Chalena, 55
Velasco Alvarado, Juan, 49–50, 203n24
Vergara Figueroa, Abilio, 55
Villanueva, Victor Modesto, 103, 104
Viña del Mar International Song Festival, 180
violin(s): in estudiantina ensembles, 46; in regional huayno, 54

"Vírgenes de sol" (Bravo de Rueda), 45
Virrey label, 56, 115, 198n4, 198n9
Vivanco, Alejandro, 92, 94, 107–8, 120, 190n13, 191n18, 197n45, 199n16, 199nn13–14, 203n20
Vivanco, Carlos, 196n23
Vivanco, Moisés, 92, 155, 191n18, 199n13, 203n20
Volcán label, 200n24
Voz de Huamanga, La (Ayacucho radio station), 77, 169–70

Wade, Peter, 186n11
wanka, 55
Waqay, Wallpa, 170–71
War of the Pacific, 81, 83, 188n22
Warmi (Solier album), 180
Warpas, Los, 52–53
"Wayanakito" (huayno), 173
Weismantel, Mary, 21, 22, 186–87n12
Wolfman Jack, 202n11
women performers, rarity of, 90–91

yaraví, 89, 94, 103–4, 108, 189n3, 190n11
yarqa aspiy, 53
Yawar, 66, 131–32, 180
"Yerba Silvestre" (huayno), 200n25
"Yo te busqué con mis ojos" (yaraví), 104

zamba, 61
Zuidema, R. Tom, 199n15

www.ingramcontent.com/pod-product-compliance
Lightning Source LLC
Chambersburg PA
CBHW021943290426
44108CB00012B/942